PREFACE

Everyone knows *something* about families. Most people grow up in a family and get their knowledge that way. Then, as adults, people often form long-term relationships and have children. Many become divorced or suffer bereavement. People learn a lot about families from their experiences of childhood, spousehood, parenthood—even from being an ex-spouse or ex-parent.

Some people spend a lot of time making a family album or researching their family tree. Doing this, they learn about family resemblances in appearance, personality, risk of illness, and life expectancy. The more speculative even come to wonder about patterns of mate selection and child rearing. Why do people marry the partners they do, they wonder? And why do some people do such a good job of raising their children while others do such a poor job?

The mass media give us a variety of images of the family and much food for thought. For example, the most popular novels are about family life. The most popular prime-time television programs present us with pictures of conventional families, unconventional families, and everything in between. In fact, popular culture is full of images of intimate life which range from positive to negative, serious to tongue-in-cheek. And as American entertainment spreads around the world, for good or ill, these American images of the family influence viewers in the Arab world and Latin America. In this way, it shapes the ways they think about family life.

What effect do these programs have? For example, what did Arab or Japanese audiences think when they watched *Dallas*, a series (in case you

v

have forgotten) about financial and sexual intrigue in a wealthy Texan family? The answer is not obvious, but for one effort to answer this question you should read *The Export of Meaning* (Liebes and Katz, 1990).

In fact, people who seek a better society—whether they are religious or secular—often focus on the family. Their thinking is simple: change the family and you change the world. This is why many social scientists, from Sigmund Freud and Margaret Mead onward, have criticized Western European and North American family practices: they inhibit useful changes. And like Freud, anthropologist Edmund Leach has gone so far as to say that the family, with its tawdry secrets, is the source of all our discontents.

With so much attention from scholars, the media and ordinary people, the family has become a convenient political symbol. For example, the phrase "family values" has entered our political vocabulary. Family values were a "motherhood issue" in the 1992 presidential campaign. Everyone who sought election was in favor of good family life and each portrayed his opponent as falling on the wrong side of the issue. For, in truth, there are many ideas about what a "good family life" might be.

The Republican party's 1992 convention adopted an extreme position. It held that a mother who works outside the home harms her children; that single-parent households are caused by people not bothering to get married, or—if they have married—not taking their marriage seriously; and that abortion is wrong in almost all circumstances. In short, the Republican position suggested that society can only solve its many problems if people live in one particular kind of family, with father as the main (or only) wage earner and mother devoting herself to raising the children and doing housework.

This platform persuaded many voters, but not a majority. Perhaps it failed to correspond to their everyday experience of family life. Nonetheless, this "family values" outlook struck a responsive chord among many. And that resonance—evidence of nostalgia for another kind of family life—leads us to wonder whether there are grains of truth in this way of thinking. Is the fear that family life is failing justified? More generally, what should we expect of families, and how can we help families meet justifiable expectations? As social scientists and citizens, we need to take these questions seriously.

There is no denying families do many things. Indeed, families may be the most basic form of social organization. So far as we can tell, families existed before corporations and governments were ever invented. They persist even when corporations and governments fall into decay. Families are also "basic" in the sense that they support common, everyday social life. From one day to the next, they maintain the work force, produce children, and regulate sexual behavior—all tasks that government and business tend to ignore, though they assume these tasks will be carried out somehow, by somebody.

So it is important that families succeed in their "basic" tasks of social organization. Yet as we write, during the recession of the mid-1990s, people have a strong sense that the family is failing in these tasks. Open a magazine or newspaper and you are likely to find articles with titles like "Family life: not enough money, too much stress," "Divorce: a ticket to poverty for women," "Two income families on the rise," and "Marriages in decline."

Are the assumptions of these articles correct? Are we seeing a decline from family patterns that were common in "the old days"? Are the changes we see inevitable by-products of late twentieth-century living? Is the family falling apart? And if family life *is* in decline, can we expect the decline to continue, or is there evidence predicting a reversal? Or are people just wallowing in nostalgia, comparing a real present with an imaginary past? Were families *ever* really as happy and united as we like to think?

There are many urgent questions for us to answer and, as sociologists, we have a duty to answer them. The urgency is made greater still when political parties invent their own simple solutions, in hopes of gaining election. But can we trust their "answers"?

For example, was the Republican party's 1992 emphasis on family values simply an attempt to "blame the victim" by holding impoverished or broken families responsible for their social and economic troubles? As far back as Roman times, the middle classes have always viewed poor people and their families with a certain amount of contempt. Perhaps today's complaint against the family is just another occasion to tell the poor to pull themselves up by their bootstraps, by getting married, staying married, and keeping a close watch on their children.

People are understandably disturbed by poverty and homelessness, family violence, unattended children, and isolated old people. No wonder they long for a time when—in fact or fantasy—family life was more stable, more satisfying, safer, and more nurturing than it is now.

But we need facts, not dreams, to address these questions. And we need a framework within which to understand these facts. In this book, we will consider what family life used to be like in other times and what it is like in other places. We will also consider which aspects of family life have changed and which have remained the same. We will consider both the positive and negative aspects of recent changes, in the context of earlier, larger changes like industrialization.

In the end, we will lay out a variety of plausible scenarios for the "futures" of the family. There are good reasons to consider a variety of possible futures, not just one. First, a lot of uncertainty surrounds the future of family life. In large part, that is because our theories about the family are less complete and less reliable than we would like them to be. Second, our best theories show that many factors influence family life and we cannot be certain how these factors—economic, cultural, political, and otherwise—will change in the foreseeable future.

Finally, and not least, some of the future of family life is within our own hands. As a society, we can influence family life in a number of ways. One way is by better understanding how families work and how they change. Another is by planning and legislating changes that make certain kinds of family life easier and more secure. Sociology shows that no amount of legislation will keep people from behaving in ways that are against their beliefs and interests. Yet legislation can make it easier and safer for people to organize their lives in ways that already make sense to them.

So how well we understand changes in family life, and how well we adapt our laws and budgets to supporting new kinds of family life, will play a large part in determining the future of families in our lifetimes. As citizens, all of us—both the writers and readers of this book—will play a part in creating the future of family life in North America. That is precisely why we have written this book.

ACKNOWLEDGMENTS

We want to start by acknowledging the role played by Dr. Mike Murphy and Dr. Krystina Rudko, now of Statistics Canada, who first asked us to provide their Demographic Review Secretariat with an overview of the future—or is it futures?—of the family.

Second, thanks go to Nancy Roberts of Prentice Hall for expressing an early and continued interest in the book and for waiting patiently until it was really done. Thanks also go to our reviewers—now known to be Mark G. Eckel of McHenry County College, Jerry B. Clavner of Cuyahoga Community College East, Joseph M. Garza of Georgia State University, and Diane Beeson of California State University at Hayward for their suggestions and comments. We have taken them seriously and we think the book is better as a result.

Our research inspiration has come from a variety of sources. The Social Sciences and Humanities Research Council of Canada has funded our research into individualization of women's social roles. The General Social Survey, as carried out in the United States and in a different form in Canada, has provided a solid benchmark for measuring change in private lives. Most important, the researchers whose work we have read and cited here—their names may be found in the index—have shown how important yet difficult it is to get a handle on the forces that are changing family life around the world. Some of this work has been excerpted in a collection Tepperman and Wilson prepared under the title *Next of Kin: An International Reader on Changing Families*, published by Prentice Hall in 1993.

Our book has benefitted significantly from help by a number of stu-

THE FUTURES
OF THE FAMILY

Charles L. Jones
University of Toronto

Lorne Tepperman
University of Toronto

Susannah J. Wilson
Ryerson Polytechnic University

Prentice Hall, Englewood Cliffs, New Jersey 07632

Library of Congress Cataloging-in-Publication Data

Jones, Charles L.
  The futures of the family / Charles L. Jones, Lorne Tepperman,
Susannah J. Wilson.
    p.   cm.
  Includes bibliographical references and index.
  ISBN 0-13-345679-X
    1. Family.   2. Family—United States.   I. Tepperman, Lorne.
II. Wilson, S. J. (Susannah Jane)   III. Title.
HQ503.J66   1995
306.85—dc20   94-22611
                                                             CIP

Acquisitions editor: Nancy Roberts
Editorial/production supervision, interior design,
    and electronic page makeup: Mary Araneo
Buyer: Mary Ann Gloriande
Editorial assistant: Pat Naturale
Copyeditor: Henry Pels
Cover designer: Carol Ceraldi

© 1995 by Prentice-Hall, Inc.
A Simon & Schuster Company
Englewood Cliffs, New Jersey 07632

Printed in the United States of America
10 9 8 7 6 5 4 3 2 1

ISBN 0-13-345679-X

Prentice-Hall International (UK) Limited, *London*
Prentice-Hall of Australia Pty. Limited, *Sydney*
Prentice-Hall Canada Inc., *Toronto*
Prentice-Hall Hispanoamericana, S.A., *Mexico*
Prentice-Hall of India Private Limited, *New Delhi*
Prentice-Hall of Japan, Inc., *Tokyo*
Simon & Schuster Asia Pte. Ltd., *Singapore*
Editora Prentice-Hall do Brasil, Ltda., *Rio de Janeiro*

CONTENTS

dents. They include Sandra Badin, Chris Demakopoulos, Laura Garton, Mubina Jaffer, Anthony Molinaro, and Karen Wolfe, who collected relevant materials from around the world for us to assess; Frances Gilbert, who cleaned up the writing on drafts of some early chapters; and Andrew Tepperman, who did the index.

Since leaving our hands for the last time, the manuscript has been under the able supervision of Mary Araneo, its production editor. We want to thank her and also Henry Pels, the copy editor. Working with them has been smooth and easy.

Finally, we want to thank our respective families—our parents, brothers and sisters, spouses and children—for providing on-the-job instruction in the subtleties of family life.

 1

AN OVERVIEW: FAMILIES TODAY

INTRODUCTION

It is tempting to wonder about "the nature" of the family. However, we have resisted the urge to speculate wildly in this book. The questions *we* raise are about the everyday family lives of people like you. They are about the ways everyday family life has changed and how people organize their family lives in other countries. In the end, this book is about how ordinary North Americans might organize better family lives in the next century.

With a mixture of data from different times and places, we draw conclusions about what might be expected of North American families in the future. And we do all of this in a short space, knowing well that many fat books could (and should) be written on this topic.

In case you skipped the Preface, we repeat there's a good reason for studying families today. More and more people are concerned about the implications of recent changes in family life.

There has been a dramatic change in people's thinking about family life in the last forty years. In the 1950s, most North Americans expected to marry and have children. Those who didn't were seen as deviant, both in common parlance and in the sociological literature of the period. For example, Stolk and Brotherton (1981) found that over half of their sample of Australian students described single women by using negative terms like "old maid" and "spinster." Single *men* have always had a more positive image in popular culture.

But beginning in the 1960s, expectations changed. Young people demanded more freedom in their sexual behavior and lifestyle choices. It was no longer unusual for young people to cohabit or live communally. Even the vast majority, who followed a more conventional path, could (rightly) feel they were choosing to do so. And given the social philosophy of the sixties, unmarried people were now described as living "alternate," not deviant, lifestyles.

Since the 1960s, intimate relations have become fluid. In the 1990s, it is more and more common for people to cohabit (even with a same-sex partner), divorce, marry without having children or have children without marrying.

As in the past, many people remain in marriages that are, emotionally speaking, dead. They often have good practical reasons for doing so. Usually, they include a desire to spare the children, a fear of change, or a reluctance to split up family property. Still, an idealist would not consider this to be healthy family living. Today, family diversity is the "new norm" (Burke, 1986) and patterns that seemed "deviant" in the 1950s, or "alternate" in the 1960s, are accepted by most people.

Even changes in technology have played a part in this drama of everyday life. No one can talk about the present, much less the future, of marriage without considering birth control. Modern techniques of birth control are both more effective and more readily available than ever before. As well, scientific advances in procreation give people more and more control over parenting decisions. These changes have revolutionized one of the main "functions" of the family: childbearing. We will have more to say about this.

It also seems as if family life today is less stable and more stressful than in the past. Consider the divorce rate: in the early 1990s, about 52 percent of Americans and 42 percent of Canadians could expect to divorce at least once during their lifetime.

The divorce rate underestimates people's movement in and out of intimate relations. It also underestimates their loss of commitment to the relationships they stay in. But even taken as a ballpark estimate, the divorce rate is disturbingly large.

Is this high divorce rate a bad thing? Not necessarily. Most people who choose to leave a relationship feel they are gaining autonomy and getting something better than what they have. And today, more people exercise a choice about the kind of intimate relationship they will enter and stay in. People are readier to marry outside of their own social (class, ethnic, or racial) group than in the past. Unhappily married people are readier to end their marriages.

But we will also have to discuss the negative side of family change. There are social and personal costs accompanying these improvements in family life. Again, consider divorce. When one partner chooses to leave, the other partner is left behind and often suffers from isolation and depression. Likewise, divorce impoverishes ex-wives and children. We can expect that a greater flow of people in and out of marriages will hurt others, if only for short periods of time. In a fluid society, the harmful effects will be common and repeated, though (often) lasting for only short periods.

Are these harmful effects inevitable? Can people have the freedom they seek without creating emotional and economic hardship for others? Is it possible for people to leave a marriage without hurting their partners and children? And is it possible for grown-up children to enjoy the freedom they seek without ignoring the emotional and financial needs of elderly parents and relatives? Stating the problem another way, is it possible to organize our society so that people can freely enter and leave family relationships without hurting the people with fewest resources? These are, typically, women (compared with men), young children (compared with parents), and the elderly (compared with people of working age).

Such questions are difficult and challenging. All we can hope to do, in this book, is make a start towards answering them. This book describes what we see as inevitable and what we see as changeable. Our focus is on the family in North America. However, our reference points are both historical and cross-cultural.

DEFINING FAMILIES

Families vary in form over history and from one society to another. Yet, for many years sociologists used George Murdock's (1949: 1) limited definition of "family" as the benchmark. Murdock defined a family as "a social group characterized by a common residence, economic cooperation and reproduction [including] adults of both sexes, at least two of whom maintain a socially approved sexual relationship, and one or more children, own or adopted, of the sexually cohabiting adults."

Murdock's definition raises a number of issues. In the first place, Murdock ignores *power*. In fact, families are small groups whose members differ significantly in size, strength, and resources (economic and otherwise). It is this imbalance that makes *patriarchy*—control of the family by a dominant male (typically, the father)—a central fact in the history of family life in most known societies.

Power aside, Murdock's definition leaves other issues unresolved. In particular, it leaves us wondering how many of the three basic relationships must be present in a "normal" nuclear family. Most people think of families as groups of people related to one another through marriage, descent, or adoption. They would agree that childless married couples, and single parents and their children, are families. But other people have trouble thinking of consensual unions, or same-sex unions, as families with the same claim to social esteem or tax and employment benefits. Murdock doesn't help us there.

Other hard-to-resolve questions remain as well. For example, are married but separated couples still a family? Are celibate couples a family? What about two sisters who live together, or two students who share an apartment; are they all "families"? More generally, what about long-term sexual and emotional intimacy? Can you have a family without these qualities? And is every relationship that has these qualities "a family"?

When studying family life, market researchers and census takers try to sidestep these difficulties by distinguishing between "household" and "family." That distinction allows us to talk about changes in households without necessarily implying changes in families or family life.

A "household" may contain only one person or many unrelated members. Or, it may contain a nuclear family, an extended family, or multiple families (as, for example, a commune). In short, a household can contain many families, or none at all. Conversely, a family may spread across many households. But usually, families and households coincide, giving rise to "family households." In the United States, *family households* are married couples with or without children under 18, and one-parent families with children under 18. Or they may be other households composed of related individuals (for example, two sisters sharing a household, or a parent and a child 18 years old or over).

By contrast, *nonfamily households* contain unrelated individuals or people who live alone. Over this century, the number of nonfamily households has risen dramatically. Today, more people can afford to live alone. One of the biggest changes in family life has been a rise in the proportion of single-person households (Sweet and Bumpass, 1987: 340).

In North America, "home life" and "family life" suggest privacy but, even more, intimacy. Intimacy and privacy of family life demands an appropriate physical environment. In practice, this means enough room (and rooms) to separate the household from the community and one family member from another within the household. It is this modern need for privacy that makes many of us feel we want larger homes. Yet the average household size (i.e., number of people present) is smaller than ever before.

By contrast, Victorian houses were intended to serve as single-family homes with space for one or two live-in servants. When immigration was at a peak, as many as 15 people occupied these houses (Iacovetta, 1992). But today, most such houses are occupied by couples with fewer than three children, or none at all. In the same way, suburban houses that were big enough for raising four middle-class children in the 1930s now seem too small for raising two children in the 1990s (Rybczynski, 1992).

Nevertheless, households *are* smaller today. For example, census data show that the average household size has shrunk by 50 percent, from around six people in 1681 to just under three people in 1981. What's more, "complex" family households, containing a variety of people who are not part of the nuclear family, have almost vanished. For example, the proportion of two-family households dropped by 75 percent between 1931 and 1981. The proportion of households with lodgers also fell, from 14.9 percent in 1931—over one household in seven—to nearly zero fifty years later (Bradbury, 1984).

At the same time, the number of single-person households has risen more than threefold, from 7 percent of the total, since 1931. So while people argue about how much families have changed, there is no doubt that households have been totally transformed.

To repeat, people who live together are not always families, nor do family members necessarily live together. There have always been married couples who lived apart because of illness, because one partner was in prison, or for job-related reasons such as migrant labor or military service. Commuter marriages are an example of this phenomenon. Gerstel and Gross (1982) see the development of commuter marriages as a response to economic and cultural pressures that force couples to live apart.

• So, "families" are made up of people who have lived together over an extended period of time, or intend to do so. They are connected by legal contract or emotional commitment or both. Finally, they may care for one or more dependent relatives, whether children, handicapped, or aged adults.

There is always a lot of risk built into family living. Remember that households and families are small groups whose members spend a lot of time together. There are large differences in strength, age, and power between them. Some family members can more easily control the other members, in a variety of ways. After all, members depend on each other for economic and noneconomic services. Those with the most resources can exercise the most control.

In families, sexual relations are permitted and expected between certain members but forbidden between other members. Women's sexual activity has almost always been more closely controlled than men's. This is because in male-dominated societies, people have felt that families had property rights in women's reproductive capacities. They also saw marriage as the capture and possession of "erotic property" (Collins, 1982).

Sex is not the only focus of concern in family life, to be sure. Effective families keep their members under surveillance against all kinds of internal and external danger. Older family members are supposed to keep children away from drugs, alcohol, and other forms of harm. Spouses are supposed to protect one another; parents are supposed to protect their children, and vice versa. In reality, family members often fail to do their duty. However, the cultural expectations are clear on these matters.

For most of us the essential quality of family life is an emotional commitment. "Good" families are supposed to provide intimacy (close, satisfying relationships), promote children's upbringing and schooling, enhance their members' material well-being and health, and raise their self-esteem and mental adjustment (Pullium, 1989).

However these "ideal" conditions are not always realized in practice. A family relationship is no guarantee of emotional commitment. In fact, many unmarried people share a closer relationship than many couples who are formally married. As well, family members do not always support one another, economically or psychologically. Many family members even neglect or abuse other members.

In the last two decades, there have been growing reports of violence *within* the family. Some estimate that one woman in ten will be assaulted at some time in her life, others put the estimate higher. In most cases the assailant is her husband or boyfriend. Violent relationships do not begin in adulthood. Children who grow up in violent homes are more likely to enter violent partnerships. Date rape and dating physical abuse occur about as often as wife abuse. Researchers estimate that one girl in four and one boy in ten are sexually abused before the age of 16, often by friends or relatives.

These figures are alarming indeed. What if they point to a huge, almost hidden problem in everyday family life—what sociologists used to call a "social pathology"? And is this pathology growing, or has family life always been stressful and violent?

One job of the sociologist is to answer questions like these. That means distinguishing actual from idealized family patterns. We must make sure the latter do not intrude on the former when constructing definitions of "family life." Doing this means being aware of the facts. It also means knowing that cultural ideas about the family change over time, sometimes faster or slower than family life itself is changing.

In the past, people also expected a certain *sequencing* of family-related events. For example, they expected people to complete their education before marrying, marry before having children, get old before becoming a grandparent, and so on. So predictable was the pattern that sociologists spoke confidently about a "cycle" of normal family events.

Today, the timing and sequencing of events are too varied to be easily categorized. In the 1990s, a woman can be a grandmother and a mid-career professional at the same time. A child whose biological parents have joint custody can call two houses "home" and claim four (or more) sets of grandparents. A woman can safely have a first child—with or without a long-term partner—after age forty. And some middle-aged adults have to cope with the anxieties of dating.

American attitudes to marriage and family have changed to reflect these changing family patterns (Yankelovich, 1981). In a national survey, only one in five Americans stated "traditional" attitudes. This traditional group views marriage almost entirely in terms of rights, duties, and obligations. Another one in five believes life is about self-fulfillment, not duty. In this context, marriage and family life are valued so long as they do not interfere with personal growth.

The remaining three Americans in five—a majority—fall between these two extreme positions. For the majority, the quality of a relationship is more important than its structure (e.g., married versus unmarried). For these people, the important question is "What makes an intimate relationship satisfying?" regardless of what we call that relationship.

Since that is true, why do people still keep up the old forms? For example, why do so many still get married (many of them in churches dressed in white bridal gowns)? We shall discuss this question in a later chapter. But in short, getting legally married has more to do with marking a transition and/or gaining social approval than with commitment. People still find the idea of legal marriage compelling, despite what they know about the realities of marriage and divorce. Enormous numbers of Americans are neither rejecting the family (let alone other durable, close relationships) nor accepting it in a traditional form. Most are hoping to revitalize and reinterpret the family (Scanzoni 1981a, 1981b, 1987).

Traditionally, we are used to thinking of love, marriage, and family as a trinity, virtually inseparable from one another. But in the future, marriage may no longer be the type of relationship in which people spend most of their adult lives. People are already less inclined to marry than they were in the past. They are more likely to view cohabitation or even singlehood positively.

What, then, are we to mean by the word "family" in this book? We will follow Trost's (1988) definition here. He has wisely suggested that instead of concerning ourselves with traditional family processes—love, sex, childbearing, socializing, and so on—we should focus on the family's basic forms. It is easier to think about differences among family systems if we pay attention to two of the family's core relationships: "spouse-to-spouse" and "parent-to-child," or the "spousal unit" and "parent-child unit," respectively.

By this standard, a *family* is a group consisting of at least one parent-child unit and/or at least one spousal unit. Moreover, a spousal unit that does not live together still constitutes a family. We have adopted Trost's practice as the basis for organizing this book.

CHANGES IN FAMILY LIFE SINCE MID-CENTURY

Let's take a brief look at the main changes in family life and personal life during the last half-century. In this period, marriage and sexual morality changed enormously, government expanded its interest in family matters, and modern sociological research learned more about the actual workings of families.

Today, families are smaller and less stable than they were in 1940. More people are affected by divorce, more children grow up in single-parent households, and more people live together without marrying. A long decline in fertility has meant an aging population. Longer life expectancy has meant a longer time spent in old age and, often, infirmity.

The period has also seen a decline of sexual puritanism. This has been marked by the growth of cohabitation before marriage, the liberalization of divorce laws, and a rise in divorce rates. As part and parcel of this, a larger fraction of wives and mothers of young children go out to work for pay.

We will not be the first to say that family life has been changing rapidly throughout the twentieth century. Some even believe that family change—indeed, social change more generally—has picked up speed over time. They say the rate of change is accelerating, so that each year sees more change than the year before it. But is this true, or is it just another way of saying that recent changes in family life are hard to understand? Do they merely *appear* too fast and even threatening?

Like many of the questions we address in this book, this question is complex. One could even argue the opposite: that there was more change between the lives of Americans born in 1890 and their children born around 1920 than there was between the lives of Americans born in 1920 and their children born around 1950 (Caplow, 1991).

By 1920, families were still large but fertility was already declining. Divorce was rare, even in the United States, though desertion was not unknown (Snell, 1983). However, single-parent households were common, since one or both parents were likely to die young. And in the 1920s, a group of liberated young women called "the flappers" created a stir by their sexual freedom and independent outlook.

One of the most profound changes in family life has been a change in family size. Since the 1870s, fertility has declined steadily throughout the West. Today, most European and North American countries are at, or just below, population replacement levels. This means that unless there is a radical shift in fertility or immigration, Western populations will get smaller and older during the next century.

A significant blip on this trend curve was the postwar "baby boom." But the baby boom was only a temporary reversal of the long-term trend and largely confined to North America. The "boom" was also misnamed. It compressed two decades of births into a decade and a half (roughly 1947–1962), rather than explode the desired family size. So, by and large, the downward trend in fertility has never stopped.

This transition to low fertility, which began around 1870, is called the *first demographic transition*. In addition, since 1965, we have seen a new force for lower fertility in the West. Demographers have called this new phase the *second demographic transition* (Van de Kaa, 1987). Whereas the first demographic transition brought births into line with lower death rates, the second demographic transition has brought births into line with new lifestyle goals and family practices. Wherever we find the second demographic transition well advanced, we find a profusion of "alternate" family styles, women working in large numbers, and people seeking autonomy in their personal lives.

The second demographic transition is particularly far along in Northern and Western Europe. There, it has renewed concerns about depopulation and a shortage of young people. In Europe, we find the fertility rates needed to replace the population—about 2.10 lifetime births per woman—only in Ireland, Malta, Poland, Albania, Turkey, and some countries of the former U.S.S.R. None of them are highly industrialized, Protestant countries. All of them make a virtue of large family size or else limit access to birth control.

In most Protestant industrial countries, fertility rates hover around 1.5 children per woman. A continuing decline in fertility will leave Europe's population with a growth of only 6 percent between 1985 and 2025, while the whole world's population will nearly double. As a result of low fertility, by 2025 one in every five Europeans will be 65 or older. And, not to be outdone, Japan's fertility rate has dropped annually from a level of 2.14 in 1973 down to 1.57 in 1989, the lowest ever recorded there.

We can give several reasons for these recent fertility declines. Yet, as before, we are hard-pressed to assign priority to one or another factor. For example, women have been taking advantage of more access to education and employment. Largely for this reason, they have delayed marrying. When people delay marriage, they are less likely to ever marry and also, if married, likely to produce fewer children.

At the same time the costs of raising children, both economic and psychic, have risen in this century. Children are particularly expensive if they need (paid) care by someone other than the (working) mother. As well, they remain in a state of economic dependency for longer than in the past. Finally, government benefits aside, children contribute little or nothing to the family's economic well-being.

But the most important factor here is technological. During the 1960s, safe, reliable contraception became easily available to women. The first demographic transition was accomplished through a combination of unenviable strategies. They included late marriage, abstinence from sex, awkward methods of birth control, and dangerous, even illegal abortion. The second demographic transition has occurred in the midst of a liberalizing sexual revolution and new means of contraception.

Thanks to the new technology, more and more women are able to choose if and when to become parents. As a result, in the last 20 years, we have seen an overall decrease in the numbers of children born to women aged 30 and over, but an increase in first births among these same women (Grindstaff, 1984). This change reflects the planned delay of childbearing.

Women are extending their education, entering careers, and postponing marriage and/or childbearing to do so. Many are not ready to begin parenthood before their thirties and few are willing to take a lot of time off work to do so. The result: a late, brief explosion of births among women who, by world standards, are "old" first parents.

There has also been a growth in the rate of childlessness in some Western countries. A small number of childless couples are desperately eager to make use of new reproductive technology or to adopt a child. But most of them do not subscribe to the traditional goals of childbearing, or to the traditional value of pride and achievement in raising a child. In short, parents think about their children in different ways today.

At the same time, we find a dramatic rise in the rate of births to unmarried women, many of whom are still teenagers. This growth is evident in North America and parts of Europe. Teen pregnancy is rare in Sweden where childbearing among women below age 18 has almost disappeared (Hoem, 1988: 22). By contrast, the United States has the highest rate of unmarried teen pregnancy in the world.

In part, the rise in such teen births is due to an increase in the number of single teenagers. However, it mostly reflects a growing acceptance of unmarried pregnancy and single motherhood and a much smaller incidence of "shotgun marriages" or babies being given up for adoption. Some believe that the greater economic and social supports available to single mothers—AFDC, food stamps, Medicaid—also contribute to the rise. However, entitlement criteria for such benefits were tightened in the 1980s, yet teen pregnancy rates continued to rise.

Comparative research by a team at Princeton University led by Elise Jones (Jones et al., 1987) offers better explanations. Nowhere, they argue, are teenagers sent such mixed messages about sexuality as in the United States. The media bombard us all with urgent messages about the thrill of sexual love. Yet religious fundamentalists make it difficult for governments and public schools to provide children with information and contraceptive devices that would prevent unwanted pregnancies. Last but not least, for an impoverished underclass of young American women, early parenthood seems as reasonable as any other action they can imagine.

It is not only preventive techniques of contraception that have improved in the last thirty years. Sterilization and abortion also play important roles in fertility reduction today. Overall, abortions have had less impact on the American fertility rate than contraceptives (pills, condoms, and the like). However, the same is not true everywhere. For example, in Eastern Europe legal abortions have had more "fertility inhibiting" effects than almost anywhere else. In fact, Eastern European women average 1 to 2.5 legal abortions in their lifetime, in contrast to .2 and .6 in other parts of Europe.

In large part that is because contraceptive devices are scarce in Eastern

Europe. The average woman in the former Soviet Union and Rumania in the mid-1960s would have had seven abortions during her lifetime. Van de Kaa (1987) notes the dramatic rise in third and higher-order births after the repeal of legal abortion legislation in Rumania. What this shows is that abortion had been playing a large role in suppressing fertility, where other means were unavailable. Once abortion was ruled out, people abandoned their babies to the care of the state. The net result, as we learned later, was a huge number of Rumanian babies and children crammed into what were euphemistically called "orphanages."

Though less dramatic, easier access to legal abortion has also influenced fertility in the West (Krannich, 1990). Up to the 1890s, abortion was tolerated in many jurisdictions. Women who wanted to end their pregnancies could do so with the assistance of surgeons, herbalists, or midwives. Abortion was in fact legal in most American states until the 1890s. Then it became illegal for 70 years as a result of pressure exerted by social purity movements. Legalizing abortion once again made the process safer. The (legal) abortion rate rose briefly after the mid-1960s, with a more liberal interpretation of the laws, but the rate soon tapered off (Krannich, 1990: 368).

The most important factor promoting a decline in the incidence of abortion is the use of contraception, which avoids unwanted pregnancies to begin with. As in so many areas of life, preventing problems is easier, safer, and surer than remedying them. So as contraceptive knowledge and use have spread, abortion has become a less often relied-upon means of limiting fertility.

This revolution in birth control has had profound effects on relations between women and men. Before effective antibiotics and birth control methods existed, there was a strong prohibition on male-female relationships outside of marriage. People were afraid they would culminate in sexual intercourse, loss of a young woman's virginity, or even pregnancy or killer venereal diseases such as syphilis.

Where sexual purity was an issue, a double standard has always been applied. Moreover, prohibition was enforced more or less strongly in different times and places. There have always been people who broke the rule. More than that, the Victorian era is notorious for the gulf between its rigid official morality and its tacit acceptance of brothels, the sexual abuse of female servants, and large-scale street prostitution. However, as "birth control techniques became more reliable, and more widely disseminated, the strong prohibitions against sexual experimentation began to diminish" (Whicker and Kronenfeld, 1986: 67).

As the discussion to this point implies, changes in fertility, family size, and contraception have been key parts of the puzzle of family change. Another big part is women's economic independence. Indeed, it would not be an exaggeration to say that families changed dramatically as women (1) were able to control their childbearing and (2) were able to support themselves economically.

Attitude change has also had a lot to do with changing patterns of intimacy. Today, the norms against nonmarital sexuality are a lot more relaxed. In some groups, people expect sex on a first or second date. In any event, most people today view sex as a lifestyle choice, not a matter of childbearing or morality. We have seen a return to more caution in the 1990s, because of fears about HIV/AIDS. There is also a growing awareness of "safe sex" through the use of condoms. People's sexual concerns today are mainly practical, not ethical. The sexual double standard is still with us, but in a weakened form. We are unlikely to see a return to the hypocritical "purity" of earlier generations.

Cohabitation too has lost its stigma. Cohabitation, or common-law marriage, is a less stable form of union than legal marriage. For example, one study shows that women who cohabit premaritally for more than three years have higher divorce rates after marriage than women who cohabit for shorter durations.

Nevertheless, cohabitation attracts many people. It has many of the benefits of marriage without the same expectation of permanence and without as many legally binding obligations. It gives people many of the expected benefits of family life—emotional and sexual satisfaction, mutual dependency and support, for example—while retaining at least the illusion of choice and freedom. Some cohabiting relationships even produce children. The old stigma of illegitimacy, or birth out of wedlock, is largely gone, particularly when the parents are in a stable cohabiting relationship. No wonder the numbers of births out of wedlock have skyrocketed.

Remember too that not all marriages preceded by a period of cohabitation will end in divorce. If cohabitation is trial marriage, you might think that the longer the cohabitation period, the more stable the subsequent marriage. However, the evidence is that there is not much difference in divorce rates between women who had previously cohabited one year, two years, or three years. Not surprisingly, the birth of a first child within the marriage stabilizes the relationship, reducing the chance of a divorce.

Most important, people who cohabit are different from people who do not cohabit. Evidence shows that people who are willing to cohabit are also divorce-prone. If so, it is not cohabitation that causes divorce. It is the self-selection of divorce-prone people into cohabitation which creates the connection we have observed.

It may even be purely coincidental that the growth of cohabitation has coincided with later marriage, higher divorce rates, and lower rates of childbearing. More and more often, people think of spousal relations as being about love and sex, not childbearing. People have come to expect more satisfaction of their emotional and psychological needs in their relationships. Women, particularly, are less economically dependent on their partners. These shifting norms and opportunities have all contributed to a decline in the stability of married life.

Sweden

Sweden is the most extreme example of the package of changes we are discussing (Popenoe, 1987: 173). It has the lowest marriage rate and highest rate of nonmarital cohabitation (25 percent) in the industrial world. Fully 98 percent of marriages in Sweden begin with cohabitation, so that our "traditional" pattern of marriage first, then co-residence, is deviant by Swedish standards.

Sweden also has the highest proportion of single-person households. There, single living is a widely accepted part of the normal life cycle and a normal transition from one relationship to another. Nevertheless, Swedes continue to support the idea of a "nuclear family" and most people spend the largest part of their adult lives in a spousal union, not alone or cohabiting.

In 1984, 45 percent of Swedish children were born to unmarried women but the majority of these women were living with their partners. Few were single parents. Because cohabiting is socially (and legally) accepted, "having children is no longer much of an incentive to get married" (Popenoe, 1987: 176). At the same time, Sweden's divorce rate is the second highest in the industrial world, after the United States. In fact, because many cohabiting relationships end in separation, Sweden actually has the highest rate of family dissolution.

The Swedish example illustrates at least three important points. First, it shows what the second demographic transition looks like in full flight. Second, it shows that no element of the second demographic transition—whether easier sexuality, more cohabitation, or more working women—spells the end of marriage, parenthood, or family life. As we have said, the family changes its forms. However, the functions of family life—companionship, love, sex, and the like—continue to remain important to most adults.

Third, the Swedish example shows that we are dealing with a package of social, cultural, and economic changes in family life. It is almost impossible to say which change is *the ultimate cause* of all the changes. Nor can we separate this package of changes from changes in the entire fabric of modern society.

THE GOOD NEWS

So far, we have only talked about "changes." But are these good changes or bad ones? What aspects of family life have improved and what aspects have worsened in the last half of the twentieth century? This is what most people wonder when they think about the future of the family.

The good news is that people have gained more choice in their personal lives and this trend is likely to continue. At the most basic level, more people today can choose if, who, and when to marry. There is less pressure to marry, and less, if any, stigma to living alone or cohabiting. Choosing not to marry does not prevent people from being sexually active, or indeed from becoming parents. As a society, we are far more willing to accept a range of possible living arrangements than people a generation ago.

The relationship between marriage, mothering, and paid employment has changed dramatically for women. Though still imperfect, these changes give women more choices than ever before. Feminists argue that Western societies remain patriarchal, meaning that men continue to dominate male-female relations, particularly within families and households. Yet marriages are more equalitarian in the 1990s than they were in the 1950s. North American women have equal access to education and face less discrimination in the labor force than ever before. Husbands no longer have legal authority over their wives. And in attitude surveys, wives and husbands claim they make important decisions jointly.

This is *not* to say that all or even most families today enjoy an equal distribution of power. To a degree, the growth of spousal equality reflects the growth of an ideal more than a change in practice. For example, time-budget studies show that women still do the lion's share of household work, whether they work for pay or not. Yet the trend is towards more balanced relations.

In the past, some young people had a lot of freedom in the choice of a marriage partner. In practice they had few chances to meet people outside of their own community. They married someone of the same class, ethnic origin, and religious background—a circumstance sociologists call *homogamy*. But it is likely that with the increase in rates of higher education, more people are marrying outside their social class as well.

In the last generation in North America, rates of ethnic exogamy, or intermarriage, have also risen, though the incidence is still low (Richard, 1992). Finally, religious intermarriage has also become more common (Nagnur and Adams, 1987). On the other hand, this process is far from complete. Despite the general secularization of Western societies and the de-ritualization of social life, religious marriages continue to be common.

For example, the Canadian province of Quebec used to be predominantly Catholic and was comparable to Ireland in the degree to which social life was controlled by the church. In Quebec social life secularized rapidly in the 1960s. By 1990, contraception and abortion were widely practiced, almost one in two first births were to an unmarried woman, and Quebec had the highest incidence of common-law unions among all Canadian provinces.

Yet in 1985, 75 percent of legal marriages in Quebec were still performed by a religious minister (Baillargeon, 1987). Surprisingly, religious marriages are less common among older persons and Francophones, perhaps because of the Catholic church's refusal to perform remarriages after divorce. And, despite the popularity of cohabitation, more than 85 percent of young brides and grooms choose religious marriages. So religion continues to be a factor in marriage, though less important than in the past.

To the extent that people's choices are limited, they are often self-limited. For example, the vast majority of people continue to see the decision to marry as a decision to commit themselves to one sexual partner. As Andrew Greeley (1990, 1991) has argued, we find a continued growth in the variety and acceptance of spousal forms, yet we find no decrease in the strength of feelings towards exclusive intimacy within a spousal relationship.

People also choose marriage from among a wider variety of alternatives. It is unlikely that legal marriage will be the only form intimacy will take in the future, but neither is marriage likely to die out. People have more choice about when to marry—early or late—or whether to marry at all. (Even *relative* age matters less than it did in the past. Men are more likely to marry women of their own age, or even older women, instead of sticking to the traditional pattern of becoming established in a career and then finding a younger woman.)

Young people today have high rates of cohabitation before marriage. Among members of the older generation, cohabitation with a new partner is common after widowhood or divorce. People also have more choice about when to become parents or whether to parent at all.

Despite all this new freedom, parents still support their children, both when they are small and when they are struggling to establish themselves as independent adults. Adult children also support their aged parents and relatives, often at the same time as they bring up their own children. Even in prosperous North America, with its strong norms about the independence of nuclear family households, family crises or economic downturns can bring relatives together. This can even mean living in temporarily crowded multigenerational family households, if it remains financially prudent to do so. Such situations may arise after a marriage breaks up, in order to care for aging parents, or because children cannot afford to set up a separate household.

The new approach to choice even allows for previously taboo lifestyles such as open homosexuality. Today there is more social acceptance of homosexuality, and even same-sex marriages. Having said that, we should beware of assuming a linear trend to greater tolerance. Recent evidence from the U.S. General Social Survey shows a definite decline among young adults in the acceptance of homosexuality. So where homosexuality is concerned, there may be many battles ahead before acceptance is complete and same-sex couples enjoy the same status as heterosexual ones.

THE BAD NEWS

So far, many of the changes we have described sound pretty good. But in social life there is never good news without some accompanying bad news. That is because in any social system, changes to one part—even if intended and planned—normally produce changes to another part that may be unintended, unplanned, and even unwanted.

Where the family is concerned, the "bad news" concerns people with the least choice and least power. It relates mostly to the consequences of taking family protection away from the weak without replacing it with anything else.

For all its faults, the traditional nuclear family provided a measure of economic security for children. It even provided security for wives who, because of their limited or interrupted work experience, had little chance of economic independence. Today, despite all the new choices people enjoy, we continue to have an occupational structure that assumes each employee will have a homemaker to provide support. We continue to suppose that children will have parents who care for them and are able to earn an adequate living.

But what if these assumptions are wrong? The answer is that families will work badly and people will be hurt. Consider the consequences of the second demographic transition, such as the neglect of children in families where both parents work full time. And consider the high rates of child poverty in single-parent families as well as in many two-parent families. By traditional standards, these things were not supposed to happen in "real families." If they did happen, this meant that family life had broken down.

Family violence is another part of the bad news we must consider. As many as one in four American women will have suffered some sort of violent treatment from a sexual partner, at least once in their lives. Such conjugal violence is found in all sections of the population, at all socioeconomic levels, educational levels, types of religious, racial or ethnic group. Only a few studies have been carried out to estimate the psychological consequences of such violence. A Toronto study done in the early 1990s (Turner et al., 1993) showed that women's history of physical abuse by a current or recent spouse is associated with an increased risk of clinical depression in the past year.

Many types of personal harm became more common during the 1970s and 1980s. According to the General Social Survey (Niemi et al., 1989), child poverty, fear of crime, spousal violence, accusations of incestuous assault, and unemployment all increased in the United States over the same period.

But did the changes in family life we have been discussing cause these increases in personal danger and harm? And even if we think they did, should we support social policies that try to strengthen the traditional family? Even if that means discouraging cohabitation before marriage, encouraging childbearing by married women, making divorce more difficult, making it harder for mothers of young children to work outside the home, or penalizing homosexuality?

Thinking this way is illogical. You may disapprove of spousal violence and you may disapprove of divorce, and both have become more common over the last few years. But that doesn't prove one has caused the other. We have no reason to think that banning divorce will reduce the incidence of spousal violence, for example. The opposite is probably true.

Given the social changes we have discussed, there may be no policies we can make that will bring the traditional family back to life. There are only policies that will weaken or strengthen new forms of families.

So, instead of starting out with things we do not like and assuming they are due to changes in the family, it is more sensible to take family changes that are occurring and ask what consequences we would *like them to have*. This involves stating our goals explicitly, and we will do so in due course.

WHAT'S TO COME

In this chapter, we have reviewed the major family changes that have taken place since 1940 (and before). All of these changes are symptoms of the exercise of choice. They show women choosing whether and when to bear children, one or both partners in a relationship choosing to end it, and so on. It is unlikely we can escape from the "new family life" without giving up *choice*.

Understanding the changing structure of families today is the basis for making informed predictions about the future. To a large extent this means using our knowledge of trends to challenge old assumptions about family life. Our purpose is to assess these trends by placing them in historical context and comparing Western families to families around the world. We ask, what is the shape of change, and what does history suggest about the future of family life in North America?

Given recent trends, will families continue to survive in their present form? Or will they survive in forms that are varied and somewhat unfamiliar, but in forms that will be eventually accepted, both culturally and economically?

We will want to find out if there is any society that has taken the lead in preparing for, and helping families to change. If so, what society is it and what, if anything, can we learn from that society? And if we follow its lead, must we become like that society in every respect, good and bad? That may be inevitable if the new kinds of families have particular social and psychological, as well as economic, needs.

If we do *not* follow that society's lead, what kinds of families can we expect to appear in our own society? Will there be as many impoverished and socially vulnerable families as there are today? Will frustration and violence continue to be common problems of modern family life?

Can we even assume that the family will remain with us in the future, and if so, why? And if the family remains with us, can we hope to have the peaceful, loving family lives that we like to imagine? Or are current family problems a result of economic, social, political, and cultural trends of the last few centuries and, in that sense, inevitable?

Will there be an end to the finger-pointing and stigmatizing that still accompanies many kinds of personal life—behavior which prevents us from finding solutions together? Or will we continue to penalize children for the choices (and nonchoices) of their parents, and neglect society's most vulnerable members—women, elderly people, and racial minorities among them?

If we come to accept many kinds of family life in the future, will they be like families of the past? Or are we embarking on a new stage of human family life? Will we ever find, within families, the ways to increase both our personal autonomy and the emotional support we require? That is, will families come to empower us—all of us, men, women, and children? Or is family life by its nature a zero-sum game in which, if some people gain autonomy, other people must suffer emotional or economic loss?

In this book we will look at historical changes, cross-cultural differences, current Western patterns, and predictions for the future. All the while we will be asking, "What are the impacts on spousal relationships and how have parent-child relationships changed?"

It is likely that people will continue to marry and divorce. Adults of both sexes will want (or need) gainful employment and people will seek more control over their personal lives. If our thinking is correct, this may also mean a continuing growth of social isolation, poverty, and domestic violence, *unless* certain steps are taken to change the prevailing pattern. We shall have more to say about this in the last chapters of the book.

At the least, positive changes will mean we shall all have to adjust our ways of thinking about "the family." And in fact, we are doing just that all the time. We—the authors—believe that family life is, on balance, getting better. For example, it is better to have low infant mortality than high infant mortality, and a high life expectancy than a low one. It is also better to be legally a person than not, to be married to a spouse who is legally a person than to one who is not, to make family decisions in an open manner and base a family on freedom, not constraint.

And like Ellwood (1987: 3,4), we believe that "absent parents should share their income and assets with their children." Further, "people who are already doing as much work as society deems acceptable ought to be able to support their families at or above the poverty level without relying on welfare or welfare-like supports."

In the next two chapters, we explore the extent to which the changes we have described here are specific to Western families in the late twentieth century. To do this we look at family life over time and across cultures. In this way, Chapters Two and Three put our current preoccupations about family instability into historical and comparative contexts.

Chapters Four and Five focus on spousal relationships, and Chapters Six and Seven on parent-child relationships. In each we examine the evidence of change in greater detail than we have in this opening chapter. In Chapter Eight, we examine forecasts and predictions about the future of family life. In closing, we consider solutions to current and predicted problems of family life.

HISTORICAL
AND CROSS-CULTURAL
COMPARISONS

INTRODUCTION

People who see a decline in modern family life often cite studies of other societies which are thought to have had better family lives. In this chapter, we make our own foray into the historical and anthropological literature in search of "the good old days."

We start 500 years ago, around the end of the European Middle Ages, at the height of the Turkish and Chinese Empires. Then, large parts of Asia and Africa and all of the Americas were still largely undisturbed by European contact. We know something of family life in ancient Egypt, Israel, and Rome. However, this knowledge is fragmentary, often telling us the way things were supposed to be, not what people actually did. Despite the best efforts of archaeologists and historians, there are many ancient civilizations for which we have nothing better than "conjectural history" about kinship and family relations.

Comparative work on the family has followed one of two main paths. Some researchers have taken a cross-national approach, comparing family lives in different cultures at the same point in time. Others have used historical data to examine changes in the family. Both approaches face the same methodological problem: namely, the difficulty of assessing a given time or place on its own terms. When studying other times and places, it is hard to steer a sensible path between diffuse relativism on the one hand and an ethnocentric bias on the other.

Diffuse relativism is a willingness to believe informants' versions of family arrangements. It accepts as valid any system that seems to "work" in the society concerned. *Ethnocentric bias* on the other hand is a readiness to judge all other societies in terms of one's own values, be they Christian, evolutionary, feminist, patriarchal, or otherwise.

Of the two, ethnocentric bias is the more common failing. In fact, Walter (1989) finds it easy to show an ethnocentric bias in many well-known social histories of the Western family. Instead of trying to understand historical families on their own terms, many researchers have judged them by present-day standards. That's what the Victorians did 100 years ago. For example, commentators in that period described polygamy (several wives for one husband) or polyandry (several husbands for one wife) as forerunners of the monogamy rule.

Today, we know better. Fieldworkers like Nancy Levine who have lived in polyandrous societies report that after a few days, the local way of doing things seems perfectly natural and the same is true for polygamous societies (Levine, 1992).

People with an ethnocentric bias place an idealized version of current Western marital standards at the forefront of their comparison. That is why, in the 1950s, some researchers described women who worked for pay as exceptions to the rule of the non-working (read "nonpaid") housewife.

To take a contentious example, the practice of "female circumcision" is common in many central African countries (Boddy, 1989). It not only deprives women of sexual pleasure but is obviously harmful. Relativists would accept as valid the view that this activity is a form of purification. An ethnocentric viewpoint, on the other hand, would focus on the physical harm the practice of genital mutilation does and ignore its ritual meaning. The habit of judging other societies, however well-justified and widely supported in North America, carries its own problems, but so does a failure to make moral judgments.

Throughout this book we will be looking at changes in family life while trying to avoid or at least balance our biases. We will be asking how North American families differ outwardly from families in other cultures, both past and present. First, we will be asking whether families are smaller, more fragmented, and more complex now than in the past. Second, we will be asking how families differ in emotional content from earlier families.

Do people feel the same ways about their spouses and children as they used to, for example? Questions like this are the hardest to answer, because often the data we need are sketchy or nonexistent. To answer them we will have to make inferences from data fragments collected by historians and cultural anthropologists. Still, this kind of detective work has led to a large body of interesting conclusions about marriage and parent-child relations in the past.

HISTORICAL PATTERNS OF FAMILY CHANGE

How do families work in different societies? What do people expect of them? On what terms do people judge them successful or unsuccessful?

While answering such questions we must remember that the vast majority of people who ever lived have farmed the earth, herded animals, hunted, fished, or harvested wild plants. In such economies, all activities are highly gendered: women do one thing and men another. As well, children and the elderly always have a place. Since an extra pair of hands is always useful somewhere, training in economically productive activities starts at an early age.

In these societies, kinship relations are very important. Families die out if no children survive and none can be adopted. Families succeed by multiplying and prospering, increasing the number of cows or camels or sheep, or improving the yield of rice, wheat, millet, or sorghum in their fields. While romantic love is known, people seek happiness collectively, if they consciously seek it at all. Personal freedom and happiness are not the main aims of family life.

Indeed it may be difficult to even explain our notions of "freedom" to people in many other societies. There, we find far more ideas about property than ideas about freedom and happiness. Virtually all societies have customs regulating the ownership of animals, the use of certain areas of land, the right to harvest wild plants in a given location, and the practice of certain trades. Tellingly, these rules are often defined for families, clans, or descent groups, not for individuals per se.

As children reach adulthood, they can inherit property under certain conditions, not others. And when young adults marry into another family group, they take limited property rights with them. They also take on rights and duties as part of the family they marry into.

The most familiar example of such a traditional culture is ancient Israel, as described in the Old Testament. Have you ever wondered why the Old Testament contains such long genealogies, full of people begetting other people? It is because these genealogies establish the membership of descent groups. This is enormously important, since kinship is what justifies people's claims to land ownership, and land ownership is the means of survival.

Indeed, for *all* families which have property rights in land or another common asset, issues of kinship are critically important. They include rights to choose a marriage partner, whether or not divorce is permitted, rules about remarriage after widowhood or divorce, the adoption of potential heirs, and the legitimacy of children. All of these issues affect people's position in a hierarchy of rights—the position of the family in the community and the individual within the family. They all affect people's ability to participate in the society's economic activities.

Accordingly, people with less property to pass on treat kinship, marriage, and legitimacy rules less seriously. Often, they imitate the behavior of richer families. They may hope that by engaging in the propertied class's behavior, they may increase their chances of upward mobility through marriage. In these societies, as in our own, there is often more similarity between the behaviors of the poor (who have nothing to lose) and the rich (who will never lose anything) than between either and the earnest middling class of peasants and workers.

Now, a definition: A *kinship group* is a group of people who recognize a blood relationship and have positions in a hierarchy of rights over the property. As we mentioned above, this often consists of rights to cultivate land or to manage herds of animals.

KINSHIP, CLAN, AND COMMUNITY

What counts as a kinship relationship varies from one society to another. This is important, for kinship determines which of your relatives count as being useful to you. Kinship relationships may also determine who you can marry, where you are to live, and the degree to which women or men specialize in child rearing and "kin-keeping" activities.

Logically speaking, there are only so many possibilities. Some societies count relationships through the male line, so that who you are is determined by who your father is; we call such kinship systems *patrilineal*. Others count relationships through the female line and use expressions such as "coming from the same womb"; they are *matrilineal* systems. Others still count relationships through both lines; they are *bilateral* kinship systems.

If the kinship system is patrilineal, a person (of either sex) gains a position in the community just by being the child of his or her *father*. In a matrilineal kinship system, on the other hand, a person has certain property rights because of being the child of his or her *mother*. However, remember that the kinship system is independent of which sex holds more authority in society. Men can be the dominant sex even in a matrilineal society. In this case, the person whose kinship link is most important to a child is not the biological father. It is the mother's brother, as among the Ashanti in West Africa or a number of American Indian societies.

Because this is unfamiliar to us, it sounds complicated. An example may help to clarify how the system actually works. The Huron measure descent through the female line. Their system is matrilineal and a person's clan membership is reckoned through his or her mother. These matrilineal clans are *exogamous*, meaning you must marry someone from another clan. Even distant relatives on your mother's side of the family are off-limits.

Most married couples live close to the wife's mother's kin, and at one time they lived in group residences called *long houses*. Each long house would contain several nuclear families, these families being linked to each other because sisters or female cousins were the women of those families, while their male partners were from a different clan or clans. Men might still have held the power in such societies. However, many scholars have argued that the combination of matriliny and matrilocality empowers women or, at least, limits the possibilities for male dominance.

As anthropologists would say, the Huron are *matrilineal* and *matrilocal*. That does not mean they are *matriarchal*, but Huron women *are* often prominent in decision making.

Because of the clan exogamy rule, a person's kin will belong to different clans. Thus, the Huron have names to distinguish a person's relatives on the mother's side from those on the father's side. The children of a person's mother's brother and of a father's sister are classified as his or her *cross-cousins*. The children of a person's mother's sister and of a father's brother are classified as sisters and brothers (Anderson, 1982: 116; Buchler and Selby, 1968).

This kind of kinship system is also common among the peoples of Central and West Africa. As in other matrilineal societies, family property can only be inherited from the mother's side of the family. In the Ashanti tribe, for example, it is better to have a rich mother than a rich father. That is because a father's wealth goes to his sisters' children; a mother's wealth goes to her own children.

Westerners (Western Europeans and North Americans) have no special words to distinguish kin on the father's side from kin on the mother's side. For emotional purposes, it does not matter whether a first cousin, uncle, or aunt is on the mother's or father's side. However, the system is biased towards patrilineality. For example, a woman has historically taken her husband's family name, not the reverse, and this name has been passed on to the children. Also in the Western pattern, property has often been inherited in the male line. Likewise, where families settle down is usually determined by the husband's job, not the wife's.

In these terms, the kinship system of the United States can be described as mildly patrilineal. However, it also has certain *matrifocal* characteristics. Because women have been defined as the primary kin-keepers, children have stronger ties with their mothers' kin than with those of their fathers (Rosenthal, 1985; Thomson and Li, 1992: 15).

In any event, bilaterality does not mean that European systems are, or were, without strong kinship sentiments. Among Scottish clans, for example, a Macdonald woman who married a Stuart man would become attached to the Stuart clan. Her daughters would be Stuarts, with a weak connection to the Macdonalds. If a blood feud broke out between the two clans, they would side with the Stuarts, however regretfully. Similar clan systems, with well-developed rules about alliances during a blood feud, have been found in Iceland, the mountains of Albania, Papua New Guinea, and other parts of the world.

Even at the best of times, these rules produce conflicts. That is because in many such kinship systems the marriage rules are exogamous. People marry outside the kinship group, even into families with whom hostilities may arise. In such cases, the local people may wryly inform anthropologists, "We marry our enemies." Such marital alliances provide the basis by which different kin groups can unify against a common enemy, should one emerge. But people may also find their loyalties to spouse's kin and their own kin tested by a conflict between the two groups.

The basic relationships of a nuclear family—spouse-to-spouse and parent-to-child—still exist within such kinship groups. However, they are less important than in our own society. By contrast, relations with cousins, uncles, and siblings are *more* important than in our society. That is because more of these kin live close by, even if not in the same household.

As we mentioned, in most agrarian societies kinship relations have an enormous importance because they determine a person's access to economic assets such as cultivation rights. So in these societies, the kinship group's approval or disapproval exercises a strong control over people's behavior.

As agriculture becomes less important, so does the kin group. Over time, "kin life" shades into "family life" as we know it. An important example of this is what the nineteenth-century sociologist Frederic Le Play called the *stem family*. Over the centuries, the stem family maintains a small farm as a family-run enterprise, and only one of the children inherits ownership. The rest move out upon marriage or remain unmarried. At points in the family life cycle, several generations of the family may be living under the same roof. At other times, they are off on their own.

Most cultures have a saying equivalent to, "Many hands make light work" and peasant families have traditionally borne large numbers of children. Many commentators, Le Play among them, have believed that big families are happy families. They have also believed that complex family households are a symbol of success and an ideal to strive for.

Le Play, for example, believed in the virtues of the European "stem" or "extended" family, and described the "ideal typical" household of such a family as follows:

> The heir and his wife, aged 25 and 20; the father and mother, the heads of the household, married for 27 years and now aged 52 and 47; a grandfather aged 80; two unmarried kinsfolk—brothers or sisters of the head of the family; nine children, of whom the eldest are nearly as old as the brother who is the heir; and the youngest is a baby, often still at the breast; finally, two servants living on terms of complete equality with the other members of the family (cited in Flandrin, 1979: 52).

Though an ideal, this type of household was probably attained only rarely. Only rich (and lucky) families looked like this. As Pierre Bourdieu's field research in the Béarn district, between France and Spain has shown, stem family households were only possible under certain conditions. These included high fertility together with cultural and legal norms that emphasized farm inheritance by the eldest son and discouraged the marriage of younger siblings (Flandrin, 1979: 74–5).

In rural European communities of the Middle Ages, a wealthy man might have a large number of relatives, servants, and apprentices living in his household. In general, the richer the household, the larger it was. From this perspective, Berkner (1975: 734) argues that if cottagers living in nuclear family households had been rich, "they would have lived in stem families like the landed peasants because they would have had property to transmit to an heir and would have been able to retire by controlling the terms of the transfer."

But for the most part, peasants remained poor, died young, and lived out their lives in nuclear families like our own (in size and composition). People may have dreamed of spending their declining years as patriarch or matriarch of a large family, basking in power and prestige. But whatever people's ideals, most nuclear families never combined to form stem families.

COMPLEX FAMILIES AND NUCLEAR FAMILIES

Today as in the past, family households may be large because there are many children, or because grandparents, uncles, aunts, or cousins live in the same household as the parents and children who form the nuclear family. However it comes about, this kind of household is called a *complex* family household. How common are such large, complex households as compared to the smaller, simpler nuclear family?

Past and Present

Marriage in the past was based on economic cooperation between a man and woman and their kin. As well, people would marry to "raise economically valuable children" who would help support them in adulthood or old age (op. cit.: 655). High rates of fertility provided three main benefits: old-age support by children, child labor, and insurance against the risks of sickness and early death.

Of course, in some kinds of societies marriage may fulfill other social functions as well. For example, it may create political alliances between families or bestow status when a man shows he can support numerous wives. But none of this applies in "modern" societies.

Two chief forces have led to a restructuring of family ties and a redefinition of the family in modern times; they are industrialization and urbanization. Both processes have had the effect of transferring the production of goods and services from the family to the market. In this way they have decreased the importance of the family as an economic unit of production.

We see this mirrored in changes to the way people choose their mates around the world. Everywhere, young people have more say in choosing a mate. This change has been largely due to the development of a cash economy, which gives children more independence from their parents. When people are paying their own bills and don't have to wait to inherit the family farm, they can marry who they wish. Unlike a rural agricultural economy, an urban, industrial economy lets young people earn an income, pay their own bills, and choose their own mates.

This basic change has had revolutionary consequences. In short, it has individualized people's lives. Over the past few centuries, more and more people have come to define themselves as distinct from the families of which they are a part. They have developed needs and desires that often conflict with those of other family members. The decline of the family as a corporate group—a group that can control people's incomes—has meant the emergence of needs of individual members that may conflict dramatically. It is no longer true that what is good for the family as a whole is good for each of its members.

Looking backward, changes like these now seem inevitable. Not only have they liberated the individual from the family, they have also liberated the nuclear family from the extended family. But is it true, as some theories say, that the Industrial Revolution destroyed a system of extended families and put the nuclear family in its place?

Laslett (1965, 1971, 1983) and others in the Cambridge Group for the Study of Population and Social Structure have tested this hypothesis and found it wanting. In England at least, nuclear families were widespread long before the Industrial Revolution. Indeed, extended families were relatively rare. While poor peasants often had many children, they lived in modest single-room households. Only the wealthy could afford large households full of family members and servants.

• Other research suggests different factors at work. For example, Finlay et al. (1982) suggest that urbanization has had more of an effect on the spread of nuclear families than industrialization. These researchers compared households in rural and urban northern Florida during an early phase of industrial development (around 1885). They found that "At any one time, the percentage of extended households in a cross-sectional sample might be quite low, even if all families go through an extended phase" (Finlay et al., 1982: 49).

This makes perfect sense. The dominant form of family life in preindustrial (preurban) times was extended or at least proto-extended (to coin a word) because a majority of people lived in rural areas. Rural households are more likely to contain larger, extended families because they work a piece of land together. Stem families keep intact lands that are not easily divided. Typically, rural property (land rights, cattle, goats, camels, the farm cottage, the watermill) is much harder to divide up than urban property (bank accounts, stocks, business assets, and so on). So city life can be lived in small, separate families.

Whether the key factor is urbanization or industrialization, we find the same kinds of families in all urban, industrial societies. Despite cross-national variations, North American families today are very much like families we would find in modern Sweden, Germany, or Italy, for example. Given the range of variation we see in families throughout the world, the variation among families in industrial countries is relatively small. So strong are the similarities that sociologists find it useful to identify a characteristic pattern and label it the *Western Family*.

In the Western Family, a couple typically falls in love, marries, establishes its own household, and raises children. This is all in sharp contrast to the pattern we see in many parts of the world where marriages are arranged and families live in extended family households. There, love is recognized as a disruptive passion that often leads to adultery or to inappropriate marriages, thus interfering with the family's plans for increasing property and transmitting it to the next generation. In arranged marriages, love may develop over time, but that is not the primary objective.

With the passage of time, the Western Family pattern has come to prevail. Studies of family life around the world show that people have more and more control over who they will marry and where they will live (for a variety of articles on this, see Tepperman and Wilson, 1993). This growing similarity of families around the world is usually referred to as *convergence* and discussions of convergence date back 40 years or more.

For example, Goode (1956, 1963) argued that the wide variety of systems of kinship, marriage, and household organization known to anthropologists and historians would, eventually, converge on a single pattern: the nuclear family household. The economic and social forces driving this transformation are urbanization and the shift from agricultural to industrial production, as we stated earlier.

Looking backward, Goode turns out to have been half right. He failed to foresee the rise of individualism and other elements of the second demographic transition. This means he also failed to foresee changes in the traditional North American and European family: especially, that role-differentiated two-parent families would lose their numerical majority (and stranglehold on cultural views about family life).

In short, we have to appreciate how complex is the weave of causes and effects of change in family life. All of the trends we have mentioned—in marriage, cohabitation, divorce, childbearing, and women's work—occur against a backdrop of even *larger* social trends. There is no understanding family change without understanding urbanization and the decline of agriculture, the rise of service industries and the opening up of varied public roles for women, the extension of formal education and the improvement of birth control technology.

The Rise of Nuclear Families

We can see the complexity of these changes by focusing on one particularly important change: namely, the rise of nuclear families. As we mentioned, Peter and his associates in Cambridge have tested the hypothesis that the Industrial Revolution destroyed a system of large, extended families and put small, nuclear families in their place (Laslett and Wall, 1992). Their data do not support this hypothesis, at least not in England for which it had originally been proposed.

In fact, the small nuclear family was common in England long before the Industrial Revolution. Historically, extended family households have been rarer than nineteenth-century scholars like Le Play had supposed.

But that is not to say complex families were entirely lacking before industrialization. Another type of complex family we should consider is the *joint family household* formed by a group of siblings and their families. Emmanual Todd (1985) has collected evidence which shows that the patrilineal joint family was dominant in Finland and central Italy before industrialization came to these areas.

In a *joint family*, all the sons are expected to marry and bring their wives to live in a family "compound"—a sort of agricultural version of the Kennedy family's summer place at Hyannisport, Massachusetts. Or, the daughters may marry and bring husbands to live with their kin. This was the practice among the Huron and Iroquois too, when joint families lived in long houses.

This practice creates a unilineal descent group, or clan, which may contain three or even four generations of the same family. Sometimes, the clan may be forced to split up into smaller units. They do so in a way that reminds us of the rules of Mennonite farm communities which divide up when they reach a critical population size.

The classic European example of family complexity is the eighteenth-century Serbian *zadruga*. Formed by a group of brothers and their wives and children, the zadruga was "an agnatic core which might include second degree patrilateral cousins and from ten to 100 members, operating as a joint-family corporation" (Hammel, 1971: 128). The group shared a residence, and produced and consumed together.

Historically, the zadruga may have arisen because it provided military defense against members of other ethnic groups in the region. It reached its height in the Middle Ages. However, the zadruga may *never* have been the most common form of family living in the region. Today it exists only as a national symbol of the way Serbians used to live in their days of past national glory. (We shall say more of the zadruga shortly.)

Leaving aside the exotic Serbian family, we even find evidence of large and complex households in the United States. For example, Sweet and Bumpass (1987: 168) have examined changes in the percentage of nonnuclear family households over this century. Overall, the trend was towards isolation of the nuclear family. Married-couple households included few relatives other than their sons or daughters. In 1900, just over one married-couple household in six had nonnuclear family relatives living in it. By 1980, this fraction had shrunk to one household in fourteen.

Such a pattern is by no means universal; consider the differences between black and white Americans. In 1900, more black couples than white couples had nonnuclear family relatives living with them. Between 1900 and 1940, this fraction increased from 21 percent to 25 percent. By 1980, it had declined to just over 15 percent. However, it was still twice as common for blacks as for American families as a whole.

We can explain this black/white difference in terms of the high rates of black migration during the twentieth century. Migrants often live with relatives, and this rise in the incidence of complex family households among blacks may have been due to the large-scale migration (rural to urban, and south to north) of blacks over this period (Lemann, 1991). Other ethnic groups in the 1980 census with many nonnuclear family relatives in the household included the Vietnamese (over 30 percent) and Filipinos (over 25 percent)—also recent migrant groups (Sweet and Bumpass, 1987: 169).

How did, and how do, people adjust to increases in their family size and complexity? In particular, how do they experience household population density and the erosion of their privacy? Do they feel crowded?

HOUSEHOLD SIZE, CROWDING, AND PRIVACY

The notion of "crowding" must be a recent idea in human history since, historically, most people have lived in dense conditions we would consider as a gross invasion of privacy.

For example, in the seventeenth and eighteenth centuries the vast majority of French urban households had only one or two rooms, and they provided space for both living *and* work activities. Under such conditions, it was necessary either to get rid of the children or learn to live with them in close proximity. Many families chose the first option.

Usually, the youngest children were put out to nurse and the adolescents were sent to serve apprenticeships. Children too old to nurse and too young to leave home "spent the day at school or in the street, and only returned to their parents' house to sleep" (Flandrin, 1979: 95–6).

Literary descriptions of seventeenth- and eighteenth-century French or English cottages usually mention only one room as being inhabited by people. The other rooms, if any, were reserved for animals. In fact, Anderson (1990: 57–8) reports that a large fraction of Scottish families lived in only one or two rooms until the early twentieth century. You can imagine how household crowding must have affected courtship in nineteenth-century Europe. Read Shorter's (1977: 40–1) description to see how this worked.

Besides too few rooms, households often contained nonfamily people. In the nineteenth and early twentieth centuries, even modest North American households contained one or more live-in servants (Katz, 1975). Lodgers were also common between 1880 and 1921 (Anderson, 1990; Bradbury, 1984).

How did we get to the currently accepted standards of privacy? One argument is that it was the social purity movement at the end of the nineteenth century which regarded the presence of lodgers as sexually dangerous and incompatible with their notion of a small, private, and intensely moral nuclear family (Katz, 1975: 305–6). In many cases, these were the same social activists—including many early feminists—who pressed for antiabortion laws and the prohibition of alcohol.

What is the most important difference between our own ideals and assumptions about family life and those that were held in past times? Michael Katz (1975: 313) argues that the main change from traditional European ideas has been:

> the increasing erosion of [what was] a fundamental social rule which held that everyone should live within a family setting. In the nineteenth century [and in earlier centuries] young people away from home most often lived as kin or boarders in a household, not in separate apartments, and elderly widows whose children had all left home moved in with relatives or neighbors. In these circumstances households acted not only as sources of lodging and welfare but as agencies of moral instruction and social order.

For many, the large and complex family offered unique advantages. It brought together a mixed community of people with varying degrees of emotional and economic connection.

For example, a study of farmer-clockmaker households in Switzerland by Pinot (quoted in Bassand, 1990: 167) gives the following account of mealtime in such a family, and its social functions:

> Meals have the effect of assembling the entire family around the table; whether they like it or not, old people, men, women, youth, children; everybody is united. It is the unique assembly of this kind: in all other circumstances of daily life, people unite according to specific aptitudes required for their different tasks; here the men are together: there the women. As for the

children, in order to figure in the group assembled around the table and hold
an honorable rank there, the only aptitude one has to have is to be hungry. . . .
In a large family, the reunion of so many different people who have different
ways of thinking, can prove quite difficult if everyone says what he thinks fit
without a thought for his neighbor. There must be some order, and to attain to
this there is no choice; all the children must remain silent and eat what is
given to them: all these little memories do not miss a word, all these young
minds understand and think more than they are given credit for. These mere
nothings, these umpteen topics, the preoccupations of local life, the farming
problems, little by little they shape the children's minds and mark them with
the image of the place where they live and the family they are born into.

This meal-taking, or what historians call *commensality*, is different
from what members of modern Western families experience. Our families
are smaller and situated farther from uncles, aunts, grandparents, and
cousins. They all are even less likely to be involved in the same kind of economic activity. Modern societies are highly differentiated, so we are all
busy doing different things at different times.

Today the occasions on which people congregate *as family members* are
briefer, less regular, and less ceremonial. They include being in the car for a
family journey or watching the same television program. It is hard to tell
what proportion of families used to eat lunch together. However, today few
school-age children and fewer working parents come home for lunch any-
more.

The time demands of work and schooling today make commensality
difficult. Add to this the industrialization and individualization of eating.
We have all become accustomed to fast foods, whether purchased at a ham-
burger chain or as microwaveable mini-portions. Such technological mar-
vels have reduced the need for family commensality even further. Now,
eating together is largely confined to weekends, if then, and ceremonial
occasions like Thanksgiving, Christmas, Passover, Ramadan, and so on.

In short, our lives have changed from being orderly and dense, even
crowded, to being unpredictable, even chaotic and, by earlier standards,
isolated. Is this a bad thing? Has the change created instability and stress in
family life, or have instability and stress always been with us?

INSTABILITY, EMOTIONAL QUALITY, AND STRESS

Many historical novels depict the deeply unhappy childhood of the main
character—in many cases, the author himself or herself. However, critics of
modern families often claim that children were treated better in the past
than they are today and that the cure for our problems is a return to the
family values of a past time. What is the truth of this matter?

Well, let's begin by remembering that in Europe infant mortality used to be common. There is also abundant evidence that infanticide and abortion were widely practiced as a way of reducing family size. Anderson (1990: 27) shows that of British children born in 1681, about 40 percent had died by their fifth year. As late as 1861, roughly 25 percent had died by age five. So before we get overly sentimental about the past, we should remember that death was a regular feature of life and not, as today, a rare and shocking occurrence confined to the hospital or the highway.

Infant mortality rates were high in the past because of malnutrition. As well, giving birth was full of danger for both the babies and their mothers. Often, babies had to come through a mother's hips which had been deformed by vitamin deficiencies. Nor should we forget other problems of inadequate birthing and the prevalence of diseases such as tuberculosis, diphtheria, pneumonia, influenza, and even strains of measles and chicken pox that were deadlier then than they are today (Flandrin, 1979: 203).

There were also epidemics of cholera, typhus, and other killer diseases to contend with. Finally, there were many child deaths through accidents and drownings. In the truest sense therefore, death was a normal, visible family event.

Certain social practices which have since disappeared also contributed to a high death rate for infants. Consider wet-nursing. Several centuries ago, a well-off mother paid another woman to suckle her baby, usually in the wet nurse's own home, along with other babies she would be looking after.

Discussions at the time justified this practice in religious terms. Since they were not fertile while nursing, good Christians could not have sex without committing the sin of lust. So the Church could justify wet-nursing on the grounds that it gave husbands their conjugal rights and protected them from urges to relieve their lust with prostitutes. Notice that the rights of women and children were subordinated to those of husbands. That is the way it was.

Yet as Lawrence Stone has forcefully argued, the institution of wet-nursing—the unlicensed day care of its time—may have substantially raised infant and child mortality levels. And it must surely have been obvious to the people concerned that wet-nursing was dangerous. If they had felt a "modern" kind of love for their children, would they have continued the practice? And how could women have been available to sell their milk? Perhaps all of a wet-nurse's charges—her own babies included—were getting watered-down milk, another possibility that might help to account for the massive death rate.

People were more willing to risk the deaths of their children in those "good old days." And there is ample evidence that infanticide was practiced and tolerated in *some* past societies.

Constance Backhouse has shown that infanticide was shockingly common in nineteenth-century Canada and there is no reason to suppose that things were any different in the United States. Infant bodies were found down wells, in tree trunks, railway stations, and a variety of other places. In the absence of birth control, many mothers resorted to infanticide and most people apparently accepted the practice as a necessary evil.

We know that, because more infant bodies were found than women charged. Whatever the law might have said, few juries and judges were willing to convict a woman on this charge. In the rare cases when a woman was convicted, sentences were light. Even coroners colluded. Often, infant deaths were ascribed to accidental smothering when the child had in fact been killed by his or her parents.

In France and elsewhere, foundling hospitals (orphanages) served essentially as a killing ground for children. This puts a different slant on the philosopher Rousseau's proud boast, in his confessional autobiography, that he personally contributed over half a dozen children to such institutions. (Parish poorhouses and private lunatic asylums played a similar role for the old and decrepit.)

Stone (1981: 59) argues that "infanticide, by deliberate or semi-deliberate neglect or direct abandonment to almost certain death in foundling hospitals, was perhaps the most important element in family limitation by the poor in early modern Europe."

Likewise, Sherwood's (1988: 205) study of the Royal Foundling Hospital in Madrid, Spain shows extraordinarily high mortality rates in the nineteenth century, for example, 85 percent in 1844 which was not a particularly bad year. This rate of death did not come down until the beginning of hygienic practices at the end of the nineteenth century. But people had their reasons for treating children callously. For example, bastardy rates were increased by economic conditions that made it impossible for young men and their pregnant girlfriends to set up house together.

Our forebears also used abortion a lot. In the 1990s, abortion policy is still hotly debated in the United States. However, back in 1870, when there were no laws against it, the abortion rate may have been as high as one abortion for every three live births (see Kain, 1990; Sauer, 1984). By that time, abortion was mainly being used by married, native-born American women as a means of family limitation. Abortion was also common in Britain. Dianne Gittins (1982) cites estimates that between 1900 and 1936, 16 to 20 percent of all pregnancies ended in abortion.

It was only as the nineteenth century drew to a close that "social purity" movements achieved great influence in North America. They had less influence in Europe, Africa, and Asia, where many countries adopted policies that made abortion effectively a routine method of birth control. Around that time, antiabortion laws were passed in most North American jurisdictions and they remained intact until the 1960s.

DO WE THINK DIFFERENTLY FROM OUR ANCESTORS?

Today, many of these historic patterns have disappeared in Western countries. Some social groups, such as Native Americans, have markedly poorer health than the majority. Yet about 95 percent of all North American children reach adulthood, most without experiencing a death in their family. In addition, most deaths now occur in hospitals. Today, death is abnormal (except among the old), invisible, and a thing that typically occurs outside the family household. In this context, the death of a child or young adult seems particularly unjust and unexpected.

Do we value children more highly today? On the basis of their research, historians typically argue that Europeans in the past must have had a completely different outlook on their children. Of course, scholars disagree about this. As a result, there is what social historians call *the sentiments debate* about the quality of the emotions experienced and displayed by our ancestors.

On one side, Shorter (1977) argues that parents invested little love in their children and took a more instrumental, less emotional, attitude toward children than we have today. On the other side, the mothers of foundling infants often kept up an emotional relationship with their children. In some cases, they recovered their children from the foundling hospital, after they had married or otherwise obtained a measure of economic security. Thus not all illegitimate babies were left to die. There is evidence that *some* of these children were loved in the same way that we understand the term.

Looking at the historical comparison from the other point of view, it is easy to show that not all children are valued today. A great many modern children also suffer from abuse and/or from the absence of one or both parents. We shall go into this in more detail in later chapters.

AFTER CHILDHOOD

In premodern Europe, childhood gave way to adulthood in the late teens (Aries, 1962). In such a society, age categories like "adolescence" and "youth," which we have come to take for granted, did not exist. And between childhood and adulthood, most people spent time in the household of a stranger.

Katz (1975: 302–3) notes, "For centuries, apparently, it was common for young people of all social classes to spend a prolonged period sometime after puberty and before marriage as a member of a household other than their parents. . . . For the most part young women worked as servants and young men, either as servants or apprentices."

Only those who married could be considered full adult members of the society and bachelors used to perform a rite celebrating the groom's transition from what Gillis (1985) calls the "homosocial" world of single-hood to true adulthood via the privileged status of marriage.

But we should not assume that this transition to early adulthood was smooth or certain. According to Gillis (1985: 15), "[Around 1600] there were always at least a tenth of the population who never married, and the rates of mortality were such that the marrieds made up no more than about thir-ty per cent of the population at any given time."

With marriage and adulthood would come new responsibilities. In the seventeenth and eighteenth centuries, French women normally bore their first child soon after marriage—often less than nine months after the wedding day. After that, they would bear children, on the average, every 25 to 30 months until the marriage ended with the death of the woman or her husband. This often happened before a woman reached her menopause (Goubert, 1965: 469).

Infant mortality was high, and there was no guarantee that both the husband and wife would survive to middle age. This is why large families (with more than ten surviving children) were rare. The average number of children per family may have been a mere four or five, despite continual childbearing while the wife lived. So it is by no means true to say that everyone had large families before reliable contraception became available. Some people controlled their fertility in part by abstinence. Other families, as we have seen, practiced infanticide and abortion. All were subject to the high risk of infant and childhood mortality.

Now consider the way things are today. In the 1990s, when North Americans and Europeans become adults, they leave their parents' homes. Some live as single people in apartments or college dormitories. Eventually, most form a stable sexual relationship and, often, a family household. Even today, this transition is to a degree ritualized and ceremonial, involving for-mal dating and eventually a wedding ceremony. Nonetheless, there have been changes.

For example, since the 1960s there has been a rapid increase in the per-centage of young people who flout the traditional order of events by living together first in a "cohabiting" or "common law" relationship, and only getting married later, if at all.

By how much has premarital cohabitation increased? The U.S. National Survey of Families and Households shows that between 1965 and 1974, only 11 percent of first-time marriers had cohabited before tying the knot. A mere 10 to 20 years later, 44 percent of those marrying for the first time in the 1980s had cohabited first. There have been big changes, even in the recent past. This brings us to the topic of marriage, and how people's view of marriage has changed in the last few centuries. There are important lessons to be learned about family life from changes in mar-riage practices.

MARRIAGE: LEARNING FROM OTHER SOCIETIES

Arranged versus Love Marriages

Before the coming of large-scale urbanization and industrialization, people viewed marriage as something beyond the concern of the marriage partners alone. Even today, in many societies, marriage links not only a couple, but two kin groups. Each fiancé's and fiancée's family considers carefully whether the proposed match is a good one for the whole kin group.

In such societies, this familial concern with marriage choices is eminently practical. With marriage, family property—land, animals, or other group possessions—may pass to the other group as a *bride-price* (a gift from the groom's family to the bride's family) or a *dowry* (a gift from the bride's family to the groom's family), or (eventually) as an inheritance (Hughes, 1978).

As well, the bride may come to live with the groom's family of origin or the groom may come to live among the bride's kin (Gittins, 1985: 61). And if one of the newlyweds should die early, there have been societies where it was the custom for a brother or sister to replace him or her by marrying the survivor. When a husband dies among the Luo in parts of Western Kenya, a brother or other close male relative inherits the widow.

The custom of *widow inheritance* has been justified on several grounds. From a functional point of view, you can look at it as a social mechanism which ensures that a widow and her children are cared for by a member of their husband/father's clan or family. In a rural, agrarian society where tasks are sex-typed, women need men to do the heavy work and keep thieves away. (This justification is less compelling in urban situations.)

The custom also has a religious justification, since the Bible says (Deuteronomy, Chapter 25, verses 5 to 7) that if brothers live together and one of them dies, the survivor should take the widow and perform the duties of the husband. All of these arrangements emphasize that kin groups, not just individuals, are joined in marriage.

On balance, which type of marriage is likely to be more economically successful, more stable, or more happy? Is it an arranged marriage, in which the family has a major influence, or a love marriage in which it does not?

Slater (1976) provides a historical answer to this question by examining marriage practices among the propertied classes in seventeenth-century England. She draws her data from the huge volume of letters written by an upper-gentry Buckinghamshire family, the Verneys.

Slater finds propertied families like the Verneys used to arrange marriages as a way of building links to other families, in order to preserve and increase family property. Financial considerations figured prominently in these arrangements. Still, they did not rule out the possibility that spouses would develop an affectionate, enduring relationship. But romantic interests were not usually the main reason for marrying.

For upper-class families like the Verneys, the new families created by arranged marriages performed a variety of vital functions. Families served to nurture and socialize children, and much more. They were also credit institutions, levers of political power, facilitators of educational and professional advancement, and—to continue the cycle in the next generation—marriage brokers.

Remember that at this time, there were few specialized institutions that could offer the same range of advantages, so marriage had a type of importance it lacks today.

Marriage expanded the kinship network that was so important to personal and professional advancement. It provided people with a whole range of social contacts that were less available to adults who remained unmarried. For their part, the unmarried were limited to operating through their family of origin.

Lawrence Stone has studied a series of matrimonial disputes in seventeenth century England. As in any argument, the people involved developed arguments which revealed their expectations, in this case about the institution of marriage. From the norms to which Stone's litigants appealed, we can see that most English people in the property owning classes expected a marriage to be at best no more than a reasonably peaceful exchange of goods and services.

However, the upper classes were not the only ones to hold practical concerns about marriage. According to Natalie Davis (1977), family life among French peasants and artisans in the sixteenth and seventeenth centuries also relied on long-term planning of the family's patrimony. The family's reputation and wealth, present and future, depended on "good" marriages. (For a similar argument about the virtues of arranged marriage, see Ahmed (1986), on marriage in Bangladesh.)

While there is an almost universal prohibition against incest, families have often solved problems surrounding the transfer (or outflow) of property by insisting on endogamy. *Endogamy* is the requirement or preference that people marry within their own social group. In a small village of several hundred people, the "pool" of eligible partners is larger than an extended family household and almost as large as the community itself. In such small communities people are tied together by generations of marriages, so everyone is more or less distantly related to everyone else.

The same cannot be said of a larger village or town. There, a person might marry someone not even distantly connected by earlier marriage. Rules of endogamy, however, would require that person to marry within his or her own social class, caste, religious group, ethnic or racial group, or geographic region. Here too, kin group advantage remained the goal of such a marriage. Wherever family land or other immovable properties might be lost through marriage, the pressure towards endogamy was still strong.

We noted in the last chapter that the practices of arranged marriage and clan endogamy are disappearing throughout the world. Young people play a greater part in their own weddings, largely due to the growth of a cash economy. A cash economy means sons are more independent of their fathers. Young men can provide for their own marriage expenses, and their own lives. They depend less on their elders and therefore permit their elders a smaller role in planning their lives. The marriage market has been deregulated. However, it is still structured to a large degree by education and cultural levels, as well as by physical attractiveness and geography.

These recent changes have affected men far more than women. Women have gained many rights in Europe and North America. However, there are many industrializing countries where young women still have little say in choosing a spouse. Rapid industrialization and urbanization benefit men first in the acquisition of economic independence and the power to arrange their own marriages. So, recent changes have increased male prerogatives without any corresponding increases for women (see, for example, an article on how this has happened recently in Iran, by Mir-Hosseini, 1985).

However one-sided the change, male independence translates into less kin involvement in wedding ceremonies. It also means a greater emphasis on the conjugal bond, as opposed to kin ties, just as Parsons (1943) has described the American kinship system. In this way, "modernization" of the economy reduces the influence of kin over marriage and the nuclear family more generally.

There are exceptions to be sure. In Bangladesh the deterioration of economic conditions over the 1970s and 1980s brought changes in the traditional pattern of marriage (Ahmed, 1986). There, as in many Asian countries, most marriages are still arranged. Guardians continue to arrange marriages with a view to maximizing the benefit of the families involved.

As in other Muslim societies in Asia and Africa, arranged marriages in Bangladesh continue to enjoy cultural legitimacy. Supporters of the practice argue that arranged marriage maintains the existing social order, affirms and strengthens parental power over the children, keeps family traditions and value systems intact, consolidates and extends family property, enhances the value of the kinship group, and helps young people avoid the stress and uncertainty of searching for a mate (Ahmed, 1986: 51).

By contrast, love marriage is thought to disrupt family life and the kinship system. According to this way of thinking, love marriage transfers a child's loyalty away from the family of birth to a single person, and substitutes personal goals for traditional family and kin-group obligations.

We are so accustomed to valuing romantic love in our society that we may have trouble seeing what's wrong with it, from an Asian standpoint.

For example, love is blind (as the old saying goes). It may lead people to exaggerate the quality of their loved one, leading to mistakes. How much better (the argument goes) if people selected mates for solid, practical reasons, then fell in love with them afterwards.

Though both favoring arranged marriage, Muslims and Hindus in Bangladesh have different ideas on the topic. But in both groups, children are given great importance, especially if they are male. Both groups also practice child marriage, a means of forging social ties between families early in a child's life. "Where marriage is arranged, the interests of the families get priority over the interests of the couple themselves" (Ahmed, 1986: 53).

As already mentioned, guardians or parents of the spouses-to-be select the mates of their children. According to Islamic law, the young couple must give their consent, in order for the marriage to be valid. In practice, the young couple's ability to refuse cooperation is limited by their psychological and economic dependence on their parents. They more or less have to agree to the selection their parents have made in order to keep the peace, and to make sure they can inherit.

In such societies, parents use different criteria in selecting mates for their sons and daughters. In fact, in Bangladesh "socioeconomic characteristics of the potential marriage partners play a stronger role in the mating process" than they do in the West (Ahmed, 1986: 54). For example, they seek beauty and modesty in the son's bride-to-be, a secure job and good income in the daughter's husband-to-be.

Is this a good way of dealing with marriage? And if so, why is it disappearing wherever people have an opportunity to make their own choices—for example, where people can earn wages outside the family? The answer is given in research on Chinese women by Xiaohe and Whyte (1990). It compares the marital happiness of people in love marriages with that of people in arranged marriages. Their data show, unambiguously, that women in love marriages are more satisfied with their marriages than women in arranged marriages. The traditional wisdom that arranged marriages become more loving over time, while love marriages "cool down," is *not* borne out by these data.

Love marriages do cool down. Most Western research confirms that marital satisfaction declines over time. However, they remain more satisfying than arranged marriages from start to finish. So at least in this instance, we can say with certainty that the family is better off today than it was in the past.

What we have seen in this chapter is that the changes in family life are only one example, a particular spin-off, of more general social changes.

Because we have no complete general theory of social change, we can have no complete particular theory of family change. But certain predictions seem more credible, or less foolhardy, than others. At the least, it seems unlikely that the changes we have witnessed in this century will be reversed. We are no more likely to return to permanent marriage, large families, or stay-at-home moms, than we are to an agrarian economy, small-town living, or travel by horse and buggy. Certainly, there is no evidence of reversals in the post-war trends we have examined.

CONCLUSION

What can we conclude from this all-too-brief survey of the past? In particular, did earlier family forms provide people with more emotional support and stability, and less stress?

Not really. Evidence from earlier European and North American families shows that most people lived close to the level of subsistence. As a result, their social relationships were largely conditioned by the demands of producing enough to eat. They didn't have time or energy to worry about happiness, and stress was a normal part of their lives too, even if it had different origins.

Such families also denied formal rights and freedoms to women and children. At best, they provided people with either support *or* integrity, but rarely with both and, often, with neither. In any event, the old-style family is incompatible with modern life. Today people want variety, fluidity, and choice. Therefore, the idea that a pre-industrial or early industrial family will satisfy people today is a *myth*. We cannot go backward to solve the problems of the present and future.

Can we solve our present problems by adopting family practices we find in other societies? Evidence from other family forms in different parts of the world shows that some are better than ours in some respects, some better in other respects. Many are what we would consider worse. In any event, none provides everything we need for family life today.

Cross-national comparisons show that many family forms are possible and provide people with unquestionable benefits. But none is completely appropriate to our society (given our values and economy). None can be adopted as a whole for our own use. Still, we can learn a lot from other societies—if only to see how wide the range of possibilities is.

NOTES

1. The term *extended family* is used to indicate the importance of the elder generation on either the male or female side. We can call this the *vertically extended family*. However, the term is also occasionally used to refer to the importance of siblings and cousins. This type should be called the *laterally extended family*. Generally, it is possible for adoptive and fictive kinship relationships to be used in order to extend family links.

3

THINKING ABOUT CHANGING FAMILY FORMS

INTRODUCTION

There are many theories about the family and most have something to say about the way family structures have changed. Most also relate changes in the family to changes in the social position of women, children, and the old. Many also make assumptions about the proper division of labor between the sexes.

These theories differ in the kinds of evidence and the criteria they use to judge that evidence. For example, religious and cultural theorists measure family life against absolute standards laid down in sacred texts. Feminism has also contributed to the family debate in ways that could be considered morally absolute, though rarely religious. Many schools of thought coexist in modern feminism. However, most of them stress the ways that family structures and state authorities have subordinated women's interests to those of men. Some analyze laws that put women into subordinate roles or give them (merely) formal equal rights with men.

On the other side are theorists who are less concerned with moral and political, or ideological, issues. For example, the psychoanalytic theorists from Sigmund Freud to Ronald Laing focus on key family resources of power and eroticism. Social demographers, for their part, amass data on births, deaths, and marriage, then look for large patterns in human history. For example, they examine the *demographic transition* by which today's rich societies went from short life expectancies and high birth rates to long life expectancies and low birth rates.

So types of theories about the family vary widely, from one social scientific paradigm to another. And as we have already seen, family forms also vary. The net result is that making and testing theories about the family is enormously complicated. It is like trying to hit a moving target with a gun that keeps changing size, shape, and caliber. However, the task is not impossible, because whatever their approach to the topic, researchers keep seeing many of the same things. Certain things don't vary much from one place to another or, for that matter, from one period to another.

WHAT REMAINS THE SAME?

Family forms are variable, but the variation is not infinite. There are a few bases upon which all family systems rest; the problem is finding them out.

Invariant features can fall into either of two main categories: *functional* or *sociobiological*. Theories about the functions of families call attention to the needs that families—all families—must fulfill for societies and for individuals. In principle at least, these are needs that vary little from one society to another.

On the other hand, sociobiological theories point to family-making tendencies we humans share by virtue of our common animal heritage. So, for example, sociobiological theories remind us that humans have deep-seated instincts that evolved over thousands of generations. Idealists and moralists may want to reform family life to bring about a better society. However, people still have a strong desire to prefer and protect their own blood kin. A classic example is the mother protecting her young. Where better to find a reason for this than in biology?

Sociobiologists believe that people must have been programmed genetically to prefer their own kind. The result is that a maximum number of genes passes intact from generation to generation; any group programmed differently would have died out. This variant of the "selfish gene" theory predicts that sexual attraction makes people more loyal to their partners (with whom they share fewer genes) than to their brothers and sisters. It also predicts that other things being equal, children run a greater risk of neglect or abuse from stepparents than from natural parents. Generally, these predictions are supported by the available data.

Other biological givens are less controversial. For example:

- women bear children and men do not;
- it takes nine months from conception to the birth of a child;
- women can nurse children from birth for up to several years, and while nursing, they are often infertile;
- until the age of six years at least, children are dependent on adults;
- women are fertile from puberty (11 to 14 years old depending on diet) to menopause (mid-forties), while men can remain fertile into their sixties;

- a number of groups had already discovered effective means of reducing their fertility, but oral contraceptives that have been available since the 1960s make it easier for women to control whether they will conceive.

Until medical science makes further advances, family forms must take account of these and other biological limits. In short, all family life will be shaped by these factors—whatever the cultural context or period of history.

The functional perspective focuses on other kinds of limits. From that perspective, societies and individuals "need" families to carry out certain tasks: for example, to produce and socialize children. Family routines appear to suit most of us, with the result that married people are generally happier and healthier than never-married, widowed, or divorced people.

However, we do not need families to do *precisely* the same things in every society, nor to do the same thing in similar ways. In seventeenth- and eighteenth-century North America, for example, kinship played a wide variety of educational, economic, and insurance roles that we no longer associate with the family. Then, Native American tribes still relied on hunting and gathering. The immigrant colonialists were farmers, most on family farms and some with large plantations in the southeast.

In North America today, a great many things have changed. Some of the family's historic functions are carried out by private businesses or governments. The family is no longer a multipurpose kin group which revolves around property and making a living. Today it operates in a private arena concerned mainly with intangibles, like people's happiness. However, the family continues to provide most people with routine support and sustenance, and to produce and socialize children.

The most striking change in family structure is one that people have called *nuclearization*. In common everyday use, the word *family* has changed its meaning from a large kin group to a small household. Talcott Parsons calls this new form the "isolated nuclear family" and William J. Goode, the "conjugal family."

CONTINUOUS PROGRESS OR A CYCLICAL VIEW OF HISTORY

The obvious (though imperfectly understood) tie between industrialization and nuclearization has led many to conclude that the new family is better. After all, if family change is part of a package we approvingly call "progress" (or "modernity") then the nuclear family is probably a good thing. But is it? Has the history of societies been a continuous upward development?

The Victorians, who believed in "progress," thought that there *had* been a natural evolution of family forms—a general movement up the slope of civility. They were aware of problem families, no doubt. However, they thought that evolution had reached the best possible result in their own middle-class patriarchal nuclear family. Today, most people would reject this view. They dispute the notion of "progress" in general. In fact, many scholars believe that civilizations, our own included, rise and then fall.

Several generations ago, sociologist Carl Zimmerman introduced a complete model of history which included family change. He argued that before a civilization rises, the dominant family forms are extended, patriarchal, and corporate. Zimmerman calls this the "trustee family." The rise of civilizations means a growth of cities and modernization, and both promote family nuclearization. This reduces the amount of inequality between men and women and produces what Zimmerman calls the "domestic family."

According to Zimmerman, all civilizations decline sooner or later. When they do so, the family breaks down and people act in their own interests instead of their kin's. This accelerates the decline of civilization. After the breakdown, people revert to elementary forms of social life based on kinship, patriarchy, and feudalism. Then, corporate forms of familism like the "trustee family" prevail once again. In due course, a centralized state rises again, the "domestic" family type becomes more common, and the whole cycle repeats itself.

Is this theory valid? It's hard to say. As we shall see, the first part of Zimmerman's theory is similar to other theories of the way urbanization and industrialization affect families. But social scientists have had few opportunities to study the breakdown of large societies. When breakdown does occur, the people involved often have more pressing things to do than carry out sociological studies! Nevertheless, the ways that people have used kinship networks to make a living in Russia, Bosnia, Croatia, and Serbia recently, since the collapse of communism, show that his theory is largely correct.

As well, the data show that nuclearization *does* occur when people move from agrarian-based societies, live longer, and participate in a cash economy. Increasingly, they spend their lives under universalistic and individualistic, not familistic, rules. The whole process is typically called *modernization*. However, modernization theory is not without its critics. It has often been criticized for its functionalist, male, middle-class bias. However, even critics of this approach lapse into the vocabulary of modernization when discussing social change, so we had better give the theory a closer look.

MODERNIZATION THEORY

The great American theorist Talcott Parsons saw modernization as a process which produced a more rational and meritocratic allotment of rewards in society. Before modernization, the older generation had authority over the younger generation in a classical extended family. It passed on whatever advantages were available, as property, knowledge, and skills related to making a living.

In this "premodern" society, better-off parents gave their children gifts of money or influence and significant advantages through inheritance. Today, in modern society, family advantages count for little. Schooling is organized by the state, inheritances are taxed, hiring decisions are based on earned diplomas ("credentials"), and salary raises are based on performance.

In short, modernity reduces the benefits of the classical extended family. The process of modernization produces a fairer, more rational society. As a result, members of the younger generation are less willing to put up with parental authority. A generation gap opens up between parents and their children. People become much more individualistic. They seek their own goals and live by their own values. Kin play little part in shaping their lives.

Always, family life reflects and is governed by legal arrangements. That is why we can see this decline of kinship and rise of individualism in legal evolution. The cross-cultural and historical research confirms Maine's (1861) conclusions of one hundred years ago:

> The movement of progressive [i.e., modern] societies has been uniform in one respect. Through all its course it has been distinguished by the gradual dissolution of family dependency and the growth of individual obligation in its place. The Individual is steadily substituted for the Family as the unit of which the civil laws take account (Maine, 1861).

Modernization means that your parents or grandparents can do little for you after seeing you through to the end of your formal schooling. The reason for maintaining contact with them is a sentimental one. In fact, all kin relations come to be based on emotional or expressive, and not instrumental (practical) exchanges.

Thus Parsons predicts that with modernization, fewer people choose a spouse to please their parents. And more choose a spouse on highly individualistic, expressive grounds: this is the era of the "companionate marriage." Modernization also makes people more likely to move away from the neighborhood or city where their parents live and makes them interact less with their parents. By severing kin relations and work, modernization makes geographical and social mobility easier—even inevitable. It also weakens customary kinship ties. On the other hand, relations between kinfolk that survive are likely to be based on genuine emotion.

The modernization argument says that old people have authority in customary societies partly because of valuable knowledge that younger people need to learn. This gives them social value and some degree of prestige, even power. No wonder the old used to live together with (or near to) their children and grandchildren. On both sides, there was a need for the relationship. For similar reasons, the old were emotionally close to their descendants.

By contrast, the modernization thesis holds that in modern societies—the United States in particular—the old are separated from their children and grandchildren. Weakened kinship ties lead to social atomism—what some have considered a form of "social disorganization." On the other hand, separation also means freedom from the oppressive controls that family and community have historically placed on young people.

However, there are several problems with modernization theory where it deals with family and kinship. First, it implies that the majority of households in customary societies contained multigenerational extended families. But the previous chapter showed such households were rare, because of short life expectancies in these societies.

This aside, the theory makes too many assumptions about the nature of kinship obligations in the classical extended family and indeed about the classical extended family itself (Thomson, 1984; Anderson, 1990). On the other hand, the theory fails to say anything about the role of the state in defining what will be the dominant family form in any society. It assumes that social norms can persuade women to channel their wishes for self-realization narrowly into the domestic sphere, and that men's can be channelled into a career outside the home. It also ignores the important social consequences of a longer life expectancy.

Modernization theory assumes that other countries must take the path of modernization taken by the United States. It says little about the large differences in family-related social policy that exist between the United States and other equally rich countries like Sweden, France, and Japan. As a result, its predictions about the weakening of kinship ties in modern America are not supported by the data.

For example, recent survey evidence shows that transfers of money from the older generation to the younger one are common. As the bumper sticker joke says, "Money can't buy happiness, but it sure keeps the kids in touch." This fact goes against the theory in two different ways. First, it shows that people continue to have cross-generational relationships over the life course. Second, it shows that even in a society marked by expressive exchanges, these relationships are instrumental.

This is not all that the modernization theory missed. Along with many other perspectives, Parsonian functionalism failed to predict the increase in divorce rates, nonmarital cohabitation and birth rates that took place in the 1970s and 1980s. A theory that has so little to say about major changes in people's everyday lives leaves a great deal to be desired. Let's consider an alternative theory which focuses on the "functions" of the family in relation to material production.

A MATERIALIST THEORY OF FAMILY CHANGE

Gerhard and Jean Lenski have argued that the definition and functioning of "family" is determined by the daily routine through which people make their living.

They focus on how the available technology determines people's mix of activities across time and space. In simpler words, the way that people in the community make their living determines what they do with their time. Equally, it determines where they do it and with whom. These distributions are relevant for the ways in which people distinguish between home and workplace. They also influence how the positions of men and women, old people and young people will be defined in different societies.

For example, when hunting or fishing are the basic forms of production, one person has to leave home to gain valued results and somebody else has to prepare the equipment. Somebody else again has to process the catch. This division of labor changes when there is a change in the mode of production. For example, having animals to herd makes a big difference to the possibilities for organizing family life. Settled agricultural communities are again different. A family farm involves different tasks with another daily and seasonal rhythm and different chances for the inheritance of land.

Plantation agriculture also has different implications for family life, because there, the laborers have no hopes of inheriting. In many historical instances they were slaves or indentured workers. The list could go on for a long time, always emphasizing the available technology and its social organization.

The basic point is that you cannot sensibly talk about family life without also talking about work. Thus, large-scale coal mining or factory work are new ways of making a living, compared with farming and hunting. It is to be expected that family life under these kinds of regimes will be molded into new, more appropriate forms. Small-scale manufacturing in the home might involve weaving cloth, as it did in the sixteenth and seventeenth centuries. Or it might mean a "home office," as in the 1990s. Either way, it produces a family life which differs from that found in a household where adults commute to work in a factory or office.

You will notice that the explanations we have grouped under *technological materialism* overlap with those grouped under *modernization*. Indeed, they might be viewed as a specification of how modernization comes about. However, many kinds of technological change in the ways people make a living occur without any significant change in urbanization or even industrialization. Family farmers can do a little more hunting and fishing. Weaving cloth and assembling clocks can coexist with operating the family farm.

Notice also that types of explanation generally labeled *technological determinism* focus on the typical patterns of task allocation and daily interaction within families and households. Usually, modernization types of explanation have been painted with a broader brush. They have focused on broader societal institutions like the legal system and implied that whole societies know only one given family form.

BEYOND THE MODERNIZATION MODEL

Changing Experiences of Old Age

There is a common myth that in the past, families looked after the old folk and three-generation family households were common. However, the truth is more complicated.

First, few people in preindustrial societies got old; they died at what we, by present standards, would regard as an early age. It follows that people rarely knew their grandparents. Michael Anderson has shown that for British women born around 1681, the average grandmother would have died thirteen years before her last grandchild was born. This fact changed little even for grandmothers born well into the first half of the nineteenth century (Anderson, 1990: 53–4).

Second, preindustrial societies are of different types. British social historian Michael Schofield (1989: 284–5) has shown that societies vary in the degree to which social relations are based on "familistic" or "individualist-collectivist" principles.

In familistic societies, people are geographically stable and kinship plays an important role in economic and social relations. Support for the elderly is mainly a family responsibility. It is closely related to the prospect of inheriting the family's stock of capital, the family farm, and other property (the stem family argument).

However, some past societies had different expectations. In preindustrial England, for example, children expected to leave home and kinship played little part in economic and social relations. People moved from one village to another easily, and the weak and elderly were largely supported by the community (friends and neighbors).

Third, the historical evidence is that parent-child relations were brutally realistic, even in familistic societies (Schofield, 1989; Stone, 1992). Detailed legal agreements between parents and adult children even specify that one or more of the adult children will get control of the family smallholding, on condition that certain food, drink, and clothing would be provided to the parents. People were not content to leave matters like this to chance. The unhappy fate of Shakespeare's King Lear gives an indication of what might have happened, had they done so.

So it makes little sense to romanticize the parent-child bond, even in familistic societies. In this society, children are valuable because they provide labor power and are *expected* to support their aged parents. Failing to provide the degree of support the community expected would be to risk disapproval, even witchcraft or the anger of the ancestors. Children are even less valuable in an individualist-collectivist society where the community is also supposed to provide support.

Schofield argues that Western Europe in general, and England in particular, was always closer to the individualist-collectivist than to the familistic pole. Even four centuries ago, the family had no mystique. For example, the sixteenth-century Tudor King Henry VIII was famous for having six wives, one after the other. His practice of what we call *serial monogamy* was rare among the common people because they could not afford it. Today, when more people can afford it, more people do it. Accordingly, even then, the parish-based "poor law" recognized no direct obligation between child and parent. Instead, it assigned primary responsibility for relief of poverty to the community, not the family.

There have been many community systems for helping the poor and the old, the widows and orphans. Doctors used to give basic treatment to the poor at no charge. Religious orders, monasteries, the leading citizens of the local community, have all been involved in what Victorians used to call the "relief of poverty." How did systems like this develop into the vast welfare bureaucracies that exist in many developed countries?

The route is long and complex, and it required many debates about basic principles and social goals. One major debate was about whether the poor should be given money ("outdoor relief" or "welfare payments") or, on the other hand, whether they should be controlled, trained, and "improved." Remember those English institutions like the workhouse, made infamous in the novels of Charles Dickens and the reportage of George Orwell. They arose in connection with this debate. They had the support of people who thought help should be firm and demanding—a kind of nineteenth-century "tough-love."

The late nineteenth century was the golden age of institution building. Workhouses, mental hospitals, orphanages, and prisons—in the seventeenth century, modest in size and scope—developed into major organizations for "warehousing" people who previously would have lived with their kin or died in the street.

Another major debate in sociology is about what families used to do for their kin. There is an assumption, fed by moral panic, that what families used to do should set a standard for what we ought to do today. However, what families "used to do" varied considerably from one period to another. The Tudor Poor Law, which was still in effect about 250 years ago, needed revising in the face of rapid urbanization and industrialization roughly 150 years ago. The New Poor Law of 1834 and its subsequent revisions ended up with the formation of a "cradle to grave" welfare state that was fully in place about 50 years ago. But this was partly dismantled by British Prime Minister Thatcher's conservative government in the 1980s.

Written laws do not tell the whole story. At the end of the nineteenth century, the actions of magistrates and administrators—not changes in the written law—changed the way old people were looked after by their family or local government (Thomson, 1984).

Between 1870 and 1910, a group of moral and ideological "family oriented" crusaders seized control of Britain's Poor Law inspectorate and leading positions in the Charity Organization Society. Their views became dominant, so that they were able to reinterpret the provisions of the New Poor Law of 1834. In this way they could make drastic cuts in the system of cash allowances paid to the elderly.

Again, there were variations even within countries. Comparing nineteenth-century rural families in Lancashire and Ireland, Anderson argues that both societies had a strong commitment to family and wider kinship bonds. This was due

> at the structural level to the fact that it was difficult for any person in these societies to solve the problems with which life faced him without recourse to assistance from others, and that kin provided the source of assistance which gave the optimum bargain to actors in their relationships with others (Anderson, 1971: 90).

Anderson adds, however, that kin helped less where the Poor Law was in place. England had the old Poor Law and Ireland did not—at least, not until 1838. As a result, an English person who turned away a relative (and was prepared to face whatever informal sanctions the neighbors might apply) was not condemning that relative to starvation. In the end the community would provide. In Ireland, on the other hand, a poor relative turned away by kin was often in real danger of starving.

In both countries, any dependent relatives who had been taken into the household were supposed to help out in return for their keep. Luxuries like tobacco might be denied them if they failed to perform. In this respect, old women were more useful dependents than old men. Women could still carry out light domestic tasks, but old men no longer had the strength to do work that was defined as appropriate for their sex.

In rural communities, extended kinship worked well as a system of social support. Varying degrees of relationship were recognized, and social norms dictating assistance from kin allowed help to be sought from outside the immediate nuclear family. These norms put the responsibility for care on kin, instead of diffusing the responsibility too thinly over the whole community. However, any system of support for dependents will break down when too much weight is placed upon it. In Ireland, for example, many sons abandoned their parents to a lonely (if short) old age in the

1840s. Then, the desperate poverty of the potato famine forced a wholesale emigration which halved the country's population.

In short, sometimes families took care of their old. Sometimes, especially under pressing economic conditions or when relief could be obtained from the community, they did not. So, where the old and poor are concerned, communities have been coming to the rescue of families for a long time. As life expectancies increase, this pattern will probably continue and expand.

DOES THE STATE UNDERMINE FAMILY OBLIGATION?

Government transfer payments in general, and social welfare provision in particular, have a major effect on the family. In this respect, government's role extends the logic of modernization. It allows family forms to change with changes in the technology and social arrangements for making a living.

In traditional societies, the extended family used to act as the employer of last resort. It also helped out with child care, schooling, and medical bills. When government provides unemployment insurance, welfare, education, and health insurance, it takes over all these functions from the family. In this way it helps family members and, indirectly, helps "the family" to function. But it also weakens the family's hold over its members. The mere existence of alternative support systems also reduces the influence church-based and neighborhood groups have over people.

Families Within Communities and States

The last chapter showed that changes in the family have gone along with increased freedom of choice. However, the idea of people being free to choose things is a recent one. It has come into practice on a large scale only in the last 200 years, and then almost entirely by men. For a long time, women were still assumed to have the same interests as their fathers or husbands. So in legal theory, the person who could make decisions was the male head of a nuclear family household.

What this means is that for most of human history, the community (and its lieutenant, the family) has been the dominant influence on what people do. But what is community authority and how does it influence personal liberty?

Sometimes, community authority is so pervasive and benevolent that it can scarcely be seen at all. For example, many hunting and gathering peoples have rough economic equality and little state organization. This means there is little visible authority and, certainly, no inequality associated with an authority structure (as there is in our own society).

The Yanomani in the Venezuelan rain forest are one example. The !Kung bush people in the South African desert are another (Howell, 1979). Their form of social organization is often kinship based. Such a combination of economic equality and community control has been a popular ideal in modern times. In fact, many new communities have been formed in an attempt to realize the ideal. These are often called utopian communities and have often been religiously based; the Shakers ("Shaking Quakers") are one among many American examples. The Israeli kibbutz is a less utopian but more successful example of such a community.

Between the organizationally primitive small communities of hunter gatherers and the organizationally sophisticated large societies of industrial people we find a variety of different community types.

Peasant societies, for example, have existed for thousands of years and are often highly stratified. Ownership of land rights is the basis of economic inequality and land is in short supply. This form of social organization is also kinship based. It is often conservative and buttressed by religious ideas which stress the importance of customary familism. The community may be embedded in a centralized state but this rarely makes much difference to the individual. The state is often weak, remote, and has no power (or will) to change important things like land tenure.

With industrialization and "nation-building," the state becomes more important. More often than not, the centralized state takes an active role in social policy formation. There is no mechanical simplicity about the outcomes. It would be naive to suppose that human behavior can be changed by an act of Congress. However, there is no doubt that people respond to financial incentives, and often legislation, like the Civil Rights Act, can bring these about.

Ever since the early part of the nineteenth century, governments of industrial societies have been passing legislation which restricts the employment of women and children. The purpose has been to protect them. Assumptions behind such legislation were that women might work outside the home, but the proper place for mothers was at home, looking after their children. Accordingly, the hours that women might work were restricted. For example, women were denied the right to work evening and night shifts.

Assumptions have changed since the 1940s, however. During the 1980s and 1990s, some of this legislation has been struck down, on the grounds that men and women should be treated equally. Another trend in legislation has been the elimination of the "eugenics laws" of the early twentieth century. They attempted to improve the quality of future generations by sterilizing the mentally handicapped or the "feeble-minded." The net result of such changes, and others, has been to give people more freedom to lead family lives as they wished, without the state's interference but (often) with its assistance.

How different that is from what we find in other "activist" states. For example, an authoritarian society has strong community authority and an activist state, though there is no attempt to make people equal. Puritan New England, for one, tolerated little deviation from accepted family forms. In the twentieth century, Hitler's Germany had a well worked-out policy under which homosexuals, along with Jews and Gypsies, were exterminated. Around this time, several countries—among them, Germany, Vichy France, and Portugal—had pro-family policies. Women were kept in the domestic sphere, so that they could produce more children. These children were to be raised in time-honored ways, under the eye of the state.

Today, there are several Asian and North African states in which strong fundamentalist Islamic movements are bringing back the veil and other aspects of enforced domesticity for women. So we have not seen the end of authoritarian activism in the world.

However, in modern industrial societies, progressive activism is increasingly common. The European welfare states—Sweden being the most often cited example—have strong community authority and a state that tries to produce economic equality. These countries provide many health and welfare benefits which used to be provided only by the market, the family, or public charity. This would seem to increase the sum total of human freedom, both within and outside family life. However, even this system has its problems.

One problem is that state officials are all too ready to interfere in family affairs. Generally, this is in the perceived interest of the health and welfare of more vulnerable family members. However, people of good will can disagree about these things. Another problem is that once put into place, social programs become entitlements. Worse, their costs are hard to contain, since each program employs many professionals and serves many clients. One of the major political problems in Western Europe is the reshaping of the welfare state. It must take a form taxpayers can afford and still act as a social safety net for the poor and vulnerable.

Socialism provided the extreme version of this process. Soviet Russia and its Eastern European satellites set up extensive welfare programs. Usually, they underfunded them or ran them inefficiently. As a result, underground black-market systems based on kinship and friendship networks grew up to provide services that the state promised but could not deliver.

At the end of the twentieth century, debates about family policy rage on in many countries. They have mainly been about the extent to which taking care of families should be a collective (or community) responsibility. (Recall, this is a debate that began in England about 300 years ago.) Concretely, they have debated the ways in which governments, businesses, and communities should provide day care, primary and secondary education, or financial supports for families.

One familiar argument is that raising children is an investment in the next generation of adults and should therefore be subsidized from tax revenues. Take family allowances for example. At the beginning of the 1990s, these payments made to families with dependent children were available in more than 70 countries around the world, not including the United States.

Some states go even further to support and stimulate family living, out of a concern that their culture and language are threatened by low birth rates. Following pronatalist policies, they give significant financial advantages to families which have many children. Examples of this are France, the former East Germany, and the Canadian province of Quebec.

APPLYING THEORIES TO CASES

We have seen that a great many beliefs about the "good old days" are more myth than truth, or at best, equal parts of both. Combining history and sociology well depends on throwing out conjecture and replacing it with recorded history. This being so, what can we say about the facts of change in family life as they are known to historians and social scientists?

1. *Classificatory Kinship* Cultural anthropologists have carried out intensive studies of small-scale societies. But many of these societies are already changing through contact with colonial and neo-colonial regimes, to say nothing of American television programs. Occasionally, large-scale intermarriage with a different cultural group can change kinship systems (Graburn, 1971). More usually, economic changes work to change aboriginal family forms over the long term.

Economic growth changes living arrangements and other aspects of socioeconomic organization. In turn, these bring about basic changes in the structural rules. For example, when Edward Bruner (1971) lived with Native Americans in the Lone Hill reservation in North Dakota he found that the clans had diminished in importance, the youth were lax in meeting certain kinship obligations. Village organization had shifted from a close-knit unit to one of separated households.

Finally, the matrilocal extended family was no longer a residence unit, nor was the lineage a corporate group. While these Native Americans still have a matrilineal family organization for daily matters, the father's lineage is no longer important for religious purposes. With culture contact and economic change, customary ceremonial life has been more or less abandoned.

2. *The Joint Family System* Or consider the fate of the Serbian joint family system (the *zadruga*) that we discussed in the last chapter. Eugene Hammel carried out fieldwork in the Serbian province of what was then Yugoslavia, and searched for traces of this classic form of family extension.

He found a population that was highly urbanized, yet still had strong links to the rural past:

> The new urban population retains strong ties to the village. Even families resident in Belgrade for a half-century still visit relatives remaining in the country, and many wealthier families have summer homes in a village, sometimes their native village. . . . Households have decreased from the nineteenth century zadruga norm to the one-child families of the Belgrade middle class. . . . There has been a shift in the lines of corporacy, with a collapse of many functions into the nuclear family and the abandonment of others, such as political activity and some aspects of social control, to the State. Nevertheless, the ideology of kinship is much the same as it always was (Hammel, 1971: 129, 130).

By "the ideology of kinship" Hammel means that when Serbians talk about kinship linkages, they emphasize descent in the male line. Using questionnaires, he found that kin related through the male line were preferred, liked, or found most useful. Men still took precedence in Serbians' family rituals.

Hammel concludes that "The maps in people's heads really are the last thing to go." He could not know that Yugoslavia would split up into the separate states of Serbia, Croatia, and Bosnia. No one really knows which aspects of kinship have been strengthened by the hardships of economic and military dislocation. Perhaps, hard times have made Serbs go back to their historic preferences—for example, putting greater trust in kinfolk who are related to them in the male line.

3. *African-American Families* Most people in the Western Hemisphere who are of African origin had ancestors who arrived in slavery. They came from West Africa, a vast area that contains a wide variety of kinship and marriage systems. In the United States, African Americans have had different experiences from what they might have had in the Caribbean or Latin America. Naturally enough, however, American writing is about black experience in the United States. It begins with the South, before and after the Civil War, then follows the great migration from the rural South to the industrial, urbanized North.

Among families in the Western Hemisphere, those of African origin often differ from aboriginal families and those of European origin. The biggest difference is the higher incidence of single-parent families among African-Americans. Social scientists have struggled to explain this higher incidence of single-parent families in terms of sensible theories about change in family forms.

First, a common-sense demographic explanation: Harriette McAdoo shows that many problems ascribed to the black American family arise from a shortage of males in the adult black population. In 1988, there were an estimated 115 black American women in their thirties for every 100 black

American men. McAdoo says that it may be because of a dearth of men that divorced or widowed black women have to wait an average of 13 years before remarriage. By contrast, black men remarry within two years, on average (1990: 80).

Some single-parent families may also arise because of the criminal justice system. Remember that the United States has one of the world's highest incarceration rates and that more young black males, per capita, are put in jail than white males.

Other authors have focused on poor African-American families, ignoring those who are well-off and, also, poor whites. They have asked whether the culture of black Americans might be inherently "matriarchal." This is an "ethnic culture" type of explanation. If young women's families—and not their husbands—are expected to look after them, it may be considered normal for men to shirk the responsibilities of fatherhood.

Still other writers blame the system of slavery that existed in the Americas during the eighteenth and nineteenth centuries. They argue that slave owners sold husbands separately from wives and wives separately from children. As a result, whatever notions African-Americans might have had about long-term spousal commitment would have faded considerably. This is another type of "ethnic culture" explanation.

However, Sue Jewell (1988) points out that the prevalence of single-parent families among black Americans is recent. Herbert Gutman (1975: 1962) had showed that 1890 census data were consistent with 90 percent of all black families being of the nuclear type. Even in 1960, three in every four black families had a husband and wife present. Only 22 percent were headed by women and, of these single mother-headed families, only 12 percent had never married.

These figures indicate that despite a heritage of slavery, a majority of black families in the 1950s had a stable structure. However, by 1982, after 20 years of "Great Society" social programs, the divorce rate among black couples had doubled from 104 per 1,000 in 1970 to 220 per 1,000 in 1982. Just over half of black families had a husband and wife present and the share of single mother-headed families had increased to 41 percent—twice its level in 1960. Of these black, single mother-headed families in 1982, one third had never married (Jewell, 1988: 16–17). What had caused this explosion?

Jewell's explanation emphasizes the interaction between state-funded "Great Society" programs and the structure of African-American communities. She maintains that black families have always had distinctive characteristics, especially a willingness to modify family arrangements to meet the needs of their consanguine and fictive kin (1988: 15).

However, she emphasizes the customary role of mutual-aid networks, particularly those centered on the black church. She points out that:

the black mutual-aid network espoused philosophical issues inextricably related to the religious doctrine of the black church, such as mutual dependence, collective responsibility and cooperation. By contrast the government, like other institutions in the larger society, embraced an ideology of autonomy, social isolation and individualism. . . . Ostensibly, the government's resources, to which blacks were entitled, were far more abundant than those possessed by informal social-support systems (1988: 41).

In the long run, government entitlement programs provided only food stamps, not community. So the problem is partly secularization and the decline of the church-based community. But family forms must also adjust to the technology of making a living. In this case, new techniques for surviving on part-time jobs and welfare are crucial.

4. *Rising Islamic Fundamentalism* What are the consequences of these changes in the family for women? Many scholars claim that women were victimized by the European and Asian marriage customs. They were "victims" in the sense of becoming the property of their husbands, being *The Weaker Vessel* and having *A Lesser Life*, to quote the titles of two best-selling books. However, comparative research shows that this is too simple a picture. Some women have held a great deal of informal power in many societies, even in those dominated by men.

As a further examination of modernization, consider the position of women in the Islamic societies of the Eastern Mediterranean, the Persian Gulf, and North Africa. This region has had patrilineal and patriarchal extended-family structures since the beginning of recorded history.

Nahla Abdo-Zubi (1987) has described how the traditional Palestinian family had an extended structure which linked nuclear households to a kinship-based village organization called the *Hamula*. In principle, the Hamula was endogamous. The head of the Hamula was the main decision maker in the village. From the time of Turkish domination of the region, through British colonial rule, to the present Israeli administration, long-term changes affected the Palestinian extended-family structure.

For example, the life of Palestinian families in United-Nations-run refugee camps in Lebanon shows:

further individualization and nuclearization of the family, gradual replacement of endogamous marriage with exogamous marriage, less stress on bride price and most importantly, the decline in the social and political role of the Head of the Hamula (Abdo-Zubi, 1987: 61–2).

Over the 1950s, 1960s, and 1970s, many factors were both causes and consequences of greater individualization of roles. They included more women's participation in the paid labor force and in political activities, and more formal education for both sexes. A decline in the importance of brideprice and marital endogamy went along with a weakening in the villages' extended family structure.

In nearby Qatar, on the Arabian Gulf, Melikian and Al-Easa (1981) trace the link between education, family change, and economic development. Qatar has enjoyed an economic boom since the early 1950s, due to oil revenues. This boom has affected the way Qatari people live in, and think about, the family. The authors write, "Less traditional attitudes . . . have been triggered by the oil industry (industrialization), sedentarization, urbanization and by education. They are also being reinforced by the mass media and increasing contact with foreigners and exposure to different ways of life" (ibid.: 94).

The customary characteristics of the family, which Qatar retains in varying degrees, are "patriarchal, extended, patrilineal, patrilocal, endogamous and occasionally polygamous" (ibid.: 82). Melikian and Al-Easa note that the nuclear family is slowly replacing the extended type, where *extended* refers to a husband and wife, all their unmarried children, their married sons, their wives, and their children.

Also, the patriarchal system is being eroded as education—a force that helps liberate women from economic dependence on men—opens up to everyone. In this changing-yet-traditional context, marriage is considered a religious duty and is arranged by the fathers of the would-be bride and groom. The would-be groom occasionally has a say in whom he would like to marry. For example, he may point her out to his father who communicates his son's wish to *her* father. Supposedly, the bride is then "given the chance to accept or reject her suitor" (ibid.: 88). In reality, daughters have been brought up to submit to their parents', and especially their fathers', wishes, so they rarely exercise this right of rejection.

Melikian and Al-Easa surveyed college students' attitudes toward the family, arguing that "the holders of these attitudes are the future leaders in the country [so] they will in all probability be emulated and thus become the initiators and carriers of change" (ibid.: 94). They find that male students have a more old-fashioned outlook—what we should expect, since the customary system works to their advantage. Both men and women expect to get married and have a family, but there the similarity ends. The authors report "most men are practical about [marriage] while the women tended to idealize it" (ibid.: 89).

Nor is it surprising to find that men want and expect more children than women. Women in Qatar, like elsewhere, have to do more of the work related to bearing and raising children. In Qatari families, maleness and advanced age confer the most power. In the traditional household, the youngest daughter and/or wife is at the bottom of the pecking order. However, "most students of the Arab family seem to feel that the wife, in her own way, wields more authority over husband and children than is commonly recognized" (see Tillion, 1966).

The authors put forward a number of predictions for the future of the Qatari (indeed, the Arab) family. They are all consistent with theories about the effects of social and economic change on family life. Namely:

1. The extended family in its customary form will be replaced by the nuclear family.
2. Most young men would prefer, upon marriage, to live separately from their parents. However, they will continue to live nearby, at least for a time.
3. Both young men and women will insist on getting to know each other before they get married. Arranged marriages will be unacceptable to young couples.
4. Rare even at present, polygamous marriages will continue to decrease in number.
5. College-educated women will try to delay marriage until they graduate.
6. With increasing education, women will marry at an older age than their mothers did and the age differences between (educated) husbands and wives will decrease.
7. Endogamy will continue in a modified form. But there will be fewer paternal-cousin marriages and fewer marriages from within the same lineage. The shift will be towards marrying within one's tribe and one's country.
8. Young married couples will have fewer children than their parents did.
9. Women will strive for a more egalitarian partnership with their husbands.

A number of Islamic societies provide examples of rapid urbanization and industrialization and also of religious fundamentalist reactions to social change. Before Algeria gained its independence from France, the urban areas of that country were largely westernized. After independence, the regime was secular and socialist, though customary family forms were Mediterranean and Islamic—an interesting mixture of old and new.

As a result, women in Algeria have been, metaphorically, stretched between two poles. On the one hand they are officially eligible to participate in the life of the state. On the other hand, customary pressures of family and daily life force them into narrow domestic and private roles. Female emancipation was always limited to an urbanized elite. In the last few decades it has lost support because of its linkage to a failed Western model of development through industrialization.

With the rise and political success of Islamic fundamentalism after 1985, many Algerian women returned to a customary role symbolized by the wearing of the veil in public. However, the younger generations of women would not wear the heavy and constricting North African veil. Instead, they adopted a lighter and more convenient veil and, in many cases, continued to work outside the home.

The significance of this is lost unless you understand the meaning of *veils*. There are various styles of veiling in the Islamic world. As we said, many young women have opted for the *hijab*, a lighter veil which is better adapted for work and social life than the customary Algerian dress (the *haik*). The change of veils was indeed an affirmation of modernity but it was *not* a statement of secularity or atheism. Outside the West, modernization does not always mean secularization, nor does feminism always mean atheism. However, modernized women do express their religious faith in a different way:

> To express her submission to God, but without the intermediary of man can be interpreted as an affirmation of self, the beginning of the emergence of woman as an individual, in a society where the very notion of individual action is only just beginning (Hakiki-Talahite, 1992).

5. *Portuguese Fishing Families* Now consider Sally Cole's research on fishing families in the village of Vila Cha, Portugal. It shows how wives and mothers can hold a central place in a classic Mediterranean-style culture.

Poverty among the *pescadores* (fishing families) has always required women *and* men to work long hours at demanding tasks like fishing and collecting seaweed. Women make a vital contribution to the fishing industry and the result is a breed of women who are self-sufficient, "empowered," and yet devoted to family values and religion.

In this region, economic and social barriers between the fishing and the farming communities dictate marriage patterns. The area is broken into two endogamous marriage groups and it is rare for villagers to marry outside of their class. In part this is because of the incompatibility of the lifestyles of wealthy landowners and poorer fishers.

Women from the wealthier households of Vila Cha are, generally, neither willing nor able to engage in the hard work of fishing and gathering seaweed. And because *pescadore* women make a vital contribution to household finances, fishermen cannot afford to take on a partner who will be an economic liability. "Fishermen, therefore, [have] preferred to marry daughters of other fishermen, women who had been raised from childhood to the maritime woman's life of hard work" (Cole, 1991: 52).

Among *pescadores*, property (usually a house, boat, and fishing gear) is passed down through the daughters of the household. Preference is given to daughters because people think that daughters will be more inclined to look after their parents in old age. For their part, without the stability of a house, the daughters might be forced to leave the parish to start life elsewhere (Cole, 1991: 55–56).

> The effect of these practices in Vila Cha was that women owned and inherited property. . . . At marriage, a husband generally moved in with his wife and her parents. A woman would start her married life in her parents' house, but she would move out when a younger sister married and brought her husband to reside in the house. Elder married daughters frequently moved into houses adjoining or near their parents' houses, and thereby resided . . . in the neighborhood of consanguineally related women (Cole, 1991: 56).

Like other parts of the world, however, this coastal area of Portugal has been unable to resist the changes of the late twentieth century. With the introduction of fish canneries and textile factories, since the mid 1960s more and more women have left the traditional lifestyle of the maritime fisher-woman. In doing so, they have joined an unskilled, low-paid work force.

The change in lifestyles reaches farther than a simple change in work pattern. A decreasing emphasis on women's work in the fishing industry has meant less self-sufficiency and more isolation for the women of Vila Cha. Factory women have little control over their work and consequently less pride. Here is one instance where modernization has worsened the status and well-being of women. Again, we see that if you change the technology and social organization of work, you will change the nature of family life.

As you can see, no changes are unambiguously good or bad. In earlier years, the fishing women were poorer than their farming counterparts, but they had more power in the public sphere. After industrialization of the region, many women escaped the harsh life of a fishing family for the dif-ferent discipline of factory work. All changes force adjustment and compro-mise, and bring new opportunities and difficulties. Nowhere is this clearer than in the matter of divorce, which we examine in a later chapter.

CONCLUSIONS

History is complex and varied, so that the evolution of complex institutions like families and households can rarely be described as a straight-line pro-gression. Instead, social change proceeds by fits and starts. Improvements in opportunity and fairness are followed by temporary retreats to more oppressive arrangements.

However, in gross terms, we can see a gradual movement in the direc-tion of greater personal choice. People worldwide are having more say in such things as whom to marry, how many children to have and when to have them, and so on. When given the choice, people have preferred love matches to arranged marriages, have preferred to have fewer children than many children, and have preferred to set up their own households rather than to live in that of their parents.

The torrent of change stops, at least for a few years, when state power is captured by conservative or fundamentalist ideologues. Then govern-ment forces people's behavior into customary channels. But the dam almost always breaks. Government cannot prevent social and familial change for-ever.

The chapters that follow this one focus on spousal relations and parent-child relations. By making cross-national comparisons, we hope to focus more closely on the object of this book. We want to know whether the trade-offs between autonomy and security, personal freedom and collective good, are inevitable. Are there societies which have cultivated "modern" family life more compassionately and less painfully than we? If so, how have they done it, and can we do it too? In the end, what role should governments play in making family life come closest to what people want it and need it to be?

4

COUPLES, CHOICE,
AND COMMITMENT

INTRODUCTION

Spousal relations occur between couples—young couples, middle-aged couples, old couples; well-matched couples or ill-matched couples. Couples may be homosexual or heterosexual, and sexuality may play a large or small part in their relationship.

As we saw in Chapter Three, historically and cross-culturally such relationships have usually been formally sanctioned by marriage. But over the last three decades, this pattern has changed dramatically in the United States and most other Western countries. Fewer Americans marry, and for this group, marriages occur later than ever before. Far more couples (not just students and young people) cohabit, rather than marry. High divorce rates argue that marriages are increasingly unstable. Couples have fewer children, and more couples are childless by choice, but more single women have children.

These trends are not unique to the United States or Canada. In Europe, marriage rates have been falling throughout the postwar period. In Australia too, marriage rates have fallen and divorces have increased over the last two decades. Carmichael (1987: 260–261) reports evidence of disenchantment with the institution of marriage among Australian young people. He attributes this change to growing individualism and an awareness that marriage is risky, since it is so likely to end in divorce.

The end of the 1960s brought a "marriage bust" in Australia, the result of several factors. For example, easier access to abortion gave women the choice of ending a pregnancy instead of marrying the father or bearing a child outside of wedlock. A rising divorce rate may have made people skeptical about marriage and more willing to think about cohabitation instead. Cohabitation, in turn, became more socially acceptable as attitudes toward nonmarital sex liberalized and safe effective contraception became widely available.

In this chapter, we look at the changing trends in spousal relations. They include changing rates of marriage and the increase in cohabitation (or common-law marriage). We raise questions about the underlying causes of these changes. Why are marriage rates falling even though people are forming more, and earlier, spousal relationships than ever? Why don't marriages that follow a period of cohabiting last longer? Is marriage, as a traditional legal arrangement, becoming a weaker institution than it was in the past? If so, why? Do these trends signal a declining commitment to what many believe is a fundamental institution—traditional family life?

In the end, we shall argue that high rates of cohabitation and divorce, and low rates of fertility, do *not* mean that people have given up on marriage as an institution or an ideal. We believe that marriages are increasingly varied, fluid, and idiosyncratic. Yet people continue to seek intimacy, anticipate a secure and loving relationship, and want children. Indeed, most unmarried Americans *want* to marry (Sweet and Bumpass, 1992).

ARE AMERICANS AVOIDING MARRIAGE?

Before the 1960s, marriage was the social ritual by which young people were expected to declare their adulthood. Parents of "baby boomers" (children born between 1946 and 1964) epitomized this sentiment. These couples married in their early twenties, and had lots of children—about twice as many as the generation before and the generation after! And there were good reasons for this focus on early marriage and family life. In the aftermath of World War II North Americans were anxious to return to "normal" by refocusing on marriage, childbearing, and home life. The economic boom of the 1950s ensured the availability of jobs and housing.

Wedding ceremonies reinforced cultural definitions of women as property, handed over by her father to her husband. There was also an exchange of vows in ritualized language, often using sixteenth-century words from the Anglican Church's Book of Common Prayer: "Who giveth this woman?" and "With this ring, I thee wed . . . to love, honor, cherish and obey . . . and with all my worldly goods I thee endow . . . for better or for worse, for richer for poorer, in sickness and in health . . . 'til death do us part. . . ."

Such ceremonial language emphasized the sanctity and permanency of the new relationship. It also called attention to the mutual obligation between husband and wife and their separation from families of origin (Parsons, 1946). How quaint these ideas and that language seem now, only a few decades later. The fact is, we are separated from them by a momentous decade, the 1960s, that might just as well have been a century long for all the change it introduced.

Two important social movements, both begun in the 1960s, changed forever our cultural definitions of marriage and family life. One was the sexual revolution. The other was the second wave of feminism.

The sexual revolution increased openness about sexuality, particularly premarital sexuality. We cannot estimate the extent to which cultural anxiety affected premarital sexuality in the past. However, we do know that attitudes have become more liberal. Thornton (1989) measured changing attitudes toward family issues—including premarital sexuality—in the postwar period. Attitude surveys show a dramatic change in the direction of more liberal attitudes in the late 1960s and early 1970s.

For example, in 1969, 68 percent of those polled agreed that "it is wrong for people to have sex relations before marriage." By 1973, only 48 percent felt that it was wrong (Thornton, 1989: 883). A similar pattern towards increasingly liberal attitudes was reflected in questions about birth control.

Interestingly, attitudes towards extramarital affairs were far more negative. There was a shift towards more acceptance during the peak of the sexual revolution, but this reversed in the late 1970s. Young people were increasingly *intolerant* of extramarital sexuality in the late 1970s and 1980s. This more recent period also saw a decline in the belief that intimacy with only one partner was too restrictive (Thornton, 1989: 888–889). Americans have been far readier to accept premarital than extramarital sexuality.

If you believe surveys, young women have started having sex earlier, the average age for a woman's first act of premarital sex having fallen from 19 in 1960 to just under 17 in 1990. Given the current later age at marriage, young people are sexually active for between seven and ten years before marriage. Virginity at marriage is no longer a cultural expectation.

The second influence on changing attitudes was the *women's movement*. Pressures for access to higher education and better employment created new opportunities for women outside of marriage.

The possibility of economic independence for women was truly a revolutionary change. Not so long ago, marriage was thought to be incompatible with work outside the home. Employers and unions cooperated in enforcing a *marriage bar* and the related notion of a *family wage* (a single wage sufficient to support an entire family). Husbands also felt ashamed to have their wives working for pay. It implied they were poor providers.

In 1938, a Gallup poll in Britain showed broad acceptance of the marriage bar. For example, more than half (56 percent) thought that women in nonprofessional jobs should give up their jobs when they married, and only 39 percent opposed this view. The support for this view varied.

For example, many argued that teachers or doctors should not waste their professional training by giving up their jobs after marrying. Still, 48 percent of adults thought that even women trained as doctors and teachers should give up their jobs after marriage. Such attitudes were shaped by the Great Depression of the 1930s, when many came to feel that working wives took jobs away from otherwise employable family breadwinners (Wybrow, 1989).

Today, our ideas of a family wage have all but disappeared. There has been an enormous change since the 1940s in assumptions about a "woman's place." We can see this by looking at responses to the General Social Survey between 1974 and 1991. This survey asked whether people agreed or disagreed with the statement, "Women should take care of running their homes and leave running the country up to men."

Overall, most people disagree with this. However, those who were over 65 at the time of the survey were as likely to agree as to disagree. Interestingly enough, the sex differences are minor and it is age differences that are most marked. Men's ideas and assumptions have evolved along with those of women. It is also the case that many families now depend on more than one income earner—so the change in attitude reflects economic realities as much as liberal attitudes.

In sum, the sexual revolution and feminism paved the way for changes in attitudes toward sexuality, and towards a woman's place in the family and the economy. These attitudinal changes are reflected in changes in the timing, structure, and permanence of marriage. Marriage rates began to decline in the 1960s, declined rapidly in the 1970s, and have continued to decline at a slower rate since 1980.

At the same time, more couples began to live together without marrying. Cohabitation increased dramatically in the 1970s and has continued to increase, at a slower rate, since 1980. The combined effect of these two trends means that the age of marriage has increased to almost 27 for men and 25 for women. Childbearing too has been postponed, although an unprecedented number of children are born to women who are unmarried. Some people who postpone marriage and childbearing will remain single and childless, either out of desire or lack of opportunity.

Today, the typical age at first marriage for both American men and women is higher than it ever has been. Indeed, a larger than ever fraction of American adults have never married at all. This fraction, only 16 percent in 1970, had risen to 23 percent in 1990. Likewise, the proportion of adult years spent outside marriage is higher than ever before. It began to rise as the average age at first marriage increased, after 1960.

WHY MARRIAGES ARE DELAYED

Thomas Espenshade (1985) feels that the attraction of marriage *is* becoming weaker. He finds more Americans postponing marriage, fewer of them ever marrying, people spending a smaller proportion of their lives in spousal relations, and average marriages lasting a shorter average time than in the past. These trends inevitably lead to a falling rate of marriage. Let's examine two theories to explain the declines—an economic explanation and a demographic explanation.

A leading *economic argument* is that marriage rates have fallen in recent decades because marriage is less necessary for both men and women, and the alternatives to marriage are more attractive. For women, financial independence and reproductive control have begun to tip the balance in favor of singlehood or cohabitation. Combining marriage, parenthood, and labor force participation is hard work, particularly for women. No wonder many women are reluctant to take the plunge into marriage.

Indeed, many factors conspired to make marriage less appealing in women's eyes. For example, because of less job security, greater educational opportunities for women, and the rising cost of housing, couples needed to coordinate two educational and job careers. This too has played a part in persuading many people to delay marrying.

Economist Gary Becker (1991) argues that lowered "gains to marriage" are primarily due to a rise in female earnings and labor force participation, along with a decline in fertility rates. Women have less to gain from motherhood and more to gain from paid work than they did in the past. Were they to express their position in the language of an economist, women might say that their "opportunity cost" of not working for pay has risen.

This theory also explains why African-American families have become even less stable than white families. Compared to black men who have suffered enormous discrimination in employment and from the criminal justice system, black women are better educated and hold positions of higher status. On this argument, black women have even less to gain from marriage (and more to lose) than white women. Their opportunity costs are, comparatively, higher than white women's.

Social welfare programs geared to assisting female-headed single-parent families can also tip the balance against marriage, though this is not an argument against such programs. More generally, the data show that anything which provides a measure of independence and support to single women, or puts them in an economically more nearly equal economic position (compared to men), will work against marriage.

This leaves us with the conclusion that many women have remained in marriage partly for love or duty. But others, unfortunately, remained because the married state was the least of several evils. Theoretically, this is a continuation of the modernization argument. It said that nuclear families became the dominant family form because the economic and insurance functions of traditional extended families were being provided by private businesses or by government.

An interesting *demographic explanation* comes from Richard Easterlin (1980, 1987), who attributes low marriage rates and high divorce rates to rises in cohort size. Easterlin invented the idea that relative income is tied to the size of a birth cohort because this influences the scarcity or surplus of job opportunities. Using this, he argues that North American baby boomers, born between 1945 and 1965, experience more financial insecurity and earn relatively less than their parents because they belong to a particularly large birth cohort.

For that reason, they were less likely to marry and more likely, if married, to divorce. This means that on Easterlin's argument, the increase in divorce over the 1960s and 1970s gives a distorted idea of the long-term trend. That is, "the traditional family may not be going down the drain quite so fast as some think" (Easterlin, 1980: 231). If smaller cohorts experience better economic conditions (and they usually do), they ought to feel better off than their parents and divorce less often. Balakrishnan et al. (1990) make the same point for Canada.

Guttentag and Secord (1983: 231) propose a different demographic explanation that focuses on sex ratio imbalance to account for changing rates of marriage and divorce. They write, "When sex ratios are high, men are in excess supply and women are in undersupply. Young adult women are highly valued because of their scarcity, and traditional sex roles are common."

But when there is an excess of women, women feel powerless and devalued by society. Men in this situation will have a weaker commitment to women, so women will in turn develop a weaker commitment to marriage and less willingness to depend upon men.

In effect, anything that causes (or increases) an unequal sex ratio on either side works to lower the marriage rate. Assuming women marry men two years older, Guttentag and Secord find evidence to support their theory that the decline in marriages is due to a changing sex ratio.

As well, they note a greater sex ratio imbalance among blacks than whites. The reasons for this include a disproportionate number of black men in the armed forces and penal institutions, lower sex ratios (i.e., ratios of men to women) for blacks at birth, and higher than average death rates among black men due to homicide and suicide, among other things.

Along similar lines, William Julius Wilson (1987) argues there is a strong causal relationship between the shrinking pool of young marriageable black males and the dramatic rise in out-of-wedlock births and female-headed households among blacks. Other factors are relevant too, but the effects of the sex ratio are important.

To suggest that women avoid marriage because they are no longer economically bound to marry is to make a negative statement about the nature of marriage. So is the suggestion that women's rates of marriage are dominated by concerns about childbearing. Neither explanation tells us about the changing nature of personal relationships. Do people in the 1990s seek or avoid stable, emotionally committed relationships? When we look at the increased numbers of cohabiting couples, it is hard to conclude that North Americans avoid intimacy.

COHABITATION

In most Western countries, the same factors that have discouraged marriage have encouraged cohabitation. At the same time, the sexual revolution has removed the stigma that used to go with "living together" outside marriage. And women's greater access to education and jobs has reduced the incentive to marry, as we have seen.

Since the 1970s, there has been a dramatic increase in cohabitation in the United States. Between 1970 and 1980 the number of cohabitors tripled to 1.6 million unmarried couples. By 1981, the number had risen to approximately 1.8 million, about 4 percent of all couples (Spanier, 1983). Over one in every three ever-married 25- to 34-year old Americans lived together before their first marriage (Cherlin, 1989).

To take just one example, in Lane County, Oregon, premarital cohabitation increased from 13 percent in 1970 to 53 percent in 1980. Gwartney-Gibbs (1986) estimated this increase by noting addresses on marriage license applications. Cohabiting couples were those who had identical addresses prior to marriage.

The rise in cohabitation shows that people want intimate relations that are more flexible and less binding than legal marriage. For people of all ages, cohabitation offers many of the usual benefits of marriage, with less expectation of permanence and fewer legal obligations.

In most of Europe, North America, and Oceania, cohabitation has increased and marriage rates have declined. Meyer and Schulze (1983) compared several European countries and the United States and feel that the most important reason for the increase is the growth in female labor force participation. Women with strong commitments to employment are less committed to marriage and family life, and more receptive to alternate living arrangements. Women in cohabiting relationships are more highly educated than the average, and are materially less dependent on their "mates" than are less educated women.

In Canada, a Family History Survey (Burch, 1989) found about one adult Canadian in six had cohabited at one time or another. Among young people (aged 18 to 29), the proportion was higher: about one man in five and one woman in four. On Census Day at the beginning of the 1980s, about 6 percent of the couples enumerated were in a cohabiting relationship.

In Australia, cohabitation has increased, although the rates are lower than in North America (Khoo, 1987). An Australian Bureau of the Census study found that nearly 5 percent of all couples living together in Australia in 1982 were unmarried. The majority of cohabitors were young people, 70 percent under the age of 35. One-third of the cohabitors were separated or divorced from earlier spouses. Likewise, over one-third of the cohabiting couples were living with dependent children.

Australian cohabitors are younger than American cohabitors, and a smaller proportion have been married before. Khoo attributes this difference to higher divorce rates in the United States. They make the pool of previously married people larger than in Australia. At the same time, relatively more Australian than American cohabitors have children living with them. This indicates less concern about the stigma of children born out of wedlock "down under."

In Europe, the trend toward increased cohabitation had already appeared by the end of World War II (Festy, 1985). Cohabitation is most commonly found in Scandinavia, particularly Sweden where it has a long history.

Because of its long history, there are interesting differences in cohabitation practices in Scandinavia compared to the rest of Europe and the United States. In Scandinavia, cohabitation has long been accepted as an alternative or prelude to marriage. Indeed, in Sweden, a country with the world's highest rates of cohabitation, it is *unusual* for people to marry without living together first. But even in Sweden, rates of cohabitation have increased since the mid-1960s.

This increase is due to couples living together at younger ages and after a shorter period of acquaintance than previously. Hoem (1986) says that these cohabiting unions are more like extended dates, or going steady, than they are like traditional marriages.

Yet, in Denmark and Sweden, childbearing within cohabitational unions is common. In the rest of Western Europe and in the United States, cohabitation is less common and fertility is less frequent (Blanc, 1984). Now, in Sweden, pregnancy is not a strong enough reason for marrying. About two-thirds of first children are born to cohabiting, not married, couples (Hoem, 1986: 9).

The increase in nonmarital cohabitation is related to a decline or delay in remarriage among divorced people. In Norway and Sweden, nonmarital cohabitation is by far the preferred type of second union (Blanc, 1987).

We only need to look at Swedish social policy for the reason. Since 1955, paid maternity leave has been available to all Swedish women, regardless of their marital status. Other Swedish policies include no-fault divorce, free birth control devices, easy abortion, good child care, state-paid children's allowances, and state-protected child support payments.

Even the income tax system is organized in such a way that marital status is all but irrelevant. Each of these policies protects personal well-being, regardless of marital status. In effect, such laws and policies make the decision about marrying *versus* cohabiting positively unimportant.

The dramatic increase in the incidence of unmarried cohabitation has attracted considerable interest. As a result, research has been directed at discovering the characteristics of those who cohabit, the nature of cohabiting relationships, and the subsequent impact on marriage.

CHARACTERISTICS OF AMERICAN COHABITORS

In the United States, much of the early increase in cohabitation was accounted for by young people, particularly college and university students. By the mid-1970s, a national survey (Clayton and Voss, 1977) found 18 percent of young American men had lived with a woman for six months or more. A study of college students discovered that nearly four respondents in five *would* cohabit if given the opportunity. And another study found 71 percent of the men and 43 percent of the women expressing a desire to cohabit.

In the 1970s, American students said the main advantages of cohabitation were convenience, a test for compatibility, love, hope of establishing a more permanent relationship, and economics. The most frequently reported reasons for not cohabiting included parental disapproval, disapproval of a partner, conscience, and fear of pregnancy (Huang-Hickrod and Leonard, 1980).

For many, living together was a practical way of splitting expenses. Their decision to live together had nothing to do with a marriagelike commitment. For others, cohabitation was a part of the dating and mating process—a prelude to marriage.

Today, cohabitation is far more common and is no longer a college student phenomenon. Indeed, there is a negative relationship between education and cohabitation. A study of cohabiting American women in their twenties (Tanfer, 1987) found that women did not seek a permanent replacement for marriage.

For these women, cohabitation was a part of the courtship process, not a long-range lifestyle. For others, cohabitation *is* a long-term alternative. It is a marriagelike commitment without the marriage ceremony and with the marital obligations left unstated but no less real for that.

Another group of cohabitors is older, previously married people. Over 40 percent of American women cohabitors are previously married (Bumpass and Sweet, 1989). This group has its own reasons for living together instead of marrying. Some were separated but not yet divorced from a spouse, so they couldn't legally remarry. Religious beliefs prevented others from divorcing and remarrying. Finally, some widows just did not want their social security benefits reduced by remarriage (Newcombe, 1979).

In the 1970s, the most important difference between college cohabitors and noncohabitors was their degree of religiosity. Cohabitors were less religious than noncohabitors—less inhibited by traditional morality. Religion still plays an important role in the decision to cohabit.

Surprisingly, cohabitation is more common in Quebec than in any other Canadian province—even than in any of the American states—despite Quebec's history of strict Catholicism (Balakrishnan et al., 1990: 8). By age 35, 44 percent of Quebec men and 40 percent of Quebec women will have cohabited, compared to only 28 percent for either sex in the rest of Canada. This shows that religious sanctions on cohabitation and nonmarital sex have been seriously weakened since the sexual revolution of the 1960s.

Balakrishnan argues that young people in Quebec cohabit in order to avoid legal marriage, given the high rates of divorce and other legal complications experienced by earlier cohorts. In doing this, they are reacting against, as well as imitating, what they have seen. (For the same reasons, more people remain single in Quebec than in any other part of Canada.)

Another important influence on cohabitation is the nature of a person's family of orientation. Children of mothers who married young and who were pregnant at marriage were more likely to enter their own marital and nonmarital unions at an early age. Children of divorced or separated parents were also more apt to cohabit (Thornton, 1991).

EFFECT ON MARRIAGE

We know that cohabiting relationships are shorter-lived than legal marriages. However, what effect does cohabitation have on marriage? Does cohabitation make for stronger, more stable marital relationships? In fact, the relationship between cohabitation and later marital success is not clear.

In Sweden, women who cohabit premaritally have almost 80 percent higher marital dissolution rates than those who do not. Women who cohabit for three or more years prior to marriage have 50 percent higher dissolution rates than women who cohabit for shorter durations. Also, cohabitors and noncohabitors whose marriages have remained intact for eight years have identical dissolution rates after that time. The evidence strongly indicates a weaker commitment to the institution of marriage on the part of those who cohabit premaritally (Bennett, Blanc, and Bloom, 1988).

Some North American studies, like Bumpass and Sweet (1989) found that couples who had previously cohabited were more likely to have divorced after ten years than couples who had not cohabited. White's (1987) study of a large sample of ever-married Canadians found that premarital cohabitation has a positive effect on staying married. This remains when length of marriage and age at marriage are controlled.

Finally, Watson and DeMeo (1987) determined that the premarital relationship of the couples, whether of cohabitation or traditional courtship, has no long-term effect on the marital adjustment of intact couples. What can we make of these contradictory findings?

You might think that people who have cohabited will know when they are ready to commit themselves to a long-term relationship. But cohabitation proves to be no better a "screening device" for mates, or preparation for marriage, than traditional courtship. The data argue that people who are willing to cohabit are also willing to divorce. Along these lines, Balakrishnan (1987) finds that people who cohabit are less stability-minded, or conformist, than people who marry legally.

Teachman and Polonko (1990) on the other hand, argue that the effect of cohabitation is tied to the fact that cohabitants have spent more time in a relationship than noncohabitants. When the total length of the relationship is accounted for, there is no difference in marital disruption between cohabitants and noncohabitants.

It is also the case that some cohabitants have little desire to remain in a stable relationship. Nor do they plan to marry. Glick and Norton (1977) report that 63 percent of cohabiting couples in the United States remain together less than two years. Most say they do *not* intend to marry each other and, in fact, do not do so. In Canada, cohabiting unions are short-lived because, in about half the cases, they are converted into legal marriages within a few years (Burch, 1989). But in the other half, the partners do not marry—they break up instead.

American couples who cohabit *are* more unconventional in their attitudes towards sexual behavior, and women who cohabit are less conventional regarding single parenting and marital permanence. However, men who cohabit are more *conventional* about parental obligations to children; there is no evidence that cohabitants are generally more individualistic or less conventional than other adults.

Should we worry about the increased trend towards cohabitation? Is this an indication of the increasing deterioration of American family life, or a positive sign that people have more control and choice?

One of the most fundamental concerns of the New Right in America is the protection of family life and family values. Conservatives assume that independent families are, or should be, the backbone of American society. If people cohabit instead of marry, they will have less emotional and legal commitment to each other and their children, it is argued.

On the other hand, policy and law concerning cohabitation is changing rapidly. Over time, the difference between married and unmarried couples has become blurred. Sarantakos (1982) reviewed laws regarding cohabitation in 22 countries. This analysis shows that cohabitation has emerged as an institution that forces people to get married unknowingly and unwillingly. State interference is as common in cohabitation as it is in marriage. Contrary to individual assumptions, cohabitation does not offer freedom from responsibility, commitment, and state interference in the couple's personal affairs.

In sum, we could say that cohabitation is associated with a delay of marriage, a decrease in family size, and an increase in divorce risks. We are far from knowing all of the reasons cohabitation has these effects.

THE SHIFTING MEANING OF MARRIAGE

Despite changes in timing and permanence, marriage continues to be central to interpersonal life in North America. Cultural stereotypes favoring traditional family life have not changed. Typically, North Americans view married people more favorably than unmarried. They also view parents more favorably than those who have not had children, and view children with married parents more favorably than children whose parents are divorced (see, for example, Beaujot, 1991).

Marriage shapes identities of men and women, and provides a support system for child raising. The institution of marriage is supported by social policy, tax structures, and law. Despite many doubts and obstacles, the great majority of people value the institution of marriage, and want to marry.

Thornton (1989) measured changing attitudes to family issues in the postwar period. Thornton found that Americans felt less pressure to marry or to have children, or to restrict intimate relations. He also found that people are more accepting of alternative family forms. Nevertheless, Americans still "value and desire marriage, parenthood and family life for themselves" (ibid.: 873).

For Thornton, this implies an important shift in norms and values concerning intimate relationships. "Marriage may now be less important as a sanctioning institution for sex and cohabitation" (Thornton, 1989: 889). At the same time, fidelity in both marital and nonmarital relationships has increased in importance.

Indeed, some people would prefer to marry and live apart than postpone or avoid marriage. Consider so-called "commuter marriages." For some couples, this is only a short-term arrangement. For others, it becomes a lifestyle. Though commuter marriages remain rare, nothing illustrates so well people's continued commitment to the institution of marriage *despite* enormous odds and conflicting values.

COMMUTER MARRIAGE

A *commuter marriage* is a marriage between spouses who live in two separate households. Typically, couples take up separate residences after having shared a common one. Less often, couples live in two different homes from the beginning of their marriages.

Gerstel and Gross (1982) see the development of commuter marriages as more than just one more variation, among many, on the theme of new and emerging families. Real economic and cultural pressures force couples to choose this path. The main reason for keeping up a commuter marriage is career advancement. In the past, there have been other reasons. They have included war, immigration, imprisonment, and temporary seasonal work, to name a few. But modern commuter marriage is the result of long-term employment constraints on a dual-career marriage.

Today, more married women are entering professional occupations which make it hard for them to move when their husbands move, and vice versa. At the same time, tighter job markets are forcing more people to relocate. In the past, this meant that a husband's wishes prevailed. But today, more equality within marriage requires more attention be given to wives' career goals. And since dual-careerism is now built into our economy, the number of commuter marriages should increase in the future.

The problem is due to an increasing emphasis on career achievement for both men and women. This makes work a more important element in people's adult lives than ever before (Gerstel and Gross, op. cit.: 73).

Not everyone winds up in a commuter marriage. People in commuter marriages are usually well-educated and affluent professionals. According to Gerstel and Gross, over half are academics and the vast majority have completed some graduate study. Most commuter spouses are in their late thirties and over half have been married more than nine years. About half of commuter couples also have children. Obviously, commuters are not a typical cross-section of the American population but they are of particular interest to college students (and their professors).

Commuter marriages can take a variety of forms. For example, some couples live a great distance from each other, and others live close by. Some reunite regularly, others only rarely when their schedules permit it.

But whatever its form, every commuter marriage suffers from tension. To reduce the stress, commuter spouses need enough money to run two households and pay high travel costs and long distance phone bills. Just as important, they need a strong commitment to their work; they must view it as a central life concern. It helps if the couple has been married long enough to have established a shared history. Young children make commuting problems worse, so it helps to not have children, or to have children who are no longer in the home. Finally, regular weekend reunions ease the situation.

Yet, despite the stress, commuter marriages often persist for long periods of time because of the advantages they offer. They permit career gains for both spouses, a high degree of occupational mobility, simpler daily lives, and lots of control for spouses over their own schedules. Responsibility for their own domestic work also gives both spouses—especially husbands—a sense of accomplishment and confidence in their ability to live independently. As well, many commuter couples experience a keener sense of intimacy when they do reunite.

Women benefit more from commuter marriage, finding that it allows them to spend time away from their spouse while focusing on their work. By contrast, many of the commuter men report they are less able to concentrate on work once the structure of home life is missing.

Beyond that, many commuter spouses report missing everyday routines and shared intimacies. Many feel lonely, particularly around meal time. Others—especially those who do *not* reunite regularly on weekends—report a large decrease in shared leisure and sexual relations, even when they reunite with their spouses. Many find their families, colleagues, and friends have trouble accepting this commuter lifestyle. Commuters with children also report feeling they have lost influence over their children's daily lives.

Gerstel and Gross conclude that although "commuter marriage is surely a response to the tensions of conventional marriage, it also generates tensions of its own." In their view, commuter marriage is a forced choice. Though the spouses want to live together, they also want meaningful jobs and "they face a relatively inflexible occupational system."

The authors believe there will have to be reforms in employer-employee relations to better deal with the needs of couples who find themselves caught in such a relationship. Like people in other kinds of nontraditional relationships, people in commuter marriages feel that they would like more understanding and acceptance than they have received so far.

VIOLENCE IN MARITAL RELATIONSHIPS

We gain a far different picture of marriage when we shift our attention to those families which suffer from domestic violence.

Violence is not restricted to domestic situations and, in fact, you can argue that most violence takes place outside the home. Many of us have become hardened to street violence between men. However, our idealized view of how family life ought to be makes it particularly disturbing for us to witness or hear reports about physical or emotional violence within families.

We mentioned in Chapter One that family life has the potential for both physical and mental abuse. Stronger family members have the power to take out their frustrations on weaker ones. As many novelists and playwrights have shown us, the family has a "psychosocial interior," with its own history and mythology, its grudges, alliances, and jealousies. Same-sex couples are by no means immune from human frailty. However, since the vast majority of couples are heterosexual, we shall concentrate on violence between men and women.

Experts often point out that police are reluctant to intervene when the neighbors call to complain of a noisy family dispute. Many (police included) still accept the view that people who are members of the same family should be allowed to work things out for themselves, without bringing in police or social workers until there are overwhelming grounds for outside involvement.

An extreme case of this occurred in Wisconsin in the early 1990s. A young man managed to escape from the house where a serial killer had kept him for sex and torture. After his escape, he was chased by his captor, who managed to get the police to give him back on the grounds that they had been having a "lover's quarrel." Parts of his body were later found with many others in the murderer's house.

The stereotype, and it may be valid, is that most domestic violence is physical and is carried out by men upon women. We do not know the ultimate causes of spousal violence. People who work in shelters for battered women believe that (roughly) nine times out of ten it is men who abuse their partners or their children. Violence tends to occur at the same time as alcohol abuse, spillover of work stress, and poor anger control.

How Common is Violence?

The United States General Social Survey asks its respondents, "Have you ever been punched or beaten by another person?" Just over half of men (55 percent) have ever been punched or beaten, compared to less than one quarter of women (23 percent). This fits with our common-sense notion that men are more violent than women, since we assume that they exercise their violence upon each other.

Analysis of Canadian data shows that the rate of violent victimization, including incidents of pushing, slapping, grabbing, beating, and shooting is higher for men than for women. Men are also more likely to suffer nonviolent victimization. In fact, the most likely people to be victimized are male, young, single, residents of urban areas and those who are students or unemployed. Perhaps men are more reckless.

Certainly, women are more prudent than men. We can see this from responses to the General Social Survey question, "Is there any area around (your neighborhood) where you would be afraid to walk alone at night?" Over half of women (58 percent) are fearful in this way, compared to around one man in five (19 percent).

What percentage of relationships involve spouse abuse? For a long time, we just did not know. Most research on the topic was based on non-random samples of specifically selected populations of women, such as women using shelters or reporting abuse to the police. Statistics from that type of research cannot be generalized to the larger population because of the biased sampling methods.

Only a small number of surveys have been carried out with scientifically drawn national samples. The Canadian government statistics agency reported one such large random-sample survey in 1993. On its estimate, one in ten of all adult women had been victimized in the last 12 months and at least some violence was reported in all social groups, rich and poor, old and young, well-educated and poorly educated. As usual, the survey found that more women are abused by people they know than they are by strangers. Another finding is that women between 18 and 24 years old are markedly more likely to report being victims of violence.

Violence in this survey was defined in the same way as assault in the criminal code and ranged from the use of a gun or a knife, through various combinations of being hit with something, choked, sexually assaulted, kicked or hit, beaten up, slapped, threatened, or pushed and shoved.

These Canadian data concentrate on women as victims, whether the violence occurred in the home, in the street, or in the workplace. But what happens between a couple? If you ask people about physical abuse by a current or previous spouse or common-law partner, then you typically find that just over 10 percent of women report abuse, compared to just under 2 percent of men. The precise proportions depend on how the questions are asked and precisely how the researchers define physical abuse.

One question which is often raised is, "Can men be victims too?" Murray Straus and Richard Gelles whose National Family Violence Survey, carried out in the United States in 1975 and again in 1985, showed that on some definitions of violence, men are just as likely to be victims of domestic violence as are women.

TABLE 4.1 Which Canadian Women Get Hurt in Just One Year (Number of women 18 and over who have experienced violence in the past 12 months)

	Total Female Population	Total Women Victimized (past 12 months)	
Total	10,498,000	1,016,000	10%
Age group			
18–24	1,315,000	353,000	27
25–34	2,334,000	331,000	14
35–44	2,256,000	191,000	8
45–54	1,628,000	91,000	6
55 and over	2,961,000	49,000	2

Even using responses that came only from the 2,947 women in the 1985 survey, Straus and Gelles found that men are the ones more likely to be assaulted by their partners. They also showed that between 1975 and 1985, the overall rate of domestic violence by men against women decreased, while women's violence against men increased.

What are we to make of all this? Are we in a competition to see whether men or women can claim to be the most victimized? According to the National Survey of Families and Households (Brush, 1989), much of the reported violence between married partners occurs in couples in which *both* partners are reported as perpetrators. In other words, Straus and Gelles are right when they say that women as well as men commit violent acts in married couples. However, the NSFH data indicate that the probabilities of injury for male and female respondents differ significantly. As one might expect with men usually being stronger than women, wives are more likely to be injured than are husbands, even when both partners are acting violently.

Research shows that as many women as men use verbal abuse within intimate relationships. Severe violence is uncommon in absolute terms. However, men are more likely to use it on women than women are to use it on men. There are subcultural exceptions here. Among African-American couples and among American Aboriginal people, the incidence of spousal homicide is almost as high for women as perpetrators as it is for men as perpetrators.

What are we to make of the highly unusual state of affairs among African Americans, where there is an almost balanced incidence of male-partner killing female-partner homicide as compared to female-partner killing male-partner homicide? This is gender equality indeed! In most other countries and in most other ethnic groups in North America, it is more common for women to be killed by their male partners than for men to be killed by their female partners.

The only North American groups that are similar to African-Americans in this respect are aboriginal peoples, many of whom live in considerable poverty. All kinds of speculations could be made to account for this. On the average, women put up with domestic violence so long as men are economically useful in cash or in kind (by bringing home a paycheck). They are more likely to fight back (or to kick the partner out), if he is not only abusive but also an economic liability.

A survey of self-reported domestic violence in Canada (Lupri, 1992, 1994) confirms and summarizes past findings elsewhere. They are that (1) younger people are more violent than older people; (2) unemployed people are more violent than employed people; but (3) poorly educated people are no more violent than highly educated people (nor are lower-income people more violent than higher-income people).

The most revealing and meaningful finding is that high rates of domestic violence are associated with high levels of domestic stress. Concretely, the more stressful events a person reports encountering in the previous year, the more likely violence will have taken place within the household.

These stressful events include the following: unemployment for more than a month, personal bankruptcy, a drop in wage or salary, taking an additional job to make ends meet, working more overtime than desired to make ends meet, new child support or alimony payments to make, a move to less expensive accommodations, taking in a boarder to make ends meet, one or more demotions at work, loss of income due to going back to a university, another important career setback, or some other important setback in economic well-being.

Reading through this list of "events," it is not hard to imagine how they might cause intense frustration. What is less clear is why these frustrating events occasionally lead to violence and in other cases do not do so. Nor is it clear why this violence should be directed against a spouse. (The best common-sense explanation of the latter is, "Because the spouse is *there*.")

We are in no position to judge how valid these self-reports really are. We are even less able to judge whether domestic violence is increasing or decreasing in North American families.

CONCLUSIONS

There can be no doubt that people worldwide are redefining marriage. The family remains the arena in which personal, emotional, and psychological growth can take place. But more than ever, marriage has come to be a voluntary act—a choice made freely by individuals. As well, what's done can be undone. Spouses are not as closely tied to each other economically as they once were, and they can opt out of marriages that do not meet their earlier expectations.

In Western countries, people are less inclined to marry than they were in the past. More people view singlehood positively. Nonmarital cohabitation offers many of the benefits of marriage, without the same expectation of permanence and without legally binding obligations.

Yet we see variations among the developed countries where marriage and divorce are concerned. For example, in Sweden, reforms have eliminated many of the traditional reasons for women to marry. Norway and other European countries have similar policies, though they have come about more slowly and recently. Nonetheless, all of the developed world is moving in the same direction.

Is the institution of marriage about to die from a lack of interest? This is not the conclusion one would reach from the data we have examined here. We see a continued increase in the acceptance of varied spousal forms. We see no decrease in the strength of feelings towards exclusive intimacy within a spousal relationship.

In general, the provision of public supports for personal life (for example, antidiscrimination laws, family assistance and welfare programs, better day care and old-age pensions) reduce people's (especially women's) need to rely on family supports. In this way, they reduce the pressure on family life. Family life can now concern itself more with companionship and love, and less with economic security, than it did in the past.

So there is no evidence that such public supports for personal life make family life more fragile or less necessary. They even reduce the likelihood of breakup and violence by reducing the strain on spousal relationships. Therefore, public supports are not an enemy of family life. In principle, they can make it better than ever. But in many countries, they have failed to do so. We will have more to say about this failure in later chapters.

At the beginning of this chapter, we asked "Why are marriage rates falling even though people are forming more, and earlier, spousal relationships than ever?" "Why is a common alternative to legal marriage—cohabitation—becoming more and more *like* legal marriage all the time?" and "Why are so many people fleeing marriage for divorce, then fleeing divorce for marriage?" The answer is that people have *not* given up on the ideal of a stable, intimate personal life. They are actively searching for ways to integrate modern family life with new ideas about personal development, on the one hand, and economic and job organization on the other.

In theory (at least), cohabitation and delays in marriage should help marriages last longer. That is because spouses who marry when they are older are less likely to divorce. But neither has shown any sign of contributing to the endurance of marriage.

One thing is certain: People today have a lot more opportunity to escape violent or otherwise dissatisfying marriages than they did in the past. And that brings us to a discussion of the rising divorce rate.

5

THE ABANDONMENT
OF COMMITMENT?

INTRODUCTION

Since the 1940s, divorce rates have increased in almost every country in the world. Even in China where divorce used to be rare, and where the state now forbids anyone to marry before their early twenties, a small but increasing number of marriages break up every year.

High rates of divorce have produced a large stock of divorced adults. Some of them remarry, some live in cohabiting relationships, and some remain without an adult partner for long periods of time. Over the past decade, divorce rates in North America have leveled off at historically high levels. It is too soon to know whether they will decrease significantly. But even if they do, it will take time for the stock of divorced adults to be reduced by remarriage or death.

High divorce rates bring newspaper headlines and articles about the decline of marriage as an institution. Putting this into context, you should know that divorce has *always* been more common in the United States than anywhere else, because the divorce laws have been more lenient. Yet even here, divorce rates increased in the 1970s and early 1980s.

As with marriage and fertility there are two kinds of statistics about divorce: statistics about divorces that have already happened (i.e., the stock of divorced people) and forecasts about what will happen if current trends continue (i.e, the outcome of continued high rates of divorce). The demographer Thomas Espenshade (1985: 208) looked at data from the mid-1970s on the stock of divorced people, and showed that about 45 percent of white women's marriages had ended in divorce. (For black women, the percentage was only slightly higher, at 47 percent.)

On the basis of current rates, Bianchi and Spain (1986: 23–4) estimate that *over half* of American marriages begun in the 1970s will end in divorce. And along similar lines, U.S. Census Bureau demographers Norton and Moorman (1986) estimate that nearly *six* out of ten Americans born between 1946 and 1955 who marry will eventually divorce. In North America and most countries of Western Europe, the best forecasts are that 40 percent to 50 percent of first marriages in the 1990s will end in divorce.

If you look at it from a life-course perspective, all marriages end sooner or later, whether by death, divorce, or desertion. Higher divorce rates mean that first marriages now last a shorter time. Along with this, the total time white females spend married, in first marriages and remarriages taken together, is lower both in the absolute number of years and relative to life expectancy. So, for example, by 1975–1980, marriages for white women had lasted an average of 22.5 years and for black women, less than 15 years. Remarriages have increased, it is true. However, this is because there are more divorced people available to remarry (Espenshade, 1985: 208).

These data support Espenshade's conclusion that marriage has been in decline as an American institution for over 30 years (ibid.: 209). Marriage is still important, but its importance has diminished, relative to other life events. We are spending less of our lives being married to one particular spouse.

This increase in divorce is due to more liberal laws which make divorces easier to get. Other countries were slower to liberalize their divorce laws, so divorce rates rose more slowly and moderately there. In Canada, for example, divorce was hard to get until 1968. In general, however, the same kinds of changes have occurred in Canada as in the United States. For example, during the 1970s and 1980s, the rates of Canadian marriage fell and the rates of divorce rose. The average age at first marriage increased too, just as in the United States (Adams and Nagnur, 1989; Devereux, 1988).

In Britain, divorce laws were liberalized in 1925 and 1937. The major reform took place in 1971, with further changes in 1984. As Haskey (1987) notes, over the long term, legal changes have made divorce easier for wives as petitioners.

Everywhere, easier divorce laws make for higher divorce rates. In turn, divorce laws are made easier in response to changes in social attitudes. What, then, are the changes in American and other countries' attitudes that have led to divorce being accepted as a normal, if regrettable, social event?

We have already seen that most families have lost their function as a "work unit," so family members are no longer held together by the chains of economic necessity. That means "more value is placed on [marriage] for emotional companionship. . . . [Therefore] the rise in divorce may not mean the decline of the marriage institution so much as the failure of this new expectation" (Moore, 1989a: 341). And this view takes us from an economic explanation to one that is more cultural and focuses on changes in people's values and expectations.

By this reckoning, divorce may be a necessary and inevitable "byproduct of a marriage system that puts a high premium on voluntary choice and that values emotional gratification above all" (Furstenberg, 1990: 380). There has been a gradual shift in marital standards from "one which required couples to remain married even if they were not in love to one which virtually demanded divorce unless they remained in love" (ibid.). The same explanation holds for lower marriage rates. High expectations produce disappointment. They also lead to doubts about the value of getting married in the first place.

WHO GETS DIVORCED?

There are a few factors which consistently predict marital stability, whatever the social context. Chief among these are the effects of age, income, and early childbearing.

Evidence from many sources indicates that arranged marriages of very young people *may* work in traditional societies, but they don't work here, and neither do love marriages. That's because young North Americans face more difficulties in life than older North Americans. Couples who face other challenges than those typically associated with marital adjustment (e.g., completing an education, finding a job) are more apt to divorce. So, for example, people who marry when they are very young, or because of pregnancy, and are forced to live in poverty, run a higher risk of divorce than other couples do.

As well, the data indicate that more women who work for pay divorce than do full-time homemakers. But here the chain of cause and effect is complicated. Generally, having a job means that a wife has more control over her marriage. Women who have financial independence are less obliged to remain in an unsatisfactory relationship.

On the other hand, people with higher education and couples with a high-income partner are *less* likely than average to divorce. And the higher a wife's level of education, the less likely she and her husband will divorce. Perhaps that is because people with more education have married later, thus avoiding the problems associated with too-early marriage.

Occasionally, married women who work for pay upset traditional role expectations and, in this way, create marital conflict. For example, in Puerto Rico, Canabal (1990) found that participation in the labor force only increased the risk of divorce for wives who had joined the labor force after marriage. Women who were employed *before* marriage were, other things being equal, no more likely to divorce than women who were homemakers.

Higher education has two opposing effects on marital stability. For the reasons we just mentioned, it pushes couples *away from* divorce. But by giving women a stronger job commitment and more economic independence, higher education also pushes them *towards* divorce. As a result, the net effect of education is unknown at this point.

So is the effect of children on a marriage. On one hand, children can create a lot of stress in marriage (see, for example, Ambert, 1992). Research has shown that parenthood produces lower levels of marital satisfaction than one finds among married people without children. Yet one of the best predictors of marital stability is having a lot of children. Couples with children, especially young children, are less apt than others to divorce, because of the effect of divorce on the children (we will say more about this in the next chapter).

Likewise, in all Western countries there is a strong correlation between divorce and infertility—an involuntary lack of children. Betzig (1989: 667) reports that "In the United States, when duration of marriage is controlled, couples with no children divorce more often than couples with one child, who divorce more often than couples with two children, who in turn divorce more often than couples with three or more children." Again, the probable reason is that couples with young children are less willing to even consider divorcing. After all, divorce is more difficult than usual when there are children to take into account.

In the end, childbearing, like education, has both stabilizing and destabilizing effects on a marriage. A lot depends on the context. Consider one particular scenario: whether the children are born before or after a couple marries.

The evidence shows that birth before marriage has a destabilizing effect on a relationship. For example, Bennett et al. (1988: 133) found that among Swedes aged 20 to 44 "women with a premarital birth have a rate of divorce that is one-half higher than women who did not give birth premaritally." On the other hand, birth after marriage has a stabilizing effect. In Sweden, divorce rates for mothers are one-quarter lower than they are for women married the same length of time who have not given birth.

These Swedish data on the effects of childbearing are consistent with results of research conducted in the United States. In both cases, the research shows people *do* stay together for the sake of the children, unless these children were unplanned and unwanted, or were born when the couple was already facing other stresses (in particular, before the spouses had completed their formal education).

Another important variable for predicting marital stability is time spent together. The risk of divorce drops slowly over the first ten years of marriage and remains at 30 percent or more over this period. After that, the risk is lower. In short, the longer a couple has lived together, the less likely they are to divorce.

Gary Becker (1991) would explain this in terms of an investment the couple has made. Couples build up "marital capital" during their lives together. The more capital they accumulate, the more difficult it becomes for them to separate. That's because the financial and emotional "costs" of breaking up are higher than they would have been a decade earlier. Perhaps, they are greater than the "benefits" they are certain of getting by breaking up.

The factors we have discussed work in similar ways in different countries. In that sense, they are stable over time and across cultures. However, historical and cross-cultural variations in divorce need to be mentioned.

First, factors external to the family exercise a powerful effect on family stability. Research in Israel by Peres and Katz (1981) shows that unending warfare with the surrounding countries has strengthened Jewish Israeli families. This is in keeping with the sociological theory that argues an external threat will strengthen the boundaries of a community or group. From this theory, we would predict that a final peace settlement in the Middle East, if it ever comes, will increase divorce rates in that part of the world.

On the other hand, influences which disrupt and even destroy community life may have disastrous effects for family life as well. There is evidence of this in research on families living in refugee camps (Williams, 1990). Beyond a certain point, adversity does *not* strengthen family life—it destroys it, just as it destroys personal well-being.

Second, as divorce becomes more common, the kinds of predictors we have been discussing are bound to become less powerful. This has already happened in America and Scandinavia. There, divorce-suppressors such as a high income or religious sentiment are ever less important. Generally, there is more "idiosyncrasy" in people's lives, as we showed in an earlier book (Jones et al., 1989). The factors influencing marriage and divorce become more numerous, and mix in less traditional ways, with the passage of time.

We must allow for the possibility—as Durkheim did with crime and Davis and Moore did with inequality—that divorce has become "normal," inevitable. Perhaps it even serves useful purposes in modern society. One such useful purpose is that divorce allows people to, once again, go in search of a "better" mate. Yet up to now, one of the main reasons people have avoided divorce (and, for that matter, marriage) is because of the perceived costs of dissolving a union. People's perceptions are valid and the costs are real enough. We shall now discuss them briefly.

POST-DIVORCE RELATIONSHIPS: COHABITATION AND REMARRIAGE

As we have mentioned, one consequence of higher divorce rates is an increase in the number of remarriages. In the United States, about 75 percent to 80 percent of divorced adults eventually remarry. In fact, Bumpass et al. (1989) find that half of the recent marriages in the United States involved at least one previously married partner.

Here again, the trend is widespread in developed countries. During the 1980s, almost a quarter of British marriages involved a divorced man. An overlapping quarter involved a divorced woman (Haskey, 1987). In Canada, remarriages are less common than in the United States or Britain (Balakrishnan et al. 1990). This is largely because of low rates of remarriage in Quebec, where the high rate of cohabitation suggests that many divorced people are cohabiting instead of remarrying. Yet even here, one in six men and women who married in 1988 had been divorced (Langlois, 1992: 139).

Balakrishnan et al. (1990), studying remarriage in Canada, found that a variety of factors—including "age at first marriage, age at first marriage dissolution, work status before marital dissolution, education, region of residence, type of separation, and age cohort"—all predict a willingness to remarry.

Whether widowed or divorced, and regardless of age, men are more likely to remarry than women. There is also a general tendency for younger people to remarry than older ones. So for women, age at divorce is inversely related to the probability of remarriage (Balakrishnan et al., 1990: 15). That is, older women are less likely to remarry than younger ones. Older women with children are least likely of all to remarry.

Among both men and women, people who are more educated and have worked before their divorce are more likely to remarry. Other things being equal, remarriage is also more likely among the widowed than among people who have divorced. And remarriages typically occur soon after widowhood, separation, or divorce. As the years pass, it becomes more and more likely that a divorced person will remain single.

Like marriage rates, American remarriage rates have recently decreased and the interval between marriages has increased (Cherlin, as cited by Furstenberg, 1990: 385). In part, this is because of increased rates of cohabitation.

This change also indicates that people remarry for reasons that are different from the reasons they married in the first place. Uhlenberg (1989: 13–14) assumes that people remarry for the *same* reasons that they married for the first time: that is, because of love, personal happiness, intimacy, and self-fulfillment. But if so, remarriage rates should look a lot more like first-marriage rates than they do.

To explain this discrepancy, Becker (1991) emphasizes the importance of practical reasons in remarriage. He believes the factors that increase the likelihood of divorce will decrease the likelihood of remarriage. For example, economic independence increases the likelihood that women will divorce and it should decrease the likelihood they will remarry out of economic need. (On the other hand, men might find economically independent women attractive remarriage prospects, from an economic point of view.)

Put in other words, people seem to be unlikely to marry for the first time for economic reasons, that is, to escape poverty and economic insecurity. They are more likely to marry a second time for these reasons. Given the "feminization of poverty" that we discuss later in this chapter, this might apply especially to women.

Whatever the reasons for remarriage, many couples have a hard time adjusting to the demands of a second family life. Let's consider these briefly.

FAMILY ADJUSTMENT TO REMARRIAGE

Researchers have found that remarriage is both psychologically and economically beneficial to parents (Pasley and Ihinger-Tallman, 1987). Where children are concerned, there is a mixture of pluses and minuses. In particular, girls have a harder time adjusting to remarriage than boys do (Allison and Furstenberg, 1989). We discuss this further in the next chapter.

On the one hand, children are better off financially once the custodial parent remarries. However, child support and visitation by the noncustodial parent often decreases. As well, remarried (or what researchers sometimes call *reconstituted*) families are different from other families in a variety of ways (Bohannon, 1985; James and Johnson, 1988).

For example, stepparents and stepsiblings often have trouble finding appropriate ways to display affection and control sexual attraction to their stepchildren and stepsiblings. They also have a hard time exercising authority over a spouse's children, forming a common family culture among two subfamilies, and relating to outside (nonbiological) kin—for example, their new in-laws.

Second marriages can run into a lot of problems. They may run an even higher risk of divorce than first marriages, for several reasons. For example, children often strain the relationship between remarried spouses (Bohannon, 1985). As we have noted, rules and roles are often ambiguous in these families, leading to what Cherlin has called an "incomplete institutionalization" of remarriages. As well, many who enter second marriages have shown themselves willing to leave an unhappy relationship in the past, so they are likelier than average to do so again (Halliday and Cherlin, 1980; Furstenberg and Spanier, 1984).

In short, explanations of the breakdown of second marriages are similar, in many respects, to explanations of the breakdown of cohabiting unions and first marriages that follow cohabiting unions. First, people who remarry (or cohabit) differ from people who marry into their first serious relationship. Second, married, remarried, and cohabiting relationships have different social and cultural meanings for people. In general, first marriages are more resistant to stress and ambiguity.

COSTS AND CONSEQUENCES OF DIVORCE

Though people usually have good reasons for divorcing, divorce hurts just about everyone. Among sociologists, there is a lot of agreement about the effects of divorce on both spouses and children. These effects include higher risks of depression and illness, and a lower life expectancy. But the effects of divorce—social, psychological, and economic—are different for women and men. We cover the effects on children in the next chapter.

For men, the psychological or emotional effects are most important. Sociologists have known this since Durkheim's landmark study of suicide nearly a century ago. Durkheim showed that men suffer far more from the effects of social and familial isolation than women do. Hence, divorce has a far stronger effect on their propensity to commit suicide.

For women, on the other hand, the *economic* effects of divorce are particularly devastating. That's because, for most women, divorce means a drop in their standard of living. This fact has not changed with the liberalization of American divorce laws in the last 25 years. If anything, the change in laws and divorce rates has made matters worse. Yet, as often happens, the laws were changed with the best of intentions—namely, a desire to rid divorce laws of their outmoded ideas about fault and blame.

There is little doubt that divorce laws affect the divorce rate. Many countries are a single jurisdiction from the point of view of family laws and most other laws. The United States is different in that family law differs from state to state. Using American data from 1960, Stetson and Wright (1975) found that more restrictive laws result in a lower rate of divorce and vice versa. As your grandmother could have told you, easier divorce laws result in higher rates of divorce.

In the 1960s and 1970s, people argued over whether or not to liberalize the divorce laws. Some feared that liberalizing the laws would result in "waves of divorces," the collapse of the family and the end of civilization as we have known it. Others felt that liberalization was necessary because divorce, however undesirable, was often inevitable. If the laws were *not* liberalized, many couples would separate nonetheless and lose all respect for the legal process. In hindsight, both fears were warranted.

More liberal laws have certainly led to higher rates of divorce. So, for example, in Canada, the divorce rates jumped dramatically following legislative changes in 1968. Canadian divorce rates had stayed constant at about 200 divorces per 100,000 married women aged 15 and over from 1952 through 1968. But after the new, easier laws came into effect, divorce rates shot up fivefold within ten years. Since then, the divorce rates have remained high but stopped growing.

A similar change occurred in the United States over the same period. There, most states had had divorce laws by the early 1900s. Though they varied, these laws typically reinforced the sex-based division of labor. They treated wives as subordinate but vulnerable people. Upon divorce, wives would typically receive alimony and custody of the children, if there were children. Husbands would remain responsible for providing financial support to their wives and children.

Before liberalization of the laws, only marital "offenses" such as adultery, cruelty, or desertion could justify a divorce. What's more, the laws worked differently for men and women. Either husband or wife could petition for divorce on the grounds of their partner's adultery, but men were more likely to do so than women. Women could also seek divorce by proving their husbands had harmed them physically, though there was once a legal doctrine that husbands had the right to subject their wives to reasonable discipline. For men, getting a divorce could mean proving that their wives had neglected them, for example, through a lack of affection or poor housekeeping. Husbands could also charge their wives with desertion if they refused to migrate. That is because husbands had the legal right to choose the location of the family home. (In those days, commuter marriages were unheard of.)

The financial terms of a divorce depended on a determination of fault. Courts only awarded alimony to the innocent spouse as a reward for "good" behavior and punishment of the other spouse for "bad" behavior. Findings of fault influenced both the property and custody awards.

Over the twentieth century, moral standards changed. Yet many couples who wished to divorce were obliged to construct a "proof" of adultery by one partner. This meant hiring a private detective who would "discover" one of the spouses in bed with someone else and then testify in court that the marital fault had occurred. This process invented a blameworthy spouse and the divorce could proceed!

Sooner or later, these domestic fictions were bound to lose their appeal. Family living had changed since the early laws had been enacted.

New laws were needed that would reflect new kinds of family life and a new morality.

The easing of divorce legislation in many countries tried to address these kinds of changes. For example, after the development of no-fault divorce in California in 1970, people could seek a divorce on the basis of "irreconcilable differences." The new laws not only eliminated a need to identify misconduct or lay blame, they got rid of the notion of fault altogether (Weitzman and Dixon, 1980).

The no-fault law aimed to "reduce the adversity, acrimony and bitterness surrounding divorce proceedings; to lessen the personal stigma attached to the divorce; and to create conditions for more rational and equitable settlements of property and spousal support" (ibid.: 345). It eliminated both the fault-based grounds for divorce and the adversary process and got down to the reality of the situation: two married people couldn't stand living together any longer.

Now, the financial aspects of the divorce were to be based on equity, equality, and economic need, not traditional sex roles and the identification of fault. "Instead of the old sex-typed division of family responsibilities, the new law has attempted to institutionalize sex-neutral obligations which fall equally upon the husband and the wife" (ibid.: 348). New laws included a joint responsibility to support any dependent children. In short, lawmakers aimed to "bring divorce legislation into line with the social realities of marital breakdown in contemporary society" (ibid.).

THE FEMINIZATION OF POVERTY

However, good intentions are not enough to create good laws. The no-fault law had ignored the persistent gender inequalities in the labor force and, often, a husband's unwillingness (or inability) to pay child support. No-fault divorce laws hold both partners responsible for their children's economic welfare in a society which pays women only 60 percent or 70 percent of what men earn and segregates women in jobs with low pay, few benefits, and little chance of advancement.

As well, working for a low wage may not make economic sense when child care outside the home costs a woman's entire salary. The law also penalizes women when it ignores their past contribution to the family as housekeepers and child rearers. Often, "a divorced woman has no rights to her former husband's retirement pension, even though her labor in the home enabled him to advance his career, and has no pension in her own right because she did not work outside of the home or had only intermittent employment" (Arendell, 1987: 132).

Today, men and women leave marriages with different earning powers and child care responsibilities. Men have a larger earning power and in most cases do *not* take custody of their children. Yet the courts have typically granted men low child maintenance payments. Even then, men have defaulted on these payments in about half of all cases (United States Bureau of the Census, 1989a). Worse still, these payments are rarely indexed to the cost of living, so they decline (in real dollar value) over time.

Arendell found that, in the United States, in 1982 "spousal support was awarded in just 17 percent of all divorces. . . . It was actually received in fewer than 6 percent of cases" (ibid.: 133). Most divorced fathers "do not comply with child-support orders" (ibid.: 130). Even when child-support orders are issued, and this is only in three to four out of five cases, they "call for payments that do not meet even half the costs of child rearing" (ibid.: 131). In Ontario, Canada, at the beginning of the 1990s, roughly three-quarters of the child and spousal support orders were in default (Hossie, 1990).

Most jurisdictions have ignored these problems, but a few have tried to solve them. For example, the state of Wisconsin has implemented a payroll deduction scheme, similar to income tax payments, for child support payments. A similar scheme is in place in Australia and was introduced in Ontario, Canada in 1993. In Great Britain, the conservative government of the early 1990s responded to public concern about young women being left literally holding the baby by irresponsible boyfriends and set up a special unit to police child support payments.

Divorce is expensive. For one thing, it often means that two housing units are required in the place of only one. But is income shared equally? Are there any maintenance checks and if there are, do any of them bounce? The research data show that on the average, men experience a rise in their standard of living and women, a decline, after divorce. In an influential early study of this pattern, Lenore Weitzman (1985) collected data on 114 men and 114 women who became divorced in Los Angeles County in 1977. The conclusion—that the economic status of a woman falls substantially after divorce—was widely discussed after the publication of her book.

Better-quality follow-up data from the Panel on Income Dynamics (Duncan and Hoffman, 1985) have confirmed Weitzman's finding. Men improve their economic status after a divorce, and do about as well as men in intact families.

By contrast, women experience a significant drop in income which lasts for several years. Eventually, most women recover economically. They return to their income level prior to the divorce, but they do less well than women in stable married families. In most cases, they recover their economic well-being only through remarriage. Women who remain unmarried continue to experience a sizable income loss even if they increase their participation in the labor force (Duncan and Hoffman, 1985).

In a later paper, Hoffman and Duncan (1988) reanalyzed Weitzman's published figures and compared them with the findings of other studies using larger and more reliable samples. They found that so far as the United States is concerned, divorce brings women an average one-third decline in economic status.

Some women do even worse than that. The exact size of the decline varies with such factors as the number of children over whom a woman has custody, their ages, the type of job (if any) the woman has, whether or not she receives any income support from the government, and the amount of child support she receives from her ex-husband. (Men are unable to claim tax relief on support payments in the United States and women do not pay taxes on the support payments they receive. This is different from Canada where, since 1942, men have been able to treat their support payments as a tax-deductible expense, though women have to pay taxes on the support income they receive.)

Remember, too, that women are less likely than men to remarry. They are more likely to have sole custody of their children, whom they must support with low wages and low support orders that are poorly enforced. All of these economic factors make the finances of female-headed single-parent families bleak indeed. The result has been a massive shift in America's most visible poverty problem from poverty among the old to poverty in female-headed single-parent families. Social scientists have dubbed this "the feminization of poverty."

If only the world were organized differently, easier access to divorce would have made ending an unhappy relationship far less painful. But in practice, no-fault divorce has reinforced inequalities between men and women. Nowhere is this more evident than in single-parent families headed by women.

Single-parent families are created by birth out of wedlock, by divorce or separation, or by widowhood. Everywhere, the proportion of single-parent female-headed families is rising and, in many countries, female-headed families face a high risk of poverty. The phrase "feminization of poverty" was first introduced to describe this economic inequity created by divorce. One observer writes, "Divorce is a primary contributor to the increase in the number of impoverished women" (Arendell, 1987: 122).

In 1985, in the United States, "although female-headed families constitute only 20 percent of all families, they represent 55 percent of all poor families. Over one-third of female-headed families live below the poverty level and many more live marginally close to the poverty level" (ibid.: 121).

It's true that at any given moment, only a small proportion of adult women are heads of single-parent families and subject to a high risk of poverty because of this. More important is the fact that a larger proportion pass *through* the status of single-parent family head during their lifetimes (see Ellwood, 1988). For example, in Canada, Maureen Moore (1989a: 345) found that by 1984, more than one woman in six had been a lone parent at some point in her life.

Moore also found that an average lone-parenting "spell" lasts a little more than five years. The period is longer for widows and shorter, on average, for women who become lone parents as a result of childbearing outside marriage. So, in effect, we are talking about a large number of "person-years" spent in the condition of single-parenthood which, as we have said, is impoverishing.

Poverty is by no means restricted to single-parent families, yet a high proportion of single-parent families are poor. Moore estimates that in Canada in 1986, 60 percent of female lone-parent families were "poor" (Moore, op cit.: 337). Yet, as custodial parents, their financial needs are high.

Nor is this "feminization of poverty" limited to North America. For example, by 1984, 13 percent of British families with dependent children were single-parent families, most of them female-headed and the result of separation or divorce. One study (Kiernan, 1988) showed that 40 percent of women who divorced during 1979–1980 had remarried within two years. Given the assumptions of the British employment and welfare systems, "Living with a partner, especially an employed partner is the major route out of poverty for lone mothers" (Kiernan, 1988: 307).

Like the British research, Moore's Canadian study found that the transition out of single parenthood (and poverty) has often depended on remarriage; Ellwood (1988: 408) finds the same thing in the United States.

Ellwood and others have argued that the key to solving these problems is a change in public policy that will reward child rearing and give realistic incentives for the poor to work. Such policy changes must come particularly in the areas of "income supplements, housing, health care, child care and care-giving support services, legal reforms in divorce laws, and retirement pension coverage" (Kiernan, 1988: 135).

Data from a variety of countries prove that such policies as these *do* prevent the feminization of poverty. They also show that in this respect, the United States has been the worst of all developed countries. Sweden has been the best, though at the cost of building a welfare bureaucracy some observers have seen as being more concerned with employee participation than with service to clients (Groulx, 1990).

International comparisons of poverty rates are always difficult. However, the Luxemburg Income Study which compared national surveys carried out in the late 1980s showed that the United States had the highest single-parent poverty rate among selected industrial countries. Fully 53 percent of single-parent families in the United States were below the poverty line, followed by Canada (45 percent), Germany (25 percent), the United Kingdom (18 percent), France (15 percent) and the Netherlands (7 percent).

Sweden had the lowest rate of all; there, only 5 percent of single-parent families were poor.

So poverty is not an inevitable result of divorce. It is mainly a result of failing to make policies that would *prevent* female and child poverty. On the other hand, divorce brings other, noneconomic problems in its wake and not all of these are likely to be solved by changes in public policy.

THE EMOTIONAL COSTS OF DIVORCE

Most families have arguments. Divorcing families sometimes argue a lot, with screaming, shouting, verbal abuse, doors slamming, tears, threats, etc. What are the typical patterns?

According to Ahrons (ibid.: 533), "divorce is a crisis of family transition which causes structural changes in the family system." Unlike other crises, the crisis of divorce does not occur suddenly. Usually, it begins with a period during which marital conflict escalates and the marital satisfaction of each spouse decreases.

Ahrons identifies five transitions a family goes through in the process of getting a divorce, jointly marking "the family's change from married to divorced status, from nuclearity to binuclearity."

During the period of "individual cognition," at least one spouse recognizes that things are not working out and are unlikely to get better. Eventually, through an exchange of information among family members, there is "the realization that the problem is essential to the system" (ibid.: 535). Gradually, family members prepare themselves, mentally and emotionally, for physical separation. In sociological jargon, they undergo "anticipatory socialization."

Nevertheless, it is often only one of the spouses who makes the decision to seek a divorce. The other has no alternative but to learn to live with that decision. Since it takes two to make a marriage work, only one of the partners has to give up on the relationship for it to founder.

Systemic separation refers to the division of property and custody rights, and to the physical separation of spouses. After this typically comes *systemic reorganization*, the process of redefining family relationships within the divorced family. When children are involved:

> [e]ach parent must establish an independent relationship with the child to pass this transition successfully, but the continuation of each parent-child relationship unit requires the continued inter-dependence of the former spouses. This paradoxical and complex process requires the clarification of roles and boundaries between parental and spousal subsystems (Ahrons, 1980: 537).

What ought to happen in a "civilized" divorce is that *family redefinition* should be achieved with the least amount of stress. On this plan, the separated parents maintain an active relationship with their children and cooperate with each other. In this way, the family is supposed to change from nuclear to "binuclear," with children serving as the focus of two separate households. "The binuclear family provides a family style which does not force the child to sever the bond with either parent, but which allows both parents to continue their parental roles post-divorce" (ibid.: 539).

Even when both partners in the relationship are trying for a civilized divorce, none of this is without a cost to the participants. Menaghan and Lieberman (1986: 326) find that the "transition to divorce brings a change in life conditions that has depressive consequences." Important changes include further economic difficulties, a perceived and actual loss in standard of living, and a reduction of close supportive relationships. More specifically, separation means the:

> loss of a valued social role, loss of an intimate relationship, loss of an adult household member, loss of a source of income and/or unpaid services, and often loss of a familiar residence, and regular daily contact with one's children (Menaghan and Lieberman, 1986: 320).

After a divorce, both spouses typically suffer a higher risk of depression, illness, and death, and these risks do not dissipate quickly. The loss of the marital role—"spouse"—affects people differently, according to their other social supports and psychological resources. But on the whole, unmarried people suffer both emotionally and economically. Often, the spouse who opposed a divorce has been caught off-guard by the other's request or threat to terminate the marriage (cf. Vaughan, 1986). This element of surprise may have additional health consequences.

One of the psychologically dislocating effects of divorce is the need to learn new roles. For example, ex-spouses must redefine their expectations of each other, and parents (both custodial and noncustodial) must renegotiate their relationship with their children. People who see the positive aspects of divorce complain that our culture provides largely negative role models for the divorcing family. Yet the popular culture has responded rapidly and provided numerous positive models. At the beginning of the 1990s there were a large number of television series about modern family forms. In them, courageous single parents—some of them divorced—struggle successfully to find new relationships and bring up their kids well. One problem with these mass media portrayals is that they take too rosy a view of life after divorce.

What past studies show is that divorce depresses people by (1) actually worsening their economic conditions, (2) making them *feel* that their living conditions have worsened, and (3) depriving them of close, confiding relationships. For example, Menaghan and Lieberman focus on depression because it is an "unambiguous indicator of negative change" as well as being easy to measure with questionnaires and interviews. They find that depressed people are no more likely than average to seek a divorce. Instead, divorce has an independent depressive effect on people. Upon divorce, both men and women experience significant reductions in happiness, or increases in depression—they feel "down"; they get "the blues." What's more, people who remain divorced for a long period of time are likely to experience more, not less, depression. As well, this depressive effect "seems to be invariably immobilizing, with even small increases diminishing adaptive psychological functioning to some degree" (ibid.).

LOSS OF THE SPOUSAL ROLE

The loss of a social role like "spouse" affects people differently depending on their other social characteristics. For example, older "divorcees are more disrupted because of their greater entrenchment in an established social order" (Menaghan and Lieberman, 1986: 320)—what we called earlier a higher investment in married capital.

This loss is more damaging to people who have few other valued roles: people who are not parents or who are unemployed. In addition, the irretrievable loss of an intimate relationship can be painful and even more disruptive for those who have few other sources of intimacy and companionship. The authors conclude that:

> The emotional and economic disadvantages encountered by the unmarried, despite their increased numbers, and the decreased stigma attached to their status help to explain the rapid movement toward remarriage that characterizes so many divorcing Americans (Menaghan and Lieberman, 1986: 326).

With increasing divorce and separation rates, we are likely to see an increase in depressive symptoms. This increase will have consequences for the health and stability of divorced spouses. In fact, it affects everyone who depends on them: children, parents, friends, and work-mates, among others.

It is widely believed that divorce also harms children, though people disagree about how such harm comes about. We shall go into this more deeply in the next chapter. Here, we shall mention that children living in one-parent families arising from divorce do worse on a variety of measures when compared with those living in two-parent families. They typically achieve lower levels of educational attainment than average, for example.

Such families are often poorer than intact families. As a result, we cannot say for certain that it is the absence of a second parent in itself that is detrimental to their educational success. Many factors are involved, including the type of neighborhood they live in, and the ways in which teachers react to children from single-parent families (Epstein, 1990: 117).

As noted, the loss of a social role affects people differently, depending on their "social characteristics." The emotional and economic disadvantages encountered by the unmarried, despite their increased numbers, and the stigma attached to their status, help to explain the rapid movement toward remarriage that characterizes so many divorcing Americans.

In summary, divorce "reduce[s] the family's economic resources, it stresses the parent-child relationship, it alters and sometimes destroys the parenting system, and it reshapes kinship ties" (Furstenberg, 1990: 398). Governmental policies have not yet adapted to the reality of divorce in North America. As we have seen, no-fault divorce, for one, has not improved the functioning of divorced families.

Yet we must keep two important points in mind in concluding this chapter on marriage and divorce. The first is that people's readiness to divorce (and unreadiness to marry) are themselves the consequence of a large-scale cultural and social change that has been decades, if not centuries, in the making. We cannot have a society based on the free choice of personal lifestyles without a free choice in the realm of marriage and divorce. With this freedom comes, inevitably, consequences that will harm *some* people. All freedom carries this potential.

Second, though changes in marriage and divorce are inevitable, their harmful consequences are *not*, at least not to the extent witnessed in North America. Remember, comparative data show that in other societies, single-parent families are less likely to suffer from poverty than they are in North America. In general, we are able to legislate changes which would make the transitions to marriage, parenthood, and divorce less painful than they are today.

CONCLUSIONS

In the chapter that follows, we examine recent trends in childbearing. These are related to changes in family formation and spousal relations we have examined in this and earlier chapters. As a result, they are related to large-scale changes in our culture, society, and economy. These changes in parenthood and parenting practices, like changes in marriage and divorce, will influence the future of the family.

6

CHILDBEARING: THE START OF PARENTHOOD

INTRODUCTION

Children are said to be poor men's riches and women's jewels—the most valued product of most people's lives and their legacies beyond the grave. Children confer immortality on their parents. They bring with them a sense of completeness, of having participated more fully in the experience of what it is to be human.

In premodern societies, births and deaths were usually in balance. Before the development of modern medicine and the spread of modern techniques of sanitation, death rates were high, but so were birth rates. As a result, the rate of *natural increase*—the difference between births and deaths, expressed as a ratio of the total population—was low. The population was young and constantly changing through birth and death, but it was not growing quickly.

Families would try to have as many children as possible. Even today, children in nonindustrial countries are an economic asset. In rural areas, they start to work at an early age as farm hands. They do chores in the home, or earn extra wages on other farms or in nearby factories. In parts of the world where old-age security, pension plans, and welfare assistance do not exist, children are the sole means of support for parents when they reach old age.

The more children a couple has, the greater likelihood they will be looked after in their "golden years." Sons are especially important. In rural South Asia, for example, they provide a sort of income insurance for the parents' old age. The failure to rear a son often is seen as a material loss. These perceptions are supported by hard evidence. Among old people who lack a surviving son, one finds higher mortality risks and a higher chance of property loss. What's more, the consequences are more severe for women than they are for men, which gives wives an even larger investment in high birth rates than it does husbands (Cain, 1986).

Likewise, in societies that practice arranged marriages, children enable a family to form economic and social ties to other families for mutual assistance. The more children one has, the more ties one will have to other families.

In some cultures, having large families is a way for people to fulfill their perceived duty to God. People view many children, especially many sons, as a blessing or sign of good fortune. Some men even view the number of children they have fathered as a sign of virility. As a result, women are often accorded prestige according to how many children (especially sons) they have borne.

However, most of these reasons for having large families are traditional. Since they have not changed for centuries, they cannot, by themselves, account for the rapid rise in world population during the last half-century or so. Therefore we must look elsewhere—to the change in death rates—for an explanation. Then we find that the population explosion did not occur because people started to have more children than before. It was because more children were surviving to adult, reproductive ages and having children of their own.

Just as birth rates have been high for most of human history, so too have death rates. The lack of proper sanitation and curative medicine, poor nutrition, recurrent famines, and warfare kept the death rate high in premodern societies. The death rate was particularly high among newborn infants and young children. Childhood diseases, which we treat so easily now with antibiotics or which have nearly disappeared due to inoculation, were feared killers in the past. Being realistic, parents could not assume that even half their children would survive to adult age.

When European medicine, nutrition, and sanitation began to improve dramatically in the eighteenth century, the death rate began to fall. More children survived to reproductive age and had children of their own, many of whom survived to reproductive age. Women no longer had to bear ten children in the hopes that four would survive. They could be confident that a majority of their children would survive. Then, they began having fewer children—only as many as they thought they could support. Historically, this pattern has been repeated countless times around the world. Demographers refer to the entire process as "the demographic transition."

THE DEMOGRAPHIC TRANSITION

The term *demographic transition* refers to the change a society undergoes, from *high* birth and death rates to *low* birth and death rates, usually during industrialization. This type of change has taken place in Europe from the onset of the Industrial Revolution up to the present day. Currently, much of the Third World is in the middle of this process.

In its most general form, the transition is brought about by a package of changes—industrialization, urbanization, and increases in literacy, among other things—called *modernization.*

During the transition period, a large growth in population occurs as a result of the temporary gap between fertility and mortality. For a while, people still have as many children as always, but many more survive. But gradually, as happened in Europe and North America in the last two centuries, members of the population come to realize they do not have to have as many children as in the past.

The reasons for this are many—for example, the burden of social security shifts from family to the government. As well, people become more rational about childbearing. Increased education, urbanization, and social and geographic mobility all reduce the economic value of children. So does the increased cost of raising a child. Finally, the changing role of women in society and the increase in female careers all reduce the willingness to bear children. So the birth rate begins to fall until, finally, it reaches approximately the same (low) level as the death rate.

Mexico provides a recent example of demographic transition theory in action. Before about 1950, Mexico was essentially a premodern society. Then, as modernization took place, mortality began to fall. Between 1950 and 1985, the population tripled and fertility started to fall around 1965. In recent years, the population has been comparatively stable. However, with the decline in fertility, the average age has risen. This has led to new problems of social planning that Mexico has never had to face before (Partida-Bush, 1990).

Modern Thailand provides another illustration of demographic transition. In rural areas that have not been modernized, fertility is high and stable. But in modernized and newly settled areas, there have been declines in fertility. They are associated with land-saving and labor-saving changes—for example, high wage rates and specialization—which have made bearing children less necessary (Hutaserani and Roumasset, 1991).

Demographic transition theory has enormous practical as well as theoretical implications. The theory describes an (apparently) universal process. It makes an important contribution to our understanding of economic development and the relationship of population to that development. Indeed, this theory is the dominant way of thinking about population today and a part of every forecast of world and Third World populations. It rightly reminds us that a low-mortality/low-fertility population type is critical if people wish to maintain a high standard of living.

Problems with the Theory

Yet research over the past 20 years has cast doubt on the theory's validity (see Coale and Watkins, 1987). Newly discovered data show that the theory does not apply as well to European history, on which it was modeled, as people once thought it did. It applies even worse to non-European, Third World countries. That is because of the theory's failure to consider many problems that are common in Third World countries today, such as the following:

1. *The permanent damage a long-term population explosion does to a nation's economy or ecosystem.* This makes transition to the final stage impossible (or even the restoration of a high-mortality/high-fertility balance). An example of this is Brazil's destruction of the Amazon rain forest, a result of both rapid population growth (and migration) and the Brazilian government's desire for a rapid increase in national revenues (through meat and lumber export).

2. *The inability of Third World countries to provide the socioeconomic factors (social security, education, urbanization, social mobility, women's careers) that make fertility reduction attractive.* Where, as in Central Africa or the Indian subcontinent (or, for that matter, among teenagers in black urban America), people have little opportunity to improve their lives by avoiding childbearing, they will have many children even if the benefit to be gained from having them is slight or short-lived.

On the other hand, mortality reductions due to modernization in poor countries are hindered by the penetration of multinational corporations (Wimberley, 1990). Expressed in another way, foreign investment may be bad for people's health, though the evidence indicates that foreign *aid* is not. The role of foreign influence has complicated the issue considerably. It was not a factor when Europe was undergoing its demographic transition.

What's more, traditional and cultural factors play a part in the persistence of large families. So mortality has fallen in Nigeria, but a high value is still placed on children. Education in Western family planning techniques will not advance unless values change (Orubuloye, 1991).

As well, in some countries there are people who have a vested political interest in having many children. A survey of Nigerian students found that members of the dominant ethnic group—the Hausa—prefer the largest families. That is partly because large numbers help them maintain their political dominance (Adebayo and Adamchak, 1991).

3. *The need of Third World countries to choose among competing social investments—to spend money on social security versus education versus health care, for example.* The theory gives no guidance as to which factors are most influential in the transition process and which should be considered top priority.

China offers a classic example of this problem. China needs reforms of almost every kind: agricultural, industrial, educational, economic, and so on. Money could be usefully invested in any of thousands of different areas of activity. Choosing, though inevitable, is almost impossible. Worse still, every year there are as many new Chinese babies born as people alive in Canada—about 25 million. To planners, these new citizens represent new demands on the public purse.

This is why China has turned to the "one child" policy. However, this poses problems. Especially in rural areas, this policy leaves parents with little security in old age, as it is difficult for one child to support two elderly parents (Goldstein and Goldstein, 1986).

This could be one reason why the policy is slow to catch on. In fact, compared to Western countries (for example, Hungary) where this policy is *not* in place, China's fraction of single-child families is low—only one family in eight. As well, in developed countries, marriage takes place at later ages and the intervals between births are longer than in China (Poston and Yu, 1986).

This shows that dramatic changes in childbearing require changes in living conditions, not merely changes in government policy. However, there is no denying that in China, the changes that have occurred have been amazingly swift.

Hungary, with the world's highest fraction of single-child families— 25 percent—has a long history of low fertility for reasons that are far from fully understood. Some rural regions of Hungary have long had a one-child system in order to keep up the tradition of peasant self-sufficiency. This system came under attack in the twentieth century, with fears of national extinction that beset many European countries (Vasary, 1989). Yet Hungarian low fertility has continued, rooted in peasant concerns about independence.

Most Third World countries have to meet these pressures of a growing population and growing demands for economic improvement. Often, as in China, the result of so many conflicting demands is a political explosion. Many of the Arab countries have the same problem of high fertility, leading to a reduction in per capita income and a young population. In fact, the mushrooming population in Arab countries has a median age that is at least ten years less than one finds in industrialized Western nations. Compounding the problem is the fact that women are not allowed to participate in the labor force (Moustafa, 1988). Only the oil-rich Arab states have avoided being hurt by these factors.

Thus, demographic transition theory more or less accurately describes Western demographic history in vague generalities. It even describes the macrodynamics of current populations. However, it is unable to illuminate the details of demographic history in a given country. As such, it is unsatisfactory in contributing to forecasting, planning social policy, or perfecting causal explanations.

THE NORTH AMERICAN PICTURE

Most North Americans would probably agree that children add a fundamental and important dimension to family life. They may also agree that the ideal family for this job is a nuclear family, preferably with both male and female adults on hand to act as care givers and role models. And, despite increased marital instability, most North American children *do* grow up in nuclear family households.

In 1990, there were about 63 million children under age 18 living in American households. Almost three-quarters lived with two parents (including biological and stepparents). Twenty-eight percent lived with only one parent—nearly always their mother. Another 3 percent lived with grandparents, uncles and aunts, older siblings, or other relatives. Only 1 child in 166 lived in a nonfamily household, with someone unrelated by blood or law (American Demographics, 1992: 6).

Today, families are smaller and childbearing is later. Women are pulled (or pushed) into the labor force by greater opportunities for education and work. Given their economic vulnerability outside of marriage, their difficulty in balancing employment and child care, and their husbands' reluctance to serve as parents, many women choose to have fewer children.

Our ideas about the place of children in family life, and who shoulders the responsibility for their care have changed dramatically over time. In the past, people did not expect all their children to survive to adulthood, so it was prudent to bear more than were needed to provide economic support for the parents in their old age. As well, children could work when they were young and older children could look after the babies.

But in the last hundred years or so, better public health has markedly reduced infant mortality rates. That means fewer children are "needed" today and children no longer go out to work. They consume expensive educations instead.

The idea of a child-centered household—especially, the idea that motherhood could be a full-time job—developed less than a century ago. Contributing factors were a decline in infant and child mortality, lower fertility, increased public opposition to child labor, and demands for compulsory education and public health reform (Ehrenreich and English, 1979). As well, the new discipline of psychology emphasized the benefits of close mother-child interaction. So, many of our current ideas about motherhood actually originated in the 1890s. In terms of world history, they are new ideas.

Lately, ideas have changed again. Since 1970, there has been an enormous increase in the proportion of mothers who work outside the home. By the beginning of the 1990s, about six in every ten adult American women worked for pay. Most important for the parent-child relationship is a dramatic change in the employment of mothers of *young* children. In the United States, about half of the mothers of preschool children, and over 60 percent of the mothers of school-aged children, are in the paid work force.

This change has consequences for the family budget, the balance of power within the family, and the availability of parents for their children. Not least, it shatters traditional notions about family life and parenthood.

Many social policies still operate on the assumption that a typical family is composed of two married adults, only one of whom is employed, plus their children. Yet the reality in the United States and in many other countries is different. For example, Canadian research shows that between 1967 and 1989:

- the proportion of families with both spouses working for pay rose from 33 percent to 62 percent; and
- the percentage of families with at least one child under six with both spouses working rose from 27 percent to 71 percent.

Changing Fertility Trends

As we said in Chapter One, Western fertility began falling in the 1870s, rose (in some countries) during the baby boom, then began to decline even more rapidly in the 1970s. Table 6.1 shows recent fertility rates for several Western countries. On average, the fertility rate is 1.8 children per woman, less than what these countries need to replace their population (or keep it at its present size).

Lower fertility reflects a combination of smaller average family sizes (that is, women having fewer children, on average) and a higher incidence of voluntary childlessness (more women having no children whatever). Of the two, smaller family size is by far the more important factor. American

TABLE 6.1 Fertility Rates for Selected Developed Countries 1970–1990

	1970	1990
Developed Regions	2.6	1.8
Australia	2.9	1.9
Canada	2.5	1.7
Japan	2.0	1.7
Sweden	2.1	1.7
United Kingdom	2.5	1.8
United States	2.6	1.8

Source: The World's Women 1970–1990; Trends and Statistics. United Nations Publications, 1991.

data from 1990 show that the average number of children under age 18 per family household (counting only married couple families with at least one child under 18) has fallen to 1.87 for white couples, 1.90 for black couples, and 2.18 for Hispanic couples.

By historical and cross-national standards, these are very small families. The trend may reverse one day, and there will always be groups which are exceptional. However, for all races and education levels, the proportion of large families has decreased over four generations (Bane, 1976). It may continue to do so.

A number of interrelated factors have caused recent fertility declines. They include the increased recognition of the emotional and economic costs of children. They also reflect important changes in women's lives: more formal education, more opportunity for paid work, easier contraception, and later ages of marriage.

THE SHIFTING COST-BENEFIT BALANCE

In view of the trend toward declining fertility, why was there a baby boom after 1950 and why did the boom stop (or "bust") in the mid-1960s? One explanation of the boom is that people were catching up on childbearing that had been severely reduced (or merely delayed) during the Depression and Second World War. By the same token, the baby bust was no more than a return to declining fertility that had begun around 1870.

Another explanation for the bust is economic. It refers to tax policies and massive inflation after 1968 which made childbearing too costly for parents. For example, Swan (1986: 747) writes, "Between 1945 and 1985, a combination of changes in the tax code plus erosion of the real value of the dependent tax exemption had 'conspired' to raise the average tax rate of a single-income family with four children by 223 percent. In contrast, two income couples without children encountered no tax rate change."

In progressive income tax systems, a tax deduction is only of use to someone who has an income and it is of most use to someone who is in a high tax bracket. The 1948 United States Income Tax Act had provided a $1,080 personal exemption for the income earner and the same amount for each dependent family member. A family tax return claiming four exemptions would have been able to deduct $4,320, a great deal of money in the early 1950s.

But over the 1960s and 1970s, inflation ate away at the value of this benefit. The benefit did not change until 1986, when the Tax Reform Act almost doubled the exemption to $2,000. This was an amount substantially less (in real dollars) than the value of the earlier exemption.

Over the same period, welfare expenditures and pensions to retired civil servants increased rapidly. Welfare payments went to the elderly (as Medicare and Medicaid) and to single-parent families (as "Aid to Families with Dependent Children"—AFDC—benefits). Poverty in old age (at least) became less of a social problem than it had been.

In summary, there used to be material incentives for people to bear children in a stable marriage. They included significant tax deductions while raising the children and inadequate financial support in old age unless the children helped out. But the tax system and old-age pension reversed all this, making children less attractive economically than they once had been.

Likewise, there were once strong material disincentives to having no children, getting divorced, or having a child out of wedlock. But successive governments changed that. They set in place a system of economic incentives that reduced the advantages of bearing children in a model working-husband/dependent-wife nuclear family.

As a result, "Between 1950 and 1977, the legitimate birth rate contracted by a third, the rate of divorce more than doubled, and the labor force participation rate of wives with young children more than trebled, as did the proportion of households headed by women with dependent children" (Swan, 1986: 748). Couples who would have previously foregone a second income in order to bring up children realized that now, doing so would gain little or no benefit from the tax system. This explains (in part) why so many rearranged their lives accordingly, by having fewer children and becoming two-earner families.

Inflation and the income tax deductions system have not been the *only* causes of these large changes in family life, but they contributed to them. Were these changes bad? Viewed positively, fewer children mean a larger proportion of wanted children. More divorces mean fewer men, women, and children trapped in hellish marriages. More mothers working outside the home mean a step towards greater equality in the relationship between husbands and wives.

However, economic and fiscal matters are far from the only reasons people do, or do not, have children. Cross-cultural research shows that children everywhere are valued mainly for psychological reasons (Walters and Walters, 1980: 814). Financial costs justify limiting family size, but we do not know how many people act on these justifications when they plan a family.

For example, comparative studies show that the reasons for wanting first children differ from the reasons for wanting second, third, and later children. "The first birth tends to symbolize values relevant to the achievement of adulthood, fulfillment of the marriage, parenthood and curiosity related motives (like the opportunity to experience pregnancy and childbirth), to re-create another life and to witness the growth and development of one's own child" (Callen, 1982: 388). The main value of a second child is to provide companionship for the first, according to this research.

In many societies, parents also prefer that their children be sons. This preference has a consequence for family size, even in North America. North American women prefer to have one child of each sex, and prefer that their first-born child be a son (Chen and Balakrishnan, 1990: 2). For this reason, couples are more likely to have a third child, and do so quickly, if they have borne two girls rather than two boys. They are least likely to bear a third child if they already have a boy and a girl (ibid.; also Krishnan, 1988a).

Rates of divorce are also highest in families with only daughters. "All children increase stability, but sons promote greater stability than daughters because they elicit a greater investment and involvement from fathers and encourage greater family-ties and interdependencies" (Morgan, Lye, and Condran, 1988: 3).

From this standpoint, the decline in family size we have witnessed demonstrates a progressive weakening of gender preferences among parents. As parents come to care less about the gender of their children, they will see less need to keep bearing children to obtain the "right" mix of boys and girls.

THE EFFECT OF MATERNAL EMPLOYMENT

Economic and job-related considerations have always influenced childbearing. What's different today is that a mother's job concerns are taken into account as well as a father's. Precise data showing the long-term trend is provided by the National Opinion Research Centre's General Social Survey. It includes a question on whether the respondent's mother worked for pay for as long as a year after she was married. As we see in Table 6.2, there has

TABLE 6.2 Percentage of Respondents' Mothers Working for Pay as Long as a Year after They Were Married

Birth Cohort	% Working for Pay	Total
1969	81.3	665
1959	76.8	3,510
1949	71.4	4,788
1939	61.8	3,290
1928	47.1	2,731
1919	34.2	2,695
1909	23.8	1,732
1898	18.3	874

Source: Authors' analysis of the Cumulative NORC General Social Survey File.

been a large change in women's work since the beginning of this century. The data show a complete reversal has taken place since 1900.

For most women, the time and effort that will go into building a career must come out of personal time and family care giving. The assumption underlying all highly paid careers is that work will take priority over everything else. But this assumption makes it hard for men or women to be good parents. Both take job risks if they tailor their employment decisions to family priorities.

Indeed, few work schedules make it easy for parents to take care of their children's routine needs (for example, appointments with the doctor or school conferences), let alone emergencies. Fuchs (1988) goes so far as to say that the only women to have really benefited from the women's movement have been white, unmarried, well-educated, and *childless*. The women's movement has given them license to delay childbearing for the sake of their careers.

Typically, the impact of a child is greater for women than men. That is because mothers typically assume more direct responsibility for child care than fathers. Interestingly, whatever the couple's intention, there is an inevitable division of labor regarding child care. Individual couples can do little in the face of gendered social expectations.

Childbearing at any age is associated with a reduction in labor force activity and earning power. Controlling for work experiences and education, women who delay childbearing until they are older than 27 earn more than those who have children after age 22 (Bloom, 1987, cited in Fuchs). So it is in women's best economic interests to delay or avoid childbearing.

Women who succeed most in the labor market are young, white, single, and highly educated. They have, additionally, postponed (or given up entirely) the opportunity of having a child (Fuchs, 1988). Women who choose to stay home to raise children find themselves economically vulnerable if their marriage fails, their spouse dies, or they decide to reenter the labor force later.

It remains more difficult for women than men to combine employment and parenting. That's why, in the United States, 90 percent of male executives aged 40 and under are fathers, but only 35 percent of female executives are mothers. So women who become parents face a no-win situation: as employed mothers, they are overworked and as full-time homemakers, they are economically vulnerable.

Child care is the "salient link" between fertility and employment. In Britain and North America, the demand for child care far outstrips the supply. As a result, there is a strong relationship between social class and the adequacy of child-care arrangements in these countries. That is, richer parents get better care for their children than poorer parents do. That's because, in these countries, child care is the responsibility of parents. State, provincial, or national governments fund child care inadequately, if at all (on these topics, see Huber and Spitze, 1983).

Who cares for the children, then? Specific arrangements vary with the age of the child as well as by ethnic background. Different countries have different schemes for government-subsidized day care. So far as the United States is concerned, most children under three are cared for at home by relatives or in the homes of nonrelatives. Children three to five are cared for by relatives or in group-care programs. School-aged children are cared for by relatives or in the homes of nonrelatives. No more than about 20 percent of all American children get institutionalized (or "professional") day care.

As the figures show, relatives (kin) still play a vital role in providing child care when mothers are out working for pay. Let's not underestimate the importance of North American kinfolk just because they are less important than extended kin in the past, or in non-Western cultures. They play a critical role in caring for many of our children. But this is not enough. Relatives and unregulated day-care services may not be able to meet the increased demand as more and more mothers enter the labor force.

Many mothers cannot afford to take time off work, even right after the birth of their child. In the United States, fewer than four employed mothers in ten receive maternity benefits. Those who do can take only a brief time off (Hofferth and Phillips, 1987: 568).

One way out of this impasse is to change the allocation of unpaid work within the household and emphasize the parental responsibility of fathers. Sweden is the best-known because most written-about example of a socially experimenting state. Since 1974, fathers have been entitled to paid parental leave after the birth or adoption of a child. The state's aim has been to ensure that child care and household chores are the shared responsibility of both parents:

> The Swedish scheme of benefits now provides a total of nine months leave from employment at nearly full salary and another three months at a strongly reduced salary that either parent is legally entitled to take. . . . Since 1980, either parent is entitled to paid absence from work in the case of family illness 60 days per year and per child. Either parent may work three-quarter time with a corresponding drop in pay as long as they have children up to the age of eight (Sandquist, 1987: 7).

Yet few Swedish fathers use their newly won rights to care for a newborn child. More often, they use "their ten days of leave with pay in connection with a delivery" and are as likely as women to stay home with a sick child.

Sandqvist (1987:8) complains about "the slow change in ingrained male attitudes and role patterns." He explains that in the eyes of most Swedish men, an extended parental leave implies role reversal—men behaving like women. This is hard for them to accept. Swedish women may also be pressed (by both sexes) to conform to the traditional role pattern of staying at home with a newborn child.

DELAYED CHILDBEARING AND INCREASED CHILDLESSNESS[1]

Most women cohabit and/or marry and most end up having at least one child. However, increasing numbers of American women are having their first child later than women did in earlier generations. As argued above, the lowest fertility exists for women with the best educational and employment opportunities.

So, for example, Grindstaff (1988) found that 30-year-old Canadian women were best off economically when they had adopted one of three strategies: they had remained single, were at least 20 when they married, or had put off childbearing until at least age 25, if they had children at all. In all cases, these successful women had avoided childbearing before age 25.

North American couples feel pressures that discourage large families on the one hand and childlessness on the other. Some remain childless by choice; others put off the decision and drift into childlessness. For others still, unwanted infertility leads to time-consuming and expensive experiments with advanced reproductive techniques or complex negotiations with adoption agencies. Matthews and Matthews (1986) estimate that about 14 percent of married women are infertile.

Since 1965, the proportion of childless marriages increased steadily. This supports the idea that the percentage of childless women will continue to increase in the future. Estimates of the number of women who will remain childless throughout their lives run as high as 30 percent (Bloom, 1982).

These increases depart from the long-term trend (Mattessich, 1979: 231). With two exceptions, rates of childlessness in America have remained stable over the past half-century. The exceptions were the 1930s Depression (when there were more childless women) and the 1950–1965 baby boom (when there were fewer childless women). Compared to the baby boom, current rates of childlessness are high.

Some voluntary childlessness is the result of a series of decisions to postpone childbirth. Occasionally, women wait until it is too late. In fact, Soloway and Smith (1987) find that after the age of 30, the "biological time clock" is a major factor in determining the time to have a child. This pressure forces women to reassess other factors in their life that have contributed to the delay of childbearing.

Not surprisingly, childless women are also less traditional in their attitudes toward family life and employment (Morgan and Waite, 1987). They also have more egalitarian relationships with their spouses. Childless couples generally put more than average emphasis on their spousal relationship (Houseknecht, 1987; Rowlands, 1982). They do not see raising children as a means of achieving success or demonstrating achievement.

In fact, voluntarily childless couples see few advantages in parenthood and recognize its costs to both intimacy and women's careers (Houseknecht, 1987: 62–63). Generally, the wives in childless couples are more committed to remaining childless than are their husbands .

Typically, childless people are more likely to have been raised by single parents. They are also less concerned with conforming to social norms than parents are and score higher on measures of self-esteem. Most important of all, childless couples are more satisfied with their marriages than other couples. Perhaps this is because they have more egalitarian relationships or because they have fewer expenses and suffer less strain. Childless couples say that the chief advantage of childlessness is "more freedom." For their part, parents say the main disadvantage of parenthood is a "loss of freedom, privacy, and time for self."

We find similar views expressed in other parts of the world. For example, in New Zealand, women give a few main reasons for their decision to remain childless. They include the career disadvantages of parenthood, the long-term commitment children require, and a lack of interest in parenting. There are also the personal advantages of greater freedom, time, and intimacy with a partner. The author reports, "For men it was mainly the long-term commitment, their greater personal freedom, greater time for self and greater time with partner, which were important" (Rowlands, 1982: 22-23).

Still, childless couples report feeling pressure from others about their decision. They feel like they are being judged as selfish, hedonistic, and inconsiderate people who dislike children. They also feel socially isolated, because they do not constitute what people commonly regard as a "family unit." In the late 1980s, dual-career couples with no children were labeled DINKs (meaning "Double Income, No Kids"), often with derision and hostility.

Will Childlessness Increase?

Some have argued that unless practical support for parents increases, the proportion of childless couples will increase. This should happen because more women will choose careers over mere jobs. Also, the pressures of combining family and work life will increase the polarization of career-centered and family-centered lifestyles. Career demands will lead more women to remain childless. That is a likelier outcome than better sharing of domestic duties within a family with children. In fact, time budget data from the last few decades (Robinson, 1991) show little increase in husbands' willingness to share the housework.

So, increasingly, family and career commitments come into conflict. Women whose main commitment is to a career are more likely to forego children and, possibly, even marriage. Likewise, commitments to family life and children largely rule out a heavy involvement in demanding careers. According to Hunt and Hunt (1982), an important consequence of this polarization is a widening gap in the standard of living between couples who parent and couples who lead a childless lifestyle.

Child-postponers are similar, in most respects, to childless people. Like people who avoid parenthood entirely, couples who postpone parenthood today tend to be white, highly educated, career-oriented city dwellers.

American statistics report that 50 percent of female postponers are in professional careers and 90 percent work for pay in a job. Krishnan (1988a) also finds that couples limit their fertility and make other family adjustments in order to buy a home. They face the dilemma that career opportunities are greatest in large cities, but because of that, home ownership is most costly there.

When asked about their worries surrounding parenthood, fathers say they worry about financial security and the difficulty of fitting a career in with their desire to parent. Women report postponing childbirth in order to advance their careers. They want to establish a work identity, maintain their freedom, develop a stable marital relationship, and wait until they are financially secure. In short, women's concerns are more numerous and complicated than those of men.

In the end, voluntarily childless couples are struggling to overcome their "disability" just as commuter couples are struggling to overcome theirs (for more on this, see Chapter Three). Both demonstrate a commitment to conventional family life in the face of difficult odds. Other couples are struggling to find a way of combining marriage and work that is less arduous. Voluntarily childless women represent one adaptation of this non-traditional kind. In all cases, families today have to cope with more varied pressures and demands.

So, as well as delaying the birth of a first child, women are reducing the total number of children they bear. They do this in response to economic and occupational pressures, as well as smaller desired family sizes. As a result, overall rates of fertility, or childbearing, have declined in all Western societies, even in those such as France, Quebec, or the former East Germany, where there have been government programs which gave substantial financial incentives for women to bear children.

On the other hand, higher-than-ever rates of teenage pregnancy demonstrate that for women with little education and limited opportunities in the paid labor force, pregnancy and early marriage offer an attractive short-term option.

BIRTHS TO UNMARRIED WOMEN

Increased access to education and employment for women and the greater availability of safe, effective contraception would lead us to expect a drop in teen pregnancy. Yet, despite the widespread availability of birth control devices, there has been an epidemic of teenage pregnancies in the United States. In recent years, the number of adolescent births has increased and rates of teenage pregnancy in America are the highest in the Western world. In fact, the American rates are more than double the rates for England or France. And over half of all children born to American teenagers are to unmarried women.

In the United States, births out of wedlock have always been common among African-American women. Recently, these rates have fallen and unmarried births among white women have increased. According to the Planned Parenthood Federation, four out of five conceptions among unmarried women are unintended. Only three out of four of these are aborted. So, according to Fuchs (1987: 68), about half of all unmarried births are unintended. As well, the proportion of teenage mothers who keep their children, instead of giving them up for adoption, has also risen—hence, a rise in single-parent families.

In Canada, the rate of childbearing by teenagers has declined steadily since 1970. Yet in Canada, as in the United States, young women who begin bearing children early are those with the smallest stake in fertility control. That is because they have the least education and fewest occupational choices. Some marry early, others have a premarital pregnancy. However, in almost all cases, they have little education, do not work for pay, and do not use contraception before a first pregnancy (Rao and Balakrishnan, 1988a).

Socially and economically, these young women are the complete opposite of women who postpone childbearing or remain childless throughout their lives (Rao, 1987; Rao and Balakrishnan, 1988b). Typically, childless married women have a better than average education, work for pay, and did not cohabit before marriage. A high family income and low religiosity are also significant correlates of childlessness (Tomes, 1985). So, teenage pregnancy reflects a particular kind of background experience and a small stake in remaining childless.

In all societies, some women have a greater stake in remaining childless than others. Yet, societies vary in the measures they take to influence young women's decisions. In Sweden, for example, educational and media materials encourage teenagers to make deliberate and responsible decisions about pregnancy and childbearing (Hoem, 1988: 25). Unemployed young Swedes are subjected to what many North Americans would regard as highly intrusive counseling and retraining programs.

As well, in Sweden, the incentives to stay in school or work are stronger than the incentives to become a mother. Rules regulating eligibility for income-related maternity benefits "make it almost necessary to complete an education and to achieve a firm foothold in the labor market before [women] have their first child" (Hoem, 1988: 26).

Why this difference? Swedish attitudes are affected by a humanist outlook on public policy which aims at giving people equal access to education regardless of their location, social background, gender, or age. In an effort to achieve full employment, Sweden offers its younger adolescents (16 to 17 years old) more education and its older adolescents (18 to 19 years old) job experience through half-time employment while pursuing either further education or a full-time job (Hoem, 1988: 5).

As well, "new contraceptives, improved education, and the recent changes in the status of women" all contribute to the postponement of a first child (Hoem, 1988: 4).

By contrast, disadvantaged young women in North America—especially the poor who are of aboriginal, African, or Hispanic descent—find that having a baby and bringing it up themselves is a good bet for emotional security. One strong motivation is having "someone to love" and a social identity as a mother.

Less charitable observers have pointed out that having a baby also provides an entitlement to social security benefits such as Aid to Families with Dependent Children (AFDC) and Medicaid. This uncharitable argument is wrong, since benefits such as these are increasingly being capped.

There is no correlation between their availability and rates of teenage single-parenthood.

Add to this the fact that in most developed countries (the United States included), half of all teenage girls and three-quarters of teenage boys are sexually active. However, only a third use contraception regularly (Oxford Analytica, 1986: 87–88). No wonder teenage pregnancies are increasing and with them, so are entries into parenthood that are not entirely prudent.

We will have more to say about these issues in the final chapter. But in the next chapter, we focus on relations between parents and their children in different kinds of families.

NOTES

1. As with other topics in sociology, it is important to avoid value-laden terms or at least, use them with great care. Couples who are happy having no children are offended by the word *childless*, since it implies they are lacking something.

   For this reason, some researchers prefer the word *childfree* (Rowland, 1982). On the other hand, children might argue that the term *childfree* has negative connotations. It suggests that people are better off free of children (as with the words *pest-free* or *caffeine-free*). Step back a little and reflect that this is another example of how family policies and even terminology become expressions of opposed social values—or of social organizations which seek to pressure the state for tax breaks.

7

PARENTING
IN DIFFERENT TYPES
OF FAMILIES

INTRODUCTION

Most of us are born into families and have some idea of what family life means. There is a great deal of variation among families and they are changing rapidly. However, whatever the family's form, a child's first emotional ties are to family members. Families provide the basic necessities of life, and often provide love, security, comfort, and emotional support as well. Sometimes, unfortunately, they provide the opposite: abuse and neglect. In these cases, the effects on child development are bound to be harmful.

Family members also teach the child the language, norms, values, and expectations of the culture or subculture to which the family belongs. They do this in a variety of ways, shaped by the society within which the family lives.

For example, the value a society places on conformity influences the overall level of control exerted on children and, also, the use of physical punishment to achieve this control. In cultures which value conformity highly, more parents use physical punishment to discipline their children. They also lecture their children and maintain closer overall control than parents in cultures which value self-reliance (Ellis and Petersen, 1992).

Yet little of what a family transmits through socialization is transmitted consciously. The child learns a great deal by observing the manner in which family members interact with one another, the roles they act out, and the attitudes and values they exemplify.

In India, for example, children are taught to be passive through a speech pattern called "causing to be overheard." One person is addressed in speech, though another person who hears—the baby—is the intended addressee. As well, children are taught the rules of the community in miniature when mothers repeat traditional stories, poems, and word games to their children (Das, 1989).

This unconscious transmission of family values continues into adolescence as well. Teenagers learn to be what they see and hear at home. So, for example, Greek high school students whose parents are alcoholics, perform worse in school, and are at greater risk of becoming alcoholics themselves, than are other students (Hyphantis, Koutras, Liakos, and Marselos, 1991). In part, this is because of a disturbed family life and the disruption of school-related behavior at home. However, it is also because drinking is being modeled as a normal or even a desirable alternative to school work.

We first learn the meaning of "woman," "wife," and "mother" by watching our own mother, for example. Later, after an opportunity to observe other versions of "woman," "wife," and "mother" in friends' homes or on television, we begin to generalize. Once generalization begins, conscious choice becomes possible. The self begins to develop more rapidly and uniquely.

So the family is important in laying down a bed of experiences on which we build or against which we fight. It is the starting point for our social knowledge, the place we experiment with our vision of the generalized other. It is in the family setting that we also form our first close attachments and learn to communicate openly.

DIFFERENT KINDS OF FAMILIES

Different kinds of socialization take place in different kinds of families, with different effects on the children. For example, controlling for socioeconomic status, Australian children in "stepfamilies" score lower on reading ability, impulse control, and self-esteem than children in two-parent (intact) or single-parent families (Amato and Ochiltree, 1987). This suggests there are parent-child interactions which disadvantage children who live in "reconstituted" families. We will say more about this later.

Social class also shapes the course of parent-child relations. For example, in urban Indian families, middle-class children have stronger ties with their parents than children from the upper or lower classes (Srivastava, 1985). These middle-class children feel they receive more emotional support from their parents and identify with their parents more than other children do. Apparently, there is no difference in the degree to which Indian parents of different classes discipline their children.

In North America, teenagers who see their parents as accepting and warm, and as less controlling, have higher self-esteem than others (Litovsky and Dusek, 1985). At the same time, parents with higher self-esteem give their child more freedom and acceptance. They also have better communication with the child as a result (Small, 1988).

In particular, mothers with high self-esteem give their children more freedom in making decisions. Generally, they communicate better, are less concerned about their children's behavior, and view their children as more independent. The result: their children are more satisfied than average with the autonomy they have been given (op. cit.).

The importance of the family's influence, for bad as well as good, cannot be overestimated. So, for example, people who were exposed to family violence as children are more likely than other people to end up committing spouse abuse as adults. In this respect, childhood experiences are a more potent influence than either chronic economic strain or acutely stressful circumstances in adulthood (Seltzer and Kalmuss, 1988).

Similarly, children who have been exposed to physical punishment are more than usually aggressive towards other family members. A particularly explosive combination is infrequent reasoning and frequent spanking by the parent. This dramatically increases the aggression level of adolescents (Larzelere, 1986).

Even something as minor as the effect of television viewing is influenced by parents. Television has a particularly strong effect on children whose parents do not try to control the TV they watch. Children whose parents watch TV with them, discuss TV with them, and/or set no rules about viewing are the most vulnerable to influences of the television. In general, less parental control increases the impact of television on adolescent family members, especially when combined with lower levels of family cohesion (Rothschild and Morgan, 1987).

However, not only do parents socialize their children; children also socialize their parents. A study of university students shows that in topic areas like sports, leisure, sexuality, drug use, and attitudes towards minorities, parents learn a great deal from their adolescent children (Peters, 1985). So the process of socialization is reciprocal. But younger people are more malleable—more easily changed through socialization—than older people.

THE EFFECT OF FAMILY SIZE

Family size is an important factor in determining the parent-child relationship. For many reasons, the fertility reduction we discussed in the last chapter is producing a different "kind" of family. Stated simply, small families work differently from large ones. As a result, single or first-born children grow up differently from later-born children.

The majority of studies show that the greater the number of children in a family, the less their average tested intelligence. The research literature also shows that, on average, first-born children have higher intelligence and achievement scores than second-borns who, in turn, perform better than later-borns.

Demographer Judith Blake has confirmed and extended previous studies on this topic. She has shown that family size has a major impact on educational attainment, even when other factors are controlled. These other factors include strong ethnic group cohesion, religio-ethnic commitment to schooling, and high parental status. None of these prove to diminish the harmful effects of a large family.

What social processes could be behind such results? Blake argues that family-size effects occur because a large number of children dilute parental resources. Robert Zajonc and Gregory Markus agree, arguing that the key explanation must relate to time allocation and parental practices. As family size increases, parents must spread their time among more children. With a fixed amount of time and money, $2n$ children will get only half as much of either as n children, other things being equal.

This line of argument assumes that the greater the amount of attention a child receives from adults, the likelier that child will learn to perform at a mental age in advance of his or her chronological age. (After all, this is what intelligence and achievement tests actually measure.)

On the average then, one child in a household with two or more adults available most of the time would be in the best developmental situation. Several children in a household with only one adult who was only intermittently available would be in the worst situation.

You would expect from this that only children would be the best off of all. Surprisingly, their scores are lower than those of eldest children who have one or two younger brothers or sisters. That is because parents often make their eldest child into a "deputy parent." In this position, a child learns from the experience of taking responsibility for and tutoring younger siblings. An only child or a youngest child will never have this experience. Other children will only have it after younger siblings have been born.

Spacing is also important, since many children are youngest in their family for only a short time. They cease to be the "baby of the family" once birth, adoption, or formation of a blended family brings in someone younger than themselves. The chances that your mother will have another child depend basically on her age: how close she is to her forties. However, you may end up with one or more half-siblings in the household if she forms a new relationship after divorce or widowhood.

Thus, sibship (or family) size operates essentially by diluting parental resources. It also affects parental time allocation and parental practices, given the structural constraints of household size, composition, and child-spacing by age.

Zajonc and Markus originally put forward their theory for conventional husband-wife families. The theory should be extended to take account of day-care and preschooling arrangements which have become common in the 1990s. It should also allow us to make predictions for single-parent family households, blended families, and other new family forms. And that brings us to the topic of divorce and remarriage, and how these events also affect childhood development.

EFFECTS OF DIVORCE

In the past, it was common for unhappily married couples to stay together, not only because wives were dependent and divorce was difficult, but also "for the sake of the children." Most people believed that divorce harms children. But in what way does it harm them? Is the harm associated with divorce any worse than the harm associated with living in a family where the parents have a very poor relationship with each other? Are the harmful effects long-lasting? And what can be done to minimize the risk of harm, if any?

Researchers disagree least about the *effects* of divorce on children, which we will discuss shortly; but they disagree a lot about the reasons for these effects. Divorce is hard on both spouses and it can be a very nasty experience for children. Before divorce there are often fights or unbearable tension. During divorce, the parents often try to get the children to take sides. Afterwards, there may be a dramatic loss of income. The effect of many of these experiences might very well depend on the age and sex of the child as well as on his or her social support network. For this reason, it is almost impossible to know for sure how these experiences might affect the development of children.

After divorce, there are new social roles with new labels. One parent—usually the mother—is assigned custody of any dependent children and retains the right to occupy the matrimonial home. The other parent is the noncustodial parent. He or she has visiting rights which are normally specific and limited. The noncustodial parent—usually the father—normally undertakes to make regular child support payments. However, these payments often become erratic or dry up completely, particularly if the noncustodial parent starts a new common-law relationship or remarries.

Many researchers doubt that it is divorce in itself, or even the economic consequences of divorce, which harm children. After all, parent-child ties are often strong among children from single-parent families, though the tie with the noncustodial biological parent is weaker (Furstenberg, 1988; Peterson and Zill, 1986). Nor is the death of a parent necessarily harmful.

After all, widowhood does children less harm than divorce. (Or perhaps this is because modern-day widows experience less financial loss than divorcees. On average, widows are older and better off financially than divorced women.)

One theory is that the negative effects of divorce on children are mostly due to their greater risk of poverty and to the stigma that is attached to divorce. Not so long ago, the single-parent family was commonly viewed as being an inherently bad environment for children. The new ideology of the 1970s cast itself as liberal and tolerant and tried to challenge this assumption and the resulting stigma. Writers and commentators in this tradition rejected the theory that unwed motherhood *by itself* necessarily damaged children.

For example, Herzog and Sudia (cited in McLanahan, 1991: 11) argued that "many of the differences between mother-only and two-parent families could be explained by differences in family socioeconomic status as opposed to differences in culture or personality traits." They, and other researchers, even emphasized the positive qualities of mother-only families (see also Sudia, 1973).

This type of argument removes much of the responsibility from parents. Instead, it blames the flaws in social assistance and employment that lead to hard times for unwed mothers. The more conservative or realistic point of view dismisses this as ideology. It claims that differences in one- and two-parent families really are important, over and above any simple economic differences. McLanahan points out this shift in consciousness in the 1970s did little more than "legitimate the dramatic increase in divorce and out-of-wedlock births that occurred during this same period" (op. cit.: 11).

Another factor associated with divorce that causes children problems is parental conflict. After all, divorce is preceded (and occasionally followed) by parental conflict. There is agreement in the research literature that such conflict is an important cause of childhood (and later) difficulties. For example, children from divorced families score worse on tests of emotional functioning than children from the average intact family.

Parental conflict is bad for children. Indeed, children in intact families marked by high levels of parental conflict showed even more severe emotional problems than did children in divorced families. It is for this reason that follow-up studies show children of divorced parents gradually improving their emotional functioning in the years after their parents separate. However, the speed of recovery is reduced when postdivorce conflicts persist.

In short, researchers disagree about the social processes by which the children of divorce turn out differently from the children of intact families. In the literature we find at least four broad types of explanation:

1. an economic hardship explanation, which focuses on the impoverishing effects of divorce;
2. a weak parenting explanation, which focuses on the relative absence of care provided to children by adults;
3. a family conflict explanation, which focuses on the greater exposure of children in divorced families to conflict between the parents (typically, before divorce); and
4. an inadequate stepparents explanation, which focuses on the failure of second marriages to provide as good parenting as first marriages.

Whatever the reason—often, a mixture of many reasons—children of divorced parents are disadvantaged in comparison to children living in two-parent families. They receive less parental attention and, as we mentioned in Chapter Three, they almost always suffer a decline in their standard of living after their parents divorce. As a result, children from divorced families run a higher risk of growing up in poverty. They are likely to live in less desirable neighborhoods with a greater chance of negative peer groups, to attend inferior schools, and to have limited access to good education and good jobs.

Today, a vast number of studies document the long-term effects of divorce upon children's well-being. Not all of these studies are in complete agreement with each other. In fact, you could probably find at least one of them to support almost any point of view that you like. Fortunately for our faith in the value of cumulative research, Amato and Keith (1991) have reanalyzed the basic results from 92 such studies.

Their comprehensive review and evaluation of studies in this area allows us to be confident in drawing conclusions about the correlates of divorce in North American families. We summarize their main findings below. For example, compared with children who grew up in intact families, the children of divorced parents have:

- lower educational attainment;
- less earned income; and a
- higher likelihood of being dependent on welfare.

Compared with daughters from intact families, the daughters of divorced parents are:

- more likely to bear a child out of wedlock;
- more likely to get divorced themselves; and
- more likely to become the head of a single-parent family.

Children face significant psychological adjustments when their parents separate. Much of the trauma young children experience diminishes within a year, but symptoms often reappear during adolescence and adulthood.

As well, divorce affects children differently according to gender, with boys displaying more immediate and longer-lasting behavioral symptoms such as aggression and acting out. Girls show a delayed effect. Later in adolescence and early in adulthood, they often have trouble managing sexuality and heterosexual relationships. Generally, they have problems with emotional commitment (Furstenberg, 1990: 393).

As we have noted, children of divorced parents tend to display a number of less common attitudes about marriage and marital stability. They show themselves in earlier sexual activity, higher levels of premarital pregnancy, earlier marriage, and less marital stability (McLanahan and Bumpass, 1988; McLanahan, 1991).

There is also evidence that the long-term effects of divorce on educational attainment include school problems, grade failure, higher dropout, lower attendance, and failure to complete higher education, leading to a reduction of occupational attainment and income in later life. These may result from attending inferior schools and receiving less economic support for advanced education. They may also result from the stress and uncertainty caused by marital breakup or a missing parent. Finally, when divorce was rare, teachers and others tended to stigmatize children from "broken homes." This may also have played a part, in the past at least.

Health Effects

Many children who experience a divorce or separation also suffer a deterioration in health (Mauldon, 1990). This may be due to a reduction in resources (poverty again) or stress associated with the family breakup. A reduced income reduces the level of health care available to a child. Stress may also make a child more vulnerable to infection, illness, or injury. As a result, reported illnesses are more frequent among children in families that have experienced a separation than among those who have not (Blaxter, 1990).

As to the first factor, poverty, research on children's health finds evidence of a strong link between poverty and poor health. Divorce usually reduces a family's financial well-being and forces women to seek a job (or a better job) outside the home. The loss of income and time available for the children, combined with changes in health-care coverage after divorce, all contribute to a reduction in children's health and general well-being.

Children face large psychological adjustments when their parents separate. The initial trauma is reduced within one year of separation. However, symptoms often appear, or reappear, during adolescence and adulthood. Still, if there is a significant relationship between poor health and stress, recorded illnesses should occur immediately after a divorce or separation.

To study this, Mauldon (1990) used the Child Health Supplement from the 1981 National Interview Survey. This study relies upon a parent's memory of the health problems a child experienced and the age at which they occurred. Reporting is probably least accurate for the least recent events, so the author augments her study with information from other clinical surveys.

Mauldon finds that the key factors affecting reported illness are income, race, education, number of children, and identity of the respondent.[1] On balance, the study proves that reported illnesses are more common for children in families that have experienced separation than for those who have not. (Whether or not the actual incidence is greater, or there is a health reporting bias, remains open to debate.) However, Mauldon's study does *not* prove that the stress of divorce directly depletes the health of the children involved.

For example, reported illnesses do *not* increase in the year immediately following divorce as much as they do later. This runs counter to the finding in another study that "Divorce effects are most evident immediately at the time of separation" due to the deterioration in parenting that occurs around the time of the divorce, nor that health problems diminish within a year or two after the separation (Hetherington, 1987, as cited in Furstenberg, op cit.: 392).

Mauldon (op. cit.: 443) identifies the loss of resources—or poverty—following a divorce or separation as the key cause of increased (reported) illness. "Children of college-educated, low income, separated mothers have significantly more health problems than similar children who are in intact families." When household income exceeds $10,000, separation has only a tiny effect that is not statistically significant.

In summary, divorce and other causes of single-parenthood bring economic hardship to children. We saw in the last chapter that divorce or the splitting up of a common-law couple often leaves women significantly worse off than before. Since the custody of children is usually awarded to mothers, the children share in any downward economic mobility. This is a serious problem for people who are already marginal economically. Here especially, a child's health and nutrition may be harmed. As well, the single parent may end up seeking cheaper rent in an area which is more crime-prone and has poorer schools.

But divorce does more than reduce the household income. It also changes the child's experience with adults in a "normal" nuclear family, with one adult of each sex being available on a daily basis. Said another way, divorce and single-parenthood reduce the amount of adult contact and surveillance. In particular, they reduce a child's stable exposure to an adult male.

One among the many consequences of father absence is that any young or teenage children in such families lack a male model in the home.

Father absence occurs for a period of months or years in the military in wartime. It also happens after a father leaves his family because of death, marital separation, or divorce. What are the consequences?

Social learning is known to proceed by identifying and imitating a role model. For this reason, many social commentators have hypothesized that father absence might cause a problem for a child's normal development. If no male role-model substitutes—even uncles, elder brothers, or grandfathers—are readily available, male children might develop feminine or dependent personality traits through imitating their mothers.

Others have predicted that the absence of a restraining male authority figure might make boys become overaggressive or make girls more masculine. The theorizing here has been normative and prescriptive. Often, it has assumed that healthy development requires the child to pass through a series of psychosexual stages on the way to becoming a healthy adult.

The common design has been to compare children from father-present with those from father-absent families. Researchers have observed the play of young children to assess their sex-role orientation or their level of dependency or aggression. Older children have completed questionnaires to establish their sex-role preference. Michael Stevenson and Kathryn Black reanalyzed the results from 67 such studies in order to see patterns emerge.

They find that father absence *does* influence the psychosexual development of boys, but the effects on girls are less evident. Specifically, father-present boys show more masculine traits than father-absent boys. This is what you would expect from social learning theory, which posits that learning occurs when a child imitates an adult role model. However, a word of caution is needed here. These effects are consistent across the majority of studies, but they are *small* effects. Father absence, at its worst, is not going to cause a large-scale rearrangement of sex roles.

In short, the stable presence of both male and female adult role models is assumed to be important for a child's healthy psychological development. More important, two adults are better able to look after a child than one adult. Since personalities differ, pairs of parenting adults develop into role-differentiated parenting teams. Usually, multiperson parenting teams are more effective in guiding adolescents away from deviant or predeviant behavior.

CHILDREN IN SINGLE-PARENT FAMILIES

Historical comparisons show that in both the United States and Canada, there were roughly the same proportions of single-parent families early in this century as there are in the 1990s. For example, at least one out of ten families in the United States was female-headed around 1900, with the percentage being higher among African-Americans (Morgan et al., 1993). In Canada, the proportion of families headed by a single parent was 12.2 percent in 1936. In 1986 it was 12.7 percent, and in 1991, 13.1 percent. Thus, single-parenthood is not a new, rare, or statistically volatile phenomenon.

Around 1900, divorce was very rare. Single mothers were strongly pressured to give up their children to adoption, or to have them raised in an orphanage. Back then, children were also more likely to lose a parent to death than divorce. In fact, about a quarter of all American children lost one or both parents by age 15 (Uhlenberg, 1983). After we add the estimated effects of desertion and divorce, our best guess is that about one in three of all children would have spent some time in a single-parent home by the time they had reached their mid-teens.

The children in such families were, on average, older than children in today's single-parent families (produced by divorce or by mothers never marrying). They may have been better able to cope with the problem. As the century progressed, loss of a parent due to death became less likely and loss of a parent due to divorce became more likely.

After 1936, the proportion of single-parent families declined steadily, reaching a low point in the 1940s, reflecting the improved life expectancies of parents. The proportion began to grow again until, as we write in the middle 1990s, the issue is a matter of great concern to social policy makers and moralists of all stripes.

Single-parent families come about because of bereavement (i.e., widowhood), divorce, or childbearing by a single mother who decides to bring up the child on her own. What has changed in the last 90 or so years is the balance, or composition, of different causes of single-parenthood.

Even with the recent increase in divorce rates "almost no children have gone to relatives, foster homes or institutions" (Bane, 1976: 557). As well, the experience of living in a single-parent family is often a transitional one. The average length of time a child spends in such a family today is roughly six years. It is less if the divorce happened when the child was young, since in that case, the mother is likelier to remarry (Bumpass, 1984, as cited in Furstenberg, 1990: 384).

Due to the high rates of divorce in second marriages, one-third of all children whose parents remarry have already witnessed a *second* divorce by their early teens, according to the National Survey of Children. This means 15 percent of all children experience at least *two* disruptions of their parents' marriages by late adolescence—even more if (unrecorded) cohabitation is taken into account (Furstenberg, 1990: 384).

Today, rates of union dissolution and teenage pregnancy are particularly high for African-Americans and aboriginal Americans. The concern about single-parent families may also hide a concern (however veiled) about racial differences. Ever since the 1970s, American policy discussions about single-parent families have implied, if not stated, a concern over what to do about inner-city African-American families.

Currently, guesses about how many children will ever live in a single-parent family range from three children in four (Hofferth, 1985), to three children in five (Bumpass, 1984; Glick, 1984), to four or five children in ten (Furstenberg, 1990:383). The estimates are highest for black children, of whom demographers expect that fewer than one in five "born in the 1980s [will] spend their entire childhood with both of their parents" (op. cit.: 383).

Some of these estimates are more precise and revealing than others. For example, Ellwood (1987) has used an excellent longitudinal study of five thousand American families (the Panel Study on Income Dynamics) to show how family structure influences the probability of a childhood spent in longer or shorter periods of poverty.

Focusing on the first ten years of childhood, Ellwood shows that it is unusual for children to spend all of their first ten years in a female-headed single-parent family. Only 6 percent of all children do so. However, this group includes almost half of all the children who are "long-term poor." That is, they have been living below the poverty line for at least seven of their first ten years.

This finding underlines the point that long-term female-headed single-parent families run a high risk of long-term poverty. Yet being in a two-parent family by no means guarantees protection against poverty. Ellwood also finds that 44 percent of the children who were below the poverty line for at least one of their first ten years had always been in a two-parent family. He concludes:

> Most estimates now suggest that more than half of the children born today will spend some part of their lives in single-parent homes. Many others will experience poverty while in two-parent homes. Children born today face a double threat. They face the possibility that their families will be poor at least for some period even if they remain intact. And they face the possibility that they will spend part or all of their childhood in single-parent families, in which case they will very likely experience poverty along with whatever other hardships the situation implies. A declining minority will live their lives entirely in non-poor two-parent homes (1987: 12).

We see then that some children will experience poverty within an intact family. However, the American data show that long-term single-parenthood virtually ensures a child will spend much of his or her childhood in poverty. Many other children will experience shorter periods of single-parenthood, and shorter periods of poverty due to single-parenthood. Fewer children will experience the childhood we idealize: life above the poverty line with both parents present.

Relations with Noncustodial Fathers

Typically, mothers gain the custody of their children at divorce. This often worsens women's economic problems and emotionally distances fathers from their children. As we said in Chapter Three, far too many fathers fail to support their children either economically, with financial payments, or emotionally through parental involvement.

The 1981 National Survey of Children found that few children who had not lived with their fathers for the last ten years or more have regular contact with their fathers. Few have even seen their father in the previous year or ever visited his home. Yet this is not due to divorce per se. We know this because when the mother is the noncustodial parent (admittedly, a rare occurrence, especially for younger children), contact with children is steady and long-lasting (Furstenberg, 1990: 389). It says something about the differences between fathers and mothers.

Do men stop paying child support because of reduced contact with their children, or do they reduce contact because they have stopped paying child support (Seltzer et al., 1989)? Answering this question is by no means easy. Fathers are occasionally "pushed out of the family, . . . [but] most seem to retreat from paternal responsibility when they no longer reside with their children." Furstenberg (1990: 387–388) attributes this to men viewing "marriage and childcare as an inseparable role set . . . [where] men sever their ties with their children in the course of establishing distance from their former wives."

Remarriage hastens disengagement, especially when geographic mobility, new family demands, and economic responsibilities further erode the "tenuous bonds between noncustodial fathers and their children" (op. cit.: 388). When the noncustodial parent keeps up regular contact with his child, a pattern of "parallel parenting" develops, where "[p]arents consult infrequently, often communicate through the child, and rarely are visible to each other." This reduces parental conflict but "it creates two distinct family worlds for the child" which are hard for the child to integrate (op. cit.: 390).

Single-parent Fathers

Since fathers typically have more money than mothers do after a divorce, it would make more economic sense for children to live with their fathers. And in fact, Amato and Keith's (1991) review of the literature found that in the small proportion of cases where this happens, the children do well.

Why, then, do fathers typically have so little involvement in the routine care of their children? Is it because fathers do not want to become involved in child care? Because they have more power in the marriage, so they are able to avoid the responsibility? Or is it because most fathers lack experience and don't know what to do with children?

To a degree, the low involvement in child care by fathers is a self-fulfilling prophecy. They receive (and seek) little preparation in the ways of caring for infants or young children, feel awkward and experience failure when they try to "help." Where babies are concerned, research shows that men "tend to avoid high involvement . . . because infants do not respond to their repertoire of skills and men have difficulty acquiring the skills needed to comfort the infant" (Rossi, 1984: 8).

Rossi (1984) believes the solution is to teach fathers about parenting and encourage their participation. They will be more active as parents if they have been trained to anticipate and play this role. And, recently, more and more middle-class fathers have become involved in their partners' pregnancies and children's births. Such experiences pave the way for greater involvement by fathers as their children grow up.

What happens when death or divorce suddenly thrusts a father into full responsibility for the care of young children? Risman (1987) predicted that men who became single fathers would rise to the occasion and act like mothers to their young children.

To test this, she compared a sample of single fathers, single mothers, and dual-earner couples, measuring such things as housework and parent-child interaction. Her results support the hypothesis that variation in gender-typed behavior is a result of "situational exigencies and opportunities," not biology or socialization. Fathers *did* rise to the occasion.

Risman concludes that when situational factors change, "divorced, widowed and even married fathers are capable of providing the nurturance that young children require despite their gendered socialization" (Risman, 1987: 28).

Not infrequently, children who have lived with their mother after their parents' divorce will want to live with their father for a time during adolescence (Furstenberg, 1990: 385). In fact, in 1980, about twice as many children of divorced parents lived with their fathers at ages 15 to 17 as did children under the age of 2 (Sweet and Bumpass, 1987). On the average then, divorce does not have to mean the end of all relationships between fathers and their children. And, as the research by Risman shows, fathers can do the job if they have to.

The problems experienced by single-parent families—especially female-headed single-parent families—argue in favor of remarriage after a divorce. Yet here too the evidence on costs and benefits is ambiguous. But, then, there is a small but definite risk that the stepparent becomes part of the problem.

CHILDREN IN BLENDED OR RECONSTITUTED FAMILIES

On the whole, remarriage is good for adults but not so good for children. The research tends to indicate that steprelationships are, on average, more distant, more conflictual, and less satisfying than the corresponding relationships between children and their biological parents. Family conflict is likelier in families formed by remarriage. Bonds between children and stepparents are weaker than they are between children and their natural parents.

The blood tie is still of enormous symbolic importance. Both stepparent and child feel differently toward each other than they do toward family members to whom they are tied biologically. This is reflected in everyday language when people distinguish between their "birth mother" or "biological mother" and their "other mother." Younger children have an easier time forming close ties with a new stepparent.

Remarriage often improves the economic well-being of children but it does little for their psychological well-being. In this respect, children in remarried families turn out to be very similar to children of divorced parents who do not remarry. That is, compared with children in other types of families, they start having sexual relations early, leave home early (Goldscheider and Goldscheider, 1988), are likelier to cohabit, marry early, and begin having children early (McLanahan and Bumpass, 1988; McLanahan and Book, 1989).

It's not obvious whether these behaviors are due to the (earlier) divorce—hence, their similarities with children of divorced single parents—or to life in a reconstituted family.

In theory, remarriage after widowhood or divorce *could* benefit children by giving them a larger pool of kin to draw on for support. Unfortunately, we know little about the ways people use their kin-by-remarriage, or even whether these ties persist beyond childhood.

What we do know is that stepchildren are disproportionately at risk of abuse. The majority of blended or reconstituted families are nonviolent, and most stepparents are not abusive. However, the presence of a stepparent is one of the best epidemiological predictors of child abuse risk yet discovered.

Stepchildren are more likely to be assaulted and far more likely to be killed. Whereas children under three years of age have about seven times higher rates of "validated" sublethal physical abuse in step-plus-genetic-parent homes than in two-genetic-parent homes for example, the differential in fatal abuse was on the order of 100-fold. Subsequent Canadian studies have found that toddlers living in stephouseholds were about 40 times more likely to become registered victims of severe physical abuse than their two-genetic-parent counterparts and were two times more likely to be murdered. Recent British data tell the same story (Daly and Wilson, 1993).

Stepmothers and stepfathers are greatly overrepresented as abusers and killers. Evolutionary social theorists note that abusive stepparents typically spare their own children. This argues against the possibility that violence in stepfamilies is due to an excess of indiscriminately violent personalities among remarried persons.

We do not want to claim that children in intact families are never at risk. Indeed, accusations of sexual abuse and incest have increased enormously since 1980. Many abusers were themselves abused as children, either by their own parents or by teachers or care givers in residential schools or orphanages. The implication is that children learn by imitation.

The increased attention given to child sexual abuse raises important and difficult questions about the limits of parental authority. It calls into doubt the degree to which the family should have privacy from the community and the point at which social workers or the police should take children from their biological parents and place them in foster care. In general, most societies have been too lax about the rights of children as compared with the rights of parents.

DO CHILDREN HAVE ANY FUTURE?

In a preindustrial, agricultural society, high fertility provides parents with three main benefits: old-age support by children, child labor, and insurance against risk. But in North America, parenthood makes no economic sense. Highly educated, urban couples are unlikely to expect children to care for their parents in old age. And, as doctors and lawyers, truck drivers and assembly line workers, business executives and secretaries and shop clerks, we have no need for a child's labor power.

As women's labor force participation has increased, fertility has fallen. Another important factor accounting for the fertility decline is a change in marriage trends. Since 1971, Europeans and North Americans have been waiting longer before getting married. Couples who marry later also tend to parent later. Worldwide, couples who postpone parenthood are usually financially well-off, career-oriented city dwellers. A (recently) growing proportion of married people are choosing not to become parents at all.

All this has been made easier by the contraceptive revolution. By the mid-1960s, an improvement in contraceptives and increased access to legal abortion and sterilization all had a significant impact on family size. Sterilization became an increasingly attractive option for women who wanted to avoid the risk of unwanted pregnancy. We are far from seeing the end of this contraceptive revolution. More likely than not, the near future will bring even more dramatic improvements—more and surer ways to avoid having children.

Those who do bear children find their lives complicated by a built-in conflict between parenting and work responsibility. This carries the heaviest cost for women, who take their parenting and domestic roles more seriously than men.

The provision of public supports for personal life (for example, family assistance programs, better day care, support groups for abusive parents, counseling in schools, and family planning) help to reduce the pressure on the modern family. In this way, they all reduce the likelihood of neglect and bad parenting, family conflict and divorce, single-parenthood and impoverishment. As yet, these public measures remain fragmentary and insufficient. Domestic problems remain personal problems, not national issues.

Some want to avoid spending the money that would significantly improve the lives of children and their parents. Others genuinely fear more state involvement in family life, believing that family problems are purely personal problems.

However, a great many families have been unable to solve their problems on their own. As we have seen, these problems are structural: they are built into the very way work and family life are organized in our society. Further, there is no proof that public supports for personal life make family life more fragile or less necessary. One cannot argue that public supports are an enemy of family life. On the contrary, other societies (like Sweden) prove the opposite case.

CONCLUSION

In the last two chapters, we have spent a great deal of attention on the effects of divorce on children and spouses. But what is the impact of *this impact* on American society as a whole? Is it big enough, or important enough, to consider divorce and single-parenting a public issue, not merely a personal trouble?

A number of writers (Fuchs, 1988; Pogrebin, 1983; Preston, 1984, among others) have called our attention to the plight of large numbers of North American children. For example:

> Compared with their parents' generation, children today commit suicide at a higher rate, perform worse in school, are more likely to be obese, and show other evidence of increased physical, mental and emotional distress. The poverty rate among children is almost double the rate for adults—a situation without precedent in American history (Fuchs, 1988: 94).

Pogrebin (1983: 42) concludes that the United States is fundamentally ambivalent about its children. As a nation, it cares but it doesn't *really* care. Americans romanticize "the family," but then overlook the systemic nature of child abuse and neglect. They pay little attention to the inadequacy of public health and public education, the large numbers of children who are homeless, hungry, or poor, and the limited futures so many children face.

Will these problems solve themselves? Data suggest they will. For example, Amato and Keith (1991) find a gradual weakening of the "effects of divorce," as measured in 20 years of studies on the differences between children from divorced families and children from intact families. The effects of divorce on children appear to be shrinking.

The meaning of this finding is unclear. It *may* mean that sociologists have gotten better at measuring these effects or that divorce has a smaller (negative) impact upon children than it once did. If so, we can all breathe a sigh of relief.

However, this finding may also mean that intact families are not as effective at parenting as they used to be. If so, this is no time to stop worrying. Is the worry justifiable? Well, rising rates of crime, drug use, and teenage pregnancy, and falling rates of academic achievement on standardized tests cannot all be ascribed to a few "problem families." It is far too soon to suppose the problem has even begun to solve itself, or to imagine it ever will.

In the next chapter we will look into the crystal ball for more signs about the future.

NOTES

1. However, the findings in this study may reflect failures in reporting, not actual variations in health conditions. For example, income affects reporting. If lower-income parents are prevented from taking their child to a doctor for financial reasons, they may not have any diagnostic label for their child's illness. Also, lower-income parents may remember less about a child's illnesses since they have other more pressing poverty-related issues to contend with.

   Education also affects the reporting of illnesses since well-educated parents are better able to identify illness in a child. In this study, however, educational effects on health are not significant once income is controlled.

   Finally, family size also affects health reporting. In large families mothers may have a harder time remembering who had what when. And when the respondent is not the child's mother, fewer illnesses are reported overall.

8

THE FUTURES
OF THE FAMILY

INTRODUCTION

It seems that everywhere, family relationships are in flux. In Africa and Asia, industrialization and urbanization are destroying extended kinship networks and bringing a drastic change in the nature of family obligations. In North America, people value family life. However, they are spending a smaller and smaller fraction of their lives in anything resembling a traditional family. And American families today show more signs of stress and conflict than ever before.

• Current family trends are the result of long-term (and worldwide) changes in social life. New laws and new contraceptive technology have given rise to new sexual permissiveness. Fertility has continued to fall for over a century. Divorce rates have reached historically high levels everywhere, especially in the United States.

These long-term trends have been given a boost by recent changes in the labor force participation of mothers of young children. In turn, their behavior is the culmination of a struggle for equality with men. It began two hundred years ago with Mary Wollstonecraft, the founder of modern feminism.

The process of industrialization has set in motion irresistible, irreversible social forces that have transformed the content of everyday life. They include the development of a consumer culture, market economy, welfare-oriented state, and mobile, urban social structure. As well, new technology prolongs life, prevents unwanted births, and creates life outside the womb. In the future, it will even create new sentient creatures through genetic engineering and artificial intelligence.

Focus in on one particular aspect of this change—what we call the "individualization" of people's lives (Jones et al., 1990; also Beck-Gernsheim, 1983; Schultz, 1983; and Herlyn and Vogel, 1989). With individualization, there is more variety, fluidity, and idiosyncrasy in all of the major demographic processes: in migration, marriage, divorce, childbearing, family decision making, and the relation of work life and family life. That's because, with individualization, we expect people to be self-sufficient actors in their economic, household, leisure, and intimate relationships.

An individualization of social roles means an "empowerment" of women, through higher levels of formal education and more participation in the paid labor force. The rise of a service economy creates more employment opportunities for women and, in this way, speeds up the process. Ultimately, the growth in jobs that free people from family control is what increases the variety, fluidity, and idiosyncrasy of people's private lives.

Do families still have anything to offer people in this age of individualization? If so, what is it? Why, given the choice, do most North Americans still value and desire marriage and children?

LOVE, COMMITMENT, AND THE FAMILIAR

It is no accident that the word *familiar*, which means "close, well-known, or intimate," originates in the word *family*. Family life is our first and best source of all that is "familiar" in our lives. Further, evidence shows that people need the familiar and families will remain the best institution for providing it.

Consider the human value of the familiar. It provides everyday life with form, content, and meaning. It's true that we all, some more than others, crave the *un*familiar. That's why we travel, change jobs and spouses, and do crazy things from time to time. Yet, for most of us, the unfamiliar has appeal only against the backdrop of the familiar. A steady diet of the unfamiliar would be chaotic and (probably) harmful to health and sanity, as well as to work and economic stability.

What families do is provide us with a set of familiar faces, activities, and routines. Family routines, like all routines, *can* be extremely boring. Nonetheless, routines serve to structure the world for us. In fact, we come to love them *because* they are comfortable and predictable. We even attribute "meaning" to our routine relationships and activities. They humanize an otherwise indifferent universe.

But people don't decide to move in together because they seek the familiar. Are we driven by tradition? Or are people simply irrational, failing to act in their own best interests? Sociology has always been fascinated by the study of behavior that makes no rational sense (on this, see Parsons, 1937). When studying it closely, sociologists have usually found that behavior that seems, at first glance, to be *irrational* turns out to be *nonrational*, that is to say, guided rationally by noneconomic concerns. Seen from this perspective, family life "makes sense" in the same way as most other social, religious, and cultural customs.

This does not mean that people behave in the ways they do because these are "traditional" ways and people are locked into tradition by fear and ignorance. In fact, the data show that highly educated, otherwise enlightened Western people are just as likely to marry, raise children, and form new relationships after divorce as other people are.

It's true that highly educated, "nontraditional" people marry later, raise fewer children, and have more tolerance for a variety of intimacies (for example, homosexuality) than less educated, more traditional people do. Otherwise, we can find no difference in this respect, so the "traditionalism" theory proves invalid.

Intellectuals have always been quick to predict an end to "traditional," nonrational concerns like religion, ethnicity, and nationalism, among others; and they have usually been wrong. None of these human concerns has disappeared. Repeatedly, they have changed form and resurfaced. Today, they remain among the most important factors in people's lives. Nor can we hope to reduce them to rational economic or political concerns, mere justifications for imperialism or responses to discrimination. Anyone who is religious, feels nationalistic, or has an ethnic identity knows better than that. These things have a reality of their own.

Family life is the same as religion, ethnicity, and nationalism in that it is nonrational. There is no sign that the human need for nonrationality is going to disappear.

Yet there are also strong signs of *rationality*. People show every sign of wanting to maximize their happiness by choosing their own destinies. When people have an opportunity to choose their own lives—for example, their mates, their living arrangements, or the number of children they will bear—they exercise this choice. In doing so they often ignore customary norms and expectations.

But more personal choice also produces uncertainty and ambivalence about how, and when, to limit personal choice. Do we tolerate or celebrate the marriages of same-sex couples, support or oppose birth control awareness in teenagers, allow abortion in incest cases but not for people who prefer one sex over another? These lines are indeed difficult to draw.

Not surprisingly, there is a conservative reaction to this uncertainty. It includes making myths about current family arrangements, for example, about the growing participation of men in family life and the pleasures of family life in the "old days." Supporting this conservative reaction is a part of the population who have been spared many of the recent changes. For example, rural people are among the strongest supporters of resistance to family change.

The outcome of this struggle for and against change in family life is hard to predict. Generally, the ratio of facilitating to resistant responses will be determined by the rate at which opportunities for independence increase (for example, through a growth of jobs for women).

Anything that (1) slows down the growth of opportunities after an initial growth, or (2) increases the individualization of lives at a rate faster than the creation of new cultural "meanings" and "norms," or (3) otherwise produces uncertainty (for example, a war or environmental disaster) will support a backward-looking mythology of the family.

Coping with Uncertainty

How do people cope with the ambivalence and uncertainty of intimacy these days? Typically, they develop new social forms and invent new lifestyles. This struggle to create new rules is especially important for women, who have been kept from a wide range of choices in the past. Solutions to the problem of uncertainty include:

1. Formal changes, such as new legislation that defines marriage and its rights and obligations, supports gender equity and affirmative action for women, improves day care, and encourages childbearing and fertility control; and
2. Informal changes, such as the efforts people make to "negotiate" new social roles and norms. For example, people work out new ways of disciplining the children of their spouse's first marriage, interacting with their mother's latest lover, or getting to know a co-worker's same-sex spouse.

Out of all this effort a new culture of intimate life emerges. Social and cultural changes, in turn, bring pressure for further structural changes by government and business. For example, the growth in part-time work, work sharing, and workplace child care all reflect new ideas about the relationship between work and family life. So do pressures on employers to pay health, retirement, or death benefits to nontraditional "spouses." In turn, these changes further increase choice, uncertainty, and cultural change, so the cycle of family change continues.

With few exceptions, this cycle works similarly in all societies. (Of course, there are suppressors and enhancers at work which we will discuss later in this chapter.) Bearing that in mind, what kinds of families will result from this process of individualization?

FOUR FAMILY TYPES OF THE FUTURE

We predict there will be at least four main kinds of nuclear families, differing along two main dimensions: (1) role separability and (2) personal interchangeability.

Role separability in families refers to the separation of spousehood from parenthood. Many North American households are made up of cohabiting couples with children, or reconstituted or blended families, where spouses may or may not parent one another's children.

A second dimension, *personal interchangeability*, refers to whether or not spouses are chosen for their unique characteristics, or because they perform certain roles. People who marry for love choose a mate for his or her unique characteristics. People who marry for instrumental reasons are more interested in whether or not the mate is a good provider, or can produce healthy offspring. Personal interchangeability is well-suited to societies with high rates of mortality. By contrast, romantic marriages are unpredictable and unstable. They are a luxury best enjoyed in prosperous times.

Now we can cross-classify nuclear families along these two dimensions. Doing so yields four possibilities: we call them the (1) corporate, (2) collected, (3) concatenated, and (4) cyclical family, respectively.

The Corporate Family

The corporate family is characterized by inseparable family roles and personal interchangeability.

That means in this kind of family people can come and go without changing the essential structure of the family. The husband serves as father to the younger generation in the household—children, apprentices, and

CHART 8.1 Four Types of Family

		ROLE SEPARABILITY	
		YES	NO
	YES	Collected Family	Corporate Family
PERSONAL INTERCHANGEABILITY			
	NO	Concatenated Family	Cyclical Family

household servants—and the wife serves as mother, whoever the natural parents of these children may be.

This type includes what Zimmerman called the "trustee family" and what Ogburn called the "multifunctional autonomous family" (see Goldenberg, 1987: 131).

It is only in a society dominated by this kind of family that people can reasonably think and speak of "the family" as a well-defined social institution. The institution of "the family" is protected in religion as well as by the state. In culture and by law, "the family" has a social importance, enjoys its own resources, and commands its members' loyalties.

This kind of family emphasizes its members' duty to the group. As Sacks says, such families only exist because of choices people do *not* make:

> To be a child is to accept the authority of parents one did not choose. To be a husband or wife is to accept the exclusion of other sexual relationships. To be a parent is to accept responsibility for a future that I may not live to see (Sacks, 1991: 56-7).

In fact, this kind of family is best suited to a theocratic, undifferentiated social structure. There, the state, the law, and religion are closely tied together and lean the same way on family matters. In societies where the corporate family dominates, competing models of life—for example, notions that individuals have rights and liberties—and competing institutions (like the secular school) hold little sway.

This "corporate family" existed among the nineteenth- and early twentieth-century European and North American middle classes. As we now know, its survival was aided by hypocrisy about the keeping of mistresses, use of street prostitutes, visits to brothels, and hidden homosexuality. Today, the corporate family is still the dominant model in Western societies. However, it is gradually losing support in law and public opinion.

The Collected Family

By contrast, the collected family is characterized by separable roles and interchangeable performers. It is similar to Duberman's (1975) "reconstituted" family, which follows the remarriage of partners who have children from previous unions.

Like the corporate family, the collected family expects family members to conform to traditional notions of husband, wife, father, mother, and child. However, given the complexities of remarriage, family members concede the impossibility of compelling mates to be both good spouses *and* good parents to the resident children.

In these families, it is not the family as a whole but the component roles which are the locus of loyalty, meaning, and resources. Children are permitted to feel close to their mothers without feeling obliged to love (or call "daddy") their mother's spouse, for example. Mothers can feel they are doing their duty as a "good mother" even if they select a partner whom they have reason to believe will not excel as a parent, and so on.

Societies like our own, with a significant number of reconstituted families, are beginning to recognize the peculiar character and special needs of collected families. For example, the state increasingly delivers benefits to spouses *or* parents *or* children, not to the "family head" of earlier days. In this system, one cannot assume that the family has a "head." Nor is it thought proper to invent one for the purposes of dispensing state funds.

So, for example, in 1988, the Canadian government began to send out family allowance checks made payable to the custodial parent of a child, typically the mother. This change recognized the crucial difference between a corporate family and a collected family.

Such legal rethinking has commanded a great deal of attention over the 1980s and it is still going on in many jurisdictions. However, this change is opposed by people who live in, or idealize, corporate families. After all, it concedes that corporate families are becoming less common and, normatively, families are less important to people's lives than they once were.

The Concatenated Family

A third kind of family, the concatenated family, is exactly opposite to the corporate family, since it is characterized by separable roles and unique performances.

From the outside, the concatenated family looks like a chance event, a slow collision of individuals in time and space. Indeed, the concatenated family is nothing more than a household at a particular moment in time. Here, meanings, loyalties, and resources are vested in individuals, not roles. Families exist only through the sharing of these meanings and resources. As a result, family members must constantly affirm and renegotiate the bases for this sharing.

Here, the meaning of "spouse" or "parent" is no longer certain. It is highly idiosyncratic from one person to another, one household to another. Occasionally, definitions will mesh for long periods of time. Sometimes, a shortage of alternatives will keep the household from dissolving despite a failure of definitions that mesh.

In any event, we cannot assume that in these families, members will have a permanent commitment to "the family" or even to their current spouses and children.

The concatenated family is an extreme version of radical individualism. It assumes that people ought to have unlimited free choice in their living arrangements. This freedom is subject only to the legal protection of minors from the consequences of family breakdown and the protection of all family members from household violence. Family life is perceived as a lifestyle or consumer choice—so far as the adults are concerned, a supermarket for intimate relations.

In this system, mating is motivated mainly by considerations of the spouse's unique characteristics, which may not continue to allure. Childbearing is motivated by a sociobiological drive or by personal self-expression—a form of psychic consumption of children for personal pleasure. Under these conditions, marital dissolution will be frequent because of the high premium on varied experience. Childbearing continues but at low levels. That's because it is expensive, reduces marital satisfaction, and makes households harder to dissolve.

Not surprisingly, this family system creates an enormous number of potential kinship connections (Gross, 1987). Along with this goes a lot of confusion about parenting responsibilities and property rights. However, more mothers than fathers remain with their children in the event of a divorce. So in practice, concatenated families (with children) are mainly matrifocal. Women and children remain, men come and go.

In North America and Europe, concatenated families are still far from the average. Yet they are common in certain subgroups (for example, the poorest and wealthiest classes, and among migrant or artistic communities). They may become an increasingly common though transient experience in many people's lives. That is, many people will spend a part of their lives in concatenated families (just as they spend a part of their lives in collected or corporate families).

The Cyclical Family

Like the corporate family, the cyclical (or recycled) family features traditional (inseparable) roles. But unlike the corporate family, there is no interchangeability in the cyclical family. Instead, the performances of its members are unique. Indeed, each is a "return engagement" occurring *because of* the unique relationship of the members.

This return engagement may be a second marriage of the same people (this is rare). More often, it is a second parenthood, during which people are called upon to parent their now-adult children (occasionally called "boomerangs") a second time.

For example, in Canada since 1981, the percentage of men and women between the ages of 20 and 34 years living with parents has risen significantly. The result is a complex household that *looks* like a corporate extended family but has none of the normative power of that older arrangement.

Many reasons account for the returns of adult children. They include unemployment, insufficient income for accommodation, or the need for more education, baby-sitting help, or savings towards a house, among others. Indeed, unique family situations result from an interaction between the reasons for return and expectations of the children and parents.

For example, the parents may expect their grown children to be tidy, to follow curfews, and to be independent. The children may expect to be looked after, even to receive an allowance. Yet they violate household rules regarding the use of cars, stereo systems, home space, and so on. Naturally, conflicts arise from these differences.

Alongside these differences in expectations, problems also arise out of feelings of guilt or a desire to maintain good relations with one another (usually, parents trying to maintain good relations with their children). Norms to guide behavior in these circumstances are not yet established, so we witness what amounts to a series of unique performances.

PREDICTIONS

The history of social science is littered with predictions that have failed. In general, the science of prediction has often meant assuming that current trends will continue into the future, and often this assumption proves wrong. Yet there is nothing inherently wrong with extrapolating current trends. The trick is to distinguish between trends that carry a lot of freight and trends that can turn on a dime.

Marriage and Fertility

The vast majority of Americans will have at least one spouse, and most American women will have at least one child. Yet, for most Americans, the "imperative to marry" has weakened. Singlehood is viewed more positively than it was in the past. We predict that marriage will remain popular and people will continue to marry. However, more people will cohabit and live by themselves for longer periods of their lives.

Where marriage is concerned, we are looking at a self-fulfilling prophecy. "Insecurity about the viability of relationships may lead to behavior that, in turn, lowers the prospects that the relationship will last" (Bumpass and Sweet, 1987: 393). But there is little reason to believe people will ever completely give up on the idea of marrying.

Other patterns are also well-established. For example, the recession of the early 1990s suppressed the fertility of the generation turning 25 at the time. As well, women's labor force participation is now well entrenched and will not decline in the future. Inequalities in the household division of labor have continued to shrink, but women continue to work a double day. Divorce rates remain high. Finally, birth control methods continue to improve in effectiveness, and we can expect fewer unintended births in the future. For all these reasons, we expect families to continue to get smaller.

Once born, and barring the occurrence of wars or epidemics, we can predict that most children will progress through the average life cycle. In prosperous countries, this means they can expect to live for 70 years or more. A "fat cohort" like the baby boomers successively create a demand for schooling, housing, active sports, and less active sports. In their child-bearing years, they create a surge in fertility just by having one or two children each. And as the boomers get old, we can expect them to create a demand for retirement homes and, eventually, for cemetery plots.

Predicting fertility levels is hazardous, but we can certainly describe the kind of society which has low fertility. On reaching a steady state, this society has "few young people and relatively many old people, children growing up with few collateral relatives, parents spending not more than a tiny fraction of their lifetime in childrearing activities" (Coale, 1987: 214). The population is poised to decline in numbers. However, if it is a rich country, large north-south differences in wealth will assure a continuing stream of immigrants with their own norms and values about family behavior. We are moving to this kind of society now.

Some view the decline of the national population as a major catastrophe and propose incentives which will get people back to making babies. For example, in France, Rumania, Quebec, and what used to be East Germany, direct financial incentives have been aimed at rewarding the mothers of large families, and they have "worked" to a limited degree.

Others have proposed to let parents vote on behalf of their dependent children, in this way rewarding parenthood with extra political influence; or to transfer a part of people's compulsory social security contributions to their living parents. Under this latter plan, seniors who never had children would be denied the benefit (Demeny, 1987: 353, quoted by Namboodiri, 1988: 787).

However, proposals like this are poorly suited to the fluid family structures that exist today. They reward families, not individuals, and in this way assume the continued dominance of corporate families. To take an example, if (according to a given plan) men are to gain points for fathering children, what happens after divorce or remarriage? Many questions like this one remain to be answered.

The Four Kinds of Families

In the long term, societies which intervene in people's lives *least*—in other words, societies where family matters are treated as personal problems, not public issues—will see the corporate family continue to thrive. This will be especially true in periods of economic difficulty. Then, people will be less able or willing to risk personal independence. (For the same reason, cyclical families will become more numerous in hard times, if state supports are unavailable.)

On the other hand, concatenated and collected families will be more common in societies where family matters are treated as public issues, not personal problems. They will be more common everywhere in prosperous times than in hard times.

If history should reverse itself and states begin to take *less* interest in people's private lives, the corporate family will stage a comeback. However, this is unlikely. Given the growing individualization of lives around the world, we will not see a major shift back toward the corporate family under any economic conditions.

More likely, in the future we shall see a continuing decline of corporate families among native-born North Americans and an increase in collected families. This is not a wild prediction. The last 50 years or so have already witnessed a shift away from the corporate family, through the collected family (in the last 20 or so years), towards the concatenated family.

However, there will not be a complete shift to concatenated families. As Yankelovich (1981) notes in *New Rules*, human nature stands in the way. In the long run, superficial or transient relationships add little to people's fulfillment or satisfaction; actually, they take away from it.

Indeed, the concatenated family has little long-range survival value for society, if only because it fuels the decline in childbearing. Sociobiologically, it produces small numbers of children who are not fertile themselves. Socially, it deprives family members of familiar routine—of the form, content, and meaning we need from family life. Gone are the socialization, security, and contentment that are supposed to constitute a family's contribution to societal survival.

The main force shifting families from a corporate to a concatenated form is *social fluidity*. Other things being equal, social fluidity is greatest where conformity and regularity—the classic middle-class virtues—are unnecessary or fruitless, as they are (typically) for the rich and the poor. A dramatic change in the economy, in either direction, could move family life towards more fluidity, hence more concatenation.

Economically, the concatenated family is unstable and unpredictable. Family creation and dissolution is costly, so the concatenated lifestyle accelerates spending; it is a bad source of production and savings. Particularly in hard economic times, this family form will be dysfunctional to both family members and the economy at large.

Some observers, like Moynihan (1986), also believe that concatenated families are liable to produce and neglect children willy-nilly, leaving the state to take responsibility for their support and socialization. They also fail to provide elderly parents with care and support.

For these reasons, concatenated families will remain a deviant form confined to the richest and poorest minorities—for the most part, not a typical middle-class, middle-aged family type. Corporate families will be most common among immigrants from preindustrial societies, and in rural, traditional areas of North America. Cyclical families may become a common form of family living at a particular stage in people's lives—inevitable and brief for many North Americans between the ages of 55 and 70.

Here are a few other things we expect to see:

- In a stagnant economy, a sustained conservative reaction will lead to more corporate families.
- In a stagnant economy, the aging of the population will lead to more cyclical families.
- Because noncustodial fathers tend to disappear, an increase in collected families will lead to more concatenated families.
- Since children raised by single mothers are divorce-prone, a rise in their numbers will lead to more concatenated families.

In closing this section, we note that around the world, all societies are having to deal with roughly the same issues of family, spousehood, parenthood, and gender. They differ only in the stage of debate they have reached at this time.

So, for example, in the 1980s, gender relations in Singapore (see Quah, 1987) were at the stage where North America was in the late 1960s or early 1970s. And parts of North America today are where Sweden was in the late 1960s or early 1970s. By the same token, Sweden is where North America could well be twenty or thirty years from now. (We will have more to say about Sweden shortly.)

REMEDIES

In the future, family life will survive. But different varieties—not just the traditional corporate family—will do so. Now it is time to consider what we want to do about the problems of family life we have noted. What remedies would make family lives easier, safer, and healthier in the foreseeable future?

To speak of "remedies" for family life proves that we see certain current conditions as problematic and value certain outcomes more than others. Our "ideal family" would support its members by providing care, sympathy, and affection, as well as material help where possible. And it would do this without reducing personal freedom any more than necessary. (Of course, we recognize that to belong to any kind of family means giving up *some* freedom.)

We have said that social roles are being individualized, and rights are being vested more in people as individuals rather than as members of any collective. Because of this individualization, people feel that they have more choice in their lives and a chance to develop their own potential. This seems, to us, a good thing. So we are looking for remedies that would work *with* individualization—which is, in any event, inevitable—and reduce the problems we have identified throughout this book.

Recent remedies have attempted to rescue the traditional corporate family, though in a form that conservatives might not recognize. They have included major changes in family law and employment practices.

Family Law in North America

In the last 50 years, the legal framework of Western families has changed a lot. Some of the consequences are already before us, even taken for granted by large portions of the public. These legal changes have happened gradually, alongside a more generalized "liberation of individuals." As people's lives have individualized, the family has changed and, in fact, one could not have changed without a corresponding change in the other. On this, one observer writes:

> The interstices between "the law" and "the family" are far broader than the general term "family law" implies [. . .] Indeed, a number of writers have indicated that perhaps it is impossible to separate law and family because historically, legal process treated "the family" as the basic constituent of society which determines the relationship of individuals to the social order (Currie, 1989: 271).

As we noted in Chapter Three, divorce legislation has become more permissive in the last few decades. But it would be a mistake to think legal changes have merely made divorce easier. Other (and related) legal trends include:

1. the reflection of legal equality of the sexes, via more neutrality in our language: "Reflected in the use of terms such as 'spouses' rather than 'husband' and 'wife' or of 'parent' rather than 'father' and 'mother.' There is a systematic elimination of most of the reference to older notions of what constitutes typical or proper family roles" (ibid.: 283). Inclusion of women in legal writing reflects their inclusion in the legal process itself.
2. "a principle of individualism within the family rather than unity of legal personality" (ibid.: 284). This trend was particularly relevant in the move towards gaining property rights for women.
3. "legalization" (ibid.: 284), with state intervention establishing husbands and wives as equals in the eyes of the law. Protecting the rights of individuals within a marriage signifies "further intrusion by the state into relationships between individuals" and makes way for "the expanding body of public law which has emerged to take over functions once performed by families" (ibid.).

Combined with women's increased ability to earn an income, these legal changes produce a major "empowerment" of wives.

As Currie notes, the general legal trend has been "toward relatively free dissolution of marital ties" (ibid.: 283). Marriage has shifted from a lifetime commitment terminated only in the case of "fault" committed by ∪ party, to a contract dissolvable upon demand in the event of personal unhappiness. "The contemporary family is seen as the sphere wherein 'personal fulfillment' is sought. Once a family fails to provide for the emotional and psychological well-being of its members, the rationale for its existence is lost" (ibid.).

Most observers have been concerned with the potential damage caused by the process of divorce itself, and therefore a great deal of effort has been spent on finding remedies which will smooth the marital dissolution process.

As we have seen, some women need transitional time after a divorce to prepare to support themselves and their children. A universal application of no-fault laws, without attention to the needs of particular women, has produced hardships the framers of the new laws had not intended.

In some places in North America, divorce courts have decided that if one partner (usually the wife) stays home to look after the children, this is the result of a joint decision. Any extra income the working partner (usually the husband) receives because of this arrangement should be shared by the married couple, so long as they remain married.

On this logic, divorce should be followed by an equitable division of the family assets and appropriate child support payments. But there should also be fair compensation to the nonworking partner for the estimated future loss of income due to her interrupted career. Moreover, there should be further compensation to the nonworking partner for the estimated future income of the working partner that was due to the nonworking partner's earlier investment of support. Lawyers can find a lot of work in such situations.

There are other ways to make divorce more equitable and less harmful. For example, Furstenberg (1990) believes that "clearer normative standards regulating postmarital ties are required" (op. cit.: 399). In short, we need an etiquette or a rule book for divorce. Some people believe that a witnessed ceremony of divorce—one which emphasizes the move to a new and different system of rules and responsibilities—might be a useful rite of passage. Perhaps we should all be obliged to make agreements at the time of marriage or when the first child is born, explicitly "allocating rights and responsibilities between parents in the event that their relationship dissolves" (op. cit.: 399).

Furstenberg also cites the enactment of the Family Support Act of 1988, which standardizes "child support based on a fixed portion of the father's earnings" and garnishees (confiscates by court order) wages in cases of default, as an attempt to establish "unambiguous standards for divorcing couples . . . [since] private bargaining has not worked well to ensure the security of children" (op. cit.: 399).

Financial issues aside, there is a need to attend to the social and psy-

.vorce as well. The typical pattern is for noncustodial
reduce their level of visiting, and this means a gradual
relationships with all kin on the side of that noncustodial
.y, the father). At the same time, there is often a failure to
.egal status and obligations of stepparents.

.n our present cultural expectations, then, most collected families
into concatenated ones, with children losing many kin when their
pai.its separate or divorce. Some have argued recently for the need to
ensure the rights of grandparents to see their grandchildren in the event of
a divorce. This is only the tip of the iceberg, if we are to take family security
seriously as a social, and not merely an economic, issue.

Alternate Work Structures

Other remedies include work structures which make it easier for people to combine paid work with family obligations such as raising children. The vast majority of employed women juggle paid employment and family care for varying periods, and for most women, the process is anything but smooth. The research and debate surrounding women's "double day," or what Hochschild (1989) calls the "second shift," looks for solutions in two areas. They are domestic work sharing and a better system of social supports, most notably for dependent care.

Generally, work structures and work cultures have been largely unresponsive to the needs of two-income or single-parent families. Few challenge the assumptions that work comes first, overtime and travel are necessary, and dependent care is a family (not a work) problem. In short, "Corporations have done little to accommodate the needs of working parents and government has done little to prod them" (Hochschild (1989: 267).

The problem is a lack of systematic, long-term thinking about the problem, at least in North America:

> Throughout Europe, governments have required companies to treat the parenting of babies as a special circumstance of employment and have invested heavily in programs to support the children of working parents. In this country, recent surveys indicate almost universal popular support for parental leave. But our instincts oppose government intervention into internal business practices. We leave decisions about flexibility and the organization of work to individual companies, which means that the decisions of first-line managers in large part create our national family policy (Rodgers and Rodgers, 1989: 129).

Whether to counter the costs of absenteeism and turnover, attract employees, present a certain corporate image, or comply with government regulations, a number of companies have made changes in the last decade or so. Many have introduced alternate career paths, flextime, job sharing, and telecommuting. In principle, all of these should make it easier for employees to meet their domestic responsibilities. But what impact have these changes in work organization had upon families? Have they, in fact, met family needs?

Organizational Changes

Consider the following attempts to adjust work to the demands of family life.

1. *Part-time work and job sharing* Part-time work is the most obvious alternative to full-time work. The postwar growth in part-time work was a result of growth in the service sector, particularly in retail, trade, and personal services. Most part-time work is done by women and an increasing amount is *involuntary* (because of the unavailability of full-time work).

Inevitably, part-time work is low paid, lacks benefits, job security, or opportunities for advancement. There are few permanent part-time jobs. Many part-time jobs involve evening and weekend work. Indeed, the majority of part-time workers work only part of the year. Given the disadvantages in terms of hours, pay, and job security, part-time work is a rare choice for most parents, whether married or not.

Even if someone *were* willing to trade some of his or her income for more free time, few families could tolerate the income insecurity that accompanies part-time work.

By contrast, *job sharing* is an arrangement between two or more employees who share a full-time job, not always equally. "In effect the job is full-time, but the job holders are part-time" (Kamerman and Kahn, 1988: 245). The arrangement is a voluntary one, usually initiated by the workers involved. Their reasons may be family-related, or they may be occasioned by health or other personal concerns.

Job sharing brings part-time workers some of the advantages of full-time employment—benefits, job security, and the possibility of advancement—that are available to most. However, because of the difficulty in finding a compatible and willing partner, few people share jobs. In the United States an estimated 1% of all workers share jobs and no more than 15% of companies offer job-sharing as an option.

2. *Flextime,* or flexitime, was first used in West Germany in the late 1960s as a means of reducing traffic congestion. The idea caught on in North America in the early 1970s, but it remains more widely used in Europe than North America. Flextime may involve varying arrival and departure times, or the week's work may be compressed into three or four

days. A major benefit of flextime is that it gives employees an element of control in determining their working hours.

Most studies evaluating work flexibility find increased morale and reductions in lateness, absenteeism, and turnover. Some also report increased productivity, which in some cases is related to a more efficient use of machinery. Does flextime help people to juggle family responsibilities? Here the evidence is less clear. Daily flextime gives people too little freedom to reduce work/family conflicts significantly. On balance, flextime is a fairly minor alteration of the work environment and has relatively little effect on ingrained family practices.

3. *Home work* Women have a long history of combining (unpaid) domestic work with paid work in their homes. In recent years, as a result of advances in technology, there has been an increase in the number of home workers.

On the surface, home work seems to help workers integrate paid and domestic work. But home work does not solve the day care problem. Home workers with preschool children rely on child care by others, or work late into the night while their children are sleeping.

A related development is *telecommuting*. The term was coined in the early 1970s to describe people working at home at computer work stations. The advantages were the time saved in commuting and gains in work autonomy. While there may be some benefits to families, this was not the incentive.

In the longer run, innovations like these may actually harm families because they reduce the economic security of workers. Businesses welcome temporary and part-time work because of the lower labor costs. During the last half of the 1980s, businesses' use of "contract" workers to supplement a core group of full-time, in-house workers went from a stopgap measure to an entrenched business strategy. But when productivity alone is the driving force, an increase in temporary or contract work leaves employees in these positions (many of them women) economically vulnerable in hard times.

If flexible work policies are to have any real impact on the integration of family and work, there must first be a major reduction in the wage gap between men and women. When policies are introduced for women only, or introduced for reasons unrelated to work/family conflicts, they perpetuate a sexual division of labor at home and at work.

Such policies fail to recognize the parental duties of men and the social responsibility (that business and industry must share) of child rearing and dependent care. They also fail to challenge existing policies on career organization and promotion. So it is difficult to provide flexibility without re-creating job ghettos, or to take into account different family and personal needs without penalizing parents.

There are also indications that North Americans are beginning to establish a different balance between work and family life. The group whom the media have labeled "generation X" are less likely than their parents to sacrifice family and personal life for organizational goals. There are several reasons for this change.

First, our work lives are going to shrink as a proportion of the total years we live, for several reasons. We are going to live longer, study longer, but work the same number or fewer years than we do today. We can expect to spend ever less of our lives as workers and more as nonworkers.

Second, for most people, work will provide less autonomy—less scope for freedom and self-expression—than today. A minority will still root their identities, and dreams, in the workplace. But they will make up a smaller part of the population than they do today. The consequent meaning gap will be filled for some by religion, ethnicity, or nationalism. For others, the gap will be filled by family life.

What, if anything, can we learn from Sweden, the society which is most advanced in its individualization of people's lives *and* in its thinking about families?

Sweden: Paradise for Families?

There is a consensus among academics that Sweden has developed the most complete and sophisticated way of linking work and family life. If so, it is worth our while to examine the Swedish experiment and see whether it provides affordable remedies for the problems we face in North America.

Swedish Policies Sweden treats employment as a right and a duty. People who lose their jobs are paid while they retrain for other jobs. However, strong economic penalties (or disincentives) face people who quit their jobs. In fact, 30 percent of unemployed Swedes receive no unemployment insurance and must depend on municipal welfare programs.

Swedish health and social services provide a large budget for children's day care and care of the elderly. In part, this is a purely practical strategy. Without much immigration, Sweden needs women in the labor force. These policies free women from traditional family-care tasks and make it possible for them to work for pay.

All Swedish employment policies recognize the equality between men and women. For example, a parent (whether mother or father, adoptive or natural) "is guaranteed 9 months of 'parental leave' at nearly full pay (90% of salary), another 3 months at minimum pay, and the option of an additional 6 months at no pay" (Popenoe, 1988: 203).

As well, nontaxable parental allowances compensate for a loss of income while caring for children. They do not guarantee an improvement in living standards for families with dependent children. Parents pay for day-care programs, which are heavily subsidized by the state, on a sliding scale according to their family income. Sweden also offers everyone free medical and dental care, and free education (including postsecondary).

Because of a high level of women's rights and equality, "Sweden today is generally considered to be the most egalitarian society in the Western world" (Popenoe, op. cit.: 176). It has the highest female labor force participation in the Northern hemisphere (77 percent of all working-age women and 85 percent of all mothers with young children employed outside the home). Moreover, the average Swedish woman working full-time earns 90 percent of the salary of her male co-workers, compared with only 60 to 70 percent in North America.

How have these policies affected and reflected changes in the Swedish family?

Swedish families Before 1950, Sweden's marriage and divorce rates were similar to those of other European countries. Today, Sweden has the lowest marriage rate in the industrial world.

The rate of marriage first started dropping radically in the mid-1960s. It fell by 40 percent in the seven or eight years following 1966, with the highest decreases among young people (Trost, 1977). "By one estimate, based on projecting current trends, 36% of Swedish women born in 1955 will not have married by the time they reach age 50, compared to only 9% of women born in 1940" (Popenoe, op. cit.: 169).

As in North America, the decline in Sweden's marriage rate is largely due to an increase in cohabitation. In Sweden, "Nonmarital cohabitation is now regarded legally and culturally as an accepted alternative rather than a prelude to marriage" (ibid.: 170). Rates of cohabitation are hard to estimate precisely, but close to 25 percent of Swedish couples are cohabiting at present. Moreover, "only an estimated 2% of women marrying today have not previously cohabited with their husbands-to-be or with some other man, compared to nearly 50% of women born in 1930" (ibid.: 170).

Yet despite high rates of cohabitation before marriage, Sweden continues to have a divorce rate many believe is the highest in Europe. This high divorce rate is particularly surprising "because many of the factors traditionally associated with divorce in the United States—brief courtship and early marriages, teen pregnancies, poverty and income instability, interethnic and interfaith unions, and high residential mobility—are mitigated in Sweden" (ibid.: 173).

In Sweden as elsewhere, high rates of divorce and cohabitation have produced a large number of single-parent families. The percentage is not as high as in the United States, but by 1980, 18 percent of all households with children were headed by single parents. In fact, one out of every four families with young children in 1980 contained a single parent. And as elsewhere, single-parenthood in Sweden comes with its share of social and economic hardships. Yet the life of the unwed parent in Sweden "is not characterized by the high level of relative deprivation that is found in the United States" (ibid.: 175).

In part, this is due to the state support of informal social networks. Large-scale use of the telephone and widespread diffusion of car ownership means that people are no longer dependent on neighbors and family members, let alone social workers. Gunnarsson and Cochran (1990: 116) note that:

> In Western industrialized societies, community is based on a network of significant social ties that extend beyond the immediate neighborhood. Increasingly these are personally selected and developed bonds, rather than ties ascribed by formal roles and obligations. Supportive formal services in Sweden expand the physical distance over which social ties can be maintained, and this formal support has its greatest effects on mothers with the fewest personal resources—single mothers.

These factors aside, the increase in mothers working outside the home has had a great effect on the structure of the Swedish family, "representing a major break from the 'separate spheres' of the traditional, bourgeois family" (Popenoe, op. cit.: 177).

For this reason, Popenoe and other North Americans writing about Sweden worry about a possible "deinstitutionalization" of the family: policies which breed "disinvestment in the family, and vice versa. For those who are interested in the enhancement of family life, the question of how to break this vicious circle is one of the serious social concerns of our time" (ibid.).

Sweden has one of the highest standards of living in the world. High taxes support the many social assistance programs—including health care, child care, and education—we have mentioned. They make it less financially risky for couples to separate. It may be true that "families are most cohesive when they are forced to be so" (ibid.: 221). And because of high government subsidies for single parents, some divorced couples are even better off financially than if they had stayed married.

Swedish women are also more educated and financially independent than most other women, so they are more able (and therefore more likely) to leave an unhappy union. In fact, women begin 70 percent of all divorce proceedings in Sweden (ibid.: 223). All of this shows that the "traditional," or corporate, type of family in other societies can survive only so long as family life is based on an inequality between men and women.

Not only does the Swedish strategy work against traditional family life, it is also expensive. In recent decades, Sweden has had the highest combined sales taxes and income taxes in the world and many Swedes have objected to their "Swedish Model" welfare state (Groulx, 1990). The economic crises of 1974, 1982, and (most seriously) 1992 brought many of their concerns to a head, with critics arguing the impossibility of maintaining such high state expenditures in a period of economic decline (Cook, 1993). They claimed that extremely high marginal tax rates distort economic activity and make Sweden unable to compete economically.

Other critics raise concerns about what will happen to the quality of care when professional, bureaucratized workers take over child care and elder care functions which were traditionally within the private sphere. They argue that social programs should move in the direction of community-oriented care, deprofessionalizing and deinstitutionalizing the social services, and increasing the participation of users.

Leaving aside the cost, there are definite pluses and minuses in the Swedish situation. On the one hand, Sweden is effective in promoting gender equality, individualization, and the employment of a well-trained, healthy work force. On the other hand, it also produces large numbers of collected and concatenated families. For reasons we went into in Chapter Four, these families are not always good for people.

CLOSING COMMENTS

Given the trends we have identified, it seems likely that families will continue to survive. However, they will continue to take a variety of forms. These forms will be institutionalized, both culturally and economically.

It is hard to see how we can avoid going the route Sweden has gone. But if we follow Sweden's lead, the number of collected and concatenated families will increase. And remember, these families have particular social and psychological, as well as economic, needs.

If we do *not* follow Sweden's lead, for fiscal or other reasons, there will be fewer collected and concatenated families. But the collected and concatenated families that do exist will still be poor, as they are today. We may hold fast to the appearance of a commitment to traditional corporate families. However, a great many of these families will contain frustrated, potentially violent members.

Whatever its future, the family will remain with us and it will remain a problem. That's because the family remains an emotionally demanding, socially and economically interdependent unit in an age of growing demands for personal autonomy. We cannot imagine a change in family problems without also imagining a huge cultural and economic shift away from the economic, social, political, and cultural trends of the last few centuries.

In the long run, more and more of us will spend parts of our lives in corporate families, collected families, concatenated families, *and* cyclical families. As we all become aware of their particular needs, advantages, and disadvantages, we will become more willing and able to work on solutions together. There will be an end to the finger pointing and stigmatizing that still accompanies many kinds of personal life—behavior which prevents us from finding solutions together.

Until then, we will continue to penalize children for the choices (and nonchoices) of their parents, and bear down most heavily on other parts of the population who are already most vulnerable—women, elderly people, and racial minorities among them.

In North America and elsewhere, we have seen the effects of privatizing family life—making it mainly a personal problem, not a public issue. And we have seen the effects, in Sweden, of making family life a public issue, not merely a personal problem. Undoubtedly, neither strategy has reached its endpoint. Both systems will continue to evolve and struggle with their current problems.

In the long run, the Swedish solution will probably prevail. It is the more humane, less economically wasteful, and more socially productive solution. However, that is only a guess, not a certainty.

Only one thing *is* certain: there is no turning back. The future will contain many kinds of families, hence, the title of this book—the futures of the family. And *those* families will not be like families of the past. More than at any time in the past, our personal lives will reflect the powers of our imagination and the state's willingness to support variety.

REFERENCES

Abdo-Zubi, Nahla. *Family, women and social change in the Middle East: the Palestinian case.* Toronto: Canadian Scholars' Press, 1987.

Abu-Laban, S.M., and Sharon McIrvin (1981) "Women and aging: A futurist perspective," *Psychology of Women Quarterly,* Vol. 6, No. 1 (Fall), 85–98.

Adams, O., and D. Nagnur (1989) "Marrying and divorcing: A status report for Canada," *Canadian Social Trends,* Vol. 13 (Summer), 24–27.

Adebayo, A., and D.J. Adamchak (1991) "Ethnic affiliation and fertility attitudes of Nigerian university students," *College Student Journal,* 25 (1), March, 470–477.

Aghajanian, Akbar. "War and Migrant Families in Iran." In Lorne J. Tepperman and Susannah J. Wilson (eds.) *Next of Kin: An International Reader on Changing Families.* Englewood Cliffs, New Jersey. Prentice Hall. 1992.

Ahmed, Ashraf U. (1986) "Marriage and its transition in Bangladesh," *International Journal of Sociology of the Family,* 16, 1, Spring, 49–59. Reprinted in Lorne J. Tepperman and Susannah J. Wilson (eds.) *Next of Kin: An International Reader on Changing Families.* Englewood Cliffs, New Jersey. Prentice Hall. 1992.

Ahmed, B. (1987) "Determinants of contraceptive use in rural Bangladesh: The demand for children, supply of children, and costs of fertility regulation," *Demography,* 24, 3, 361–373.

Ahrons, Constance R. (1980) "Divorce: A crisis of family transition and change," *Family Relations,* 29, October, 533–540.

Akyeampong, Ernest B. (1987) "Involuntary part-time employment in Canada 1975–1986," *Canadian Social Trends,* Autumn, 26–9.

Aldous, Joan (1987) "New views on the family life of the elderly and the near-elderly," *Journal of Marriage and the Family,* 49 (May), 227–234.

Allison, Paul D., and Fank F. Furstenberg, Jr., "How Marital Dissolution Affects Children: Variations by Age and Sex," *Developmental Psychology,* 89, 540–549.

Amato, Paul, R., and Bruce Keith. "Parental Divorce and the Well-Being of Children: A Meta-Analysis," *Psychological Bulletin,* 1991, 110 (1): 26–46.

Amato, Paul R. "Family Processes in One-Parent Stepparent, and Intact Families: The Child's Point of View," *Journal of Marriage and the Family*, Vol. 49 (May 1987): 327–337.

Amato, P.R., and Booth, A. (1991) Consequences of parental divorce and marital unhappiness for adult well-being. *Social Forces*, 69, 3, March, 895–914.

Amato, P.R., and Keith, B. (1991) Separation from a parent during childhood and adult socio-economic attainment. *Social Forces*, 70 (1), September, 187–206.

Amato, P.R., and G. Ochiltree (1987) "Child and adolescent competence in intact, one-parent, and step-families: An Australian study," *Journal of Divorce*, 10 (3–4), spring-summer, 75–96.

Ambert, Anne-Marie. *The Effect of Children on Parents*. New York: Haworth Press. 1992.

Anderson, K. L. (1982) Huron women and Huron men: the effects of demography, kinship and the social division of labour on male/female relations among the 17th century Huron. University of Toronto: Sociology Department. Unpublished doctoral Thesis.

Anderson, Michael, 1971, *Family and Class in Nineteenth Century Lancarshire*. London: Routledge.

Anderson, Michael, "The social implications of demographic change." In F.M.L. Thompson (ed.) *The Cambridge Social History of Britain 1750–1950: Volume 2. People and Their Environment*. Cambridge University Press. 1990. Pp. 1–70.

Arendell, Terry J. (1987) "Women and the economics of divorce in the contemporary United States," *Signs*, 13, 1, 121–135. Reprinted in Lorne J. Tepperman and Susannah J. Wilson (eds.) *Next of Kin: An International Reader on Changing Families*. Englewood Cliffs, New Jersey. Prentice Hall. 1992.

Aries, P. (1962) *Centuries of Childhood* , New York: Vintage Books.

Bachrach, Christine A. "Children in Families: Characteristics of Biological, Step-, and Adopted Children," *Journal of Marriage and the Family*, Vol. 45 (February 1983): 171–179.

Baillargeon, Jean-Paul. (1987) "Les mariages religieux, 1976–1985," *Recherches sociographiques*, 28 (2–3), 341–348.

Balakrishnan, T. R., and Jiajian Chen, "Religiosity, nuptiality and reproduction in Canada," *Canadian Review of Sociology and Anthropology* 27: 316–40, August, 1990.

Balakrishnan, T.R. (1989) "Changing nuptiality patterns and their fertility implications in Canada," Pp. 229–250 in Jacques Légaré, T.R. Balakrishnan, and Roderic P. Beaujot, eds. *The Family in Crisis: A Population Crisis?* Ottawa: Royal Society of Canada.

Balakrishnan, T.R., K.V. Rao, Evelyne Lapierre-Adamcyk, and K.J. Krótki (1987) "A hazard model analysis of the covariates of marriage dissolution in Canada," *Demography*, Vol. 24, 395-406.

Ball, R.E., and L. Robbins (1986) "Marital status and life satisfaction among black Americans." *Journal of Marriage and the Family*, 48, 2, May, 389–394.

Bandura, Albert, and Richard H. Walters. *Social Learning and Personality Development*. New York: Holt Rinehart, and Winston. 1963.

Bane, Mary Jo, and David T. Ellwood, "The Dynamics of Children's Living Arrangements." Prepared for the U.S. Department of Health and Human Services (March, 1984).

Bane, M.J. (1976) *Here to Stay: American Families in the Twentieth Century*, New York: Basic Books.

Bane, Mary Jo, "Is the welfare state replacing the family?" *The Public Interest*, No. 70 (Winter 1983): 91–101.

Banfield, Edward C., with Laura Fasano (1967) *The Moral Basis of a Backward Society*. New York: Free Press. 1967.

Bassand, Michel, "Urbanization: Appropriation of Space and Culture." Pro Helvetia Swiss Lectureship. No. 7. The Graduate School and University Center: City University of New York. 1990.

Beaujot, R. (1991) *Rationales used in marriage and childbearing decisions*. Discussion Paper No. 91-7. London, Ontario: Population Studies Centre, University of Western Ontario.

Becker, Gary S. *A Treatise on the Family*. Enlarged Edition. Harvard University Press. 1991.

Beck-Gernsheim, Elisabeth, "From Living for Others to a Life of One's Own: Structural Changes in Women's Lives," *Soziale-Welt*, 1983, 34, 3, 307–340.

Beck, Ulrich. *The Risk Society: Towards a New Modernity*. Sage.

Bell, W. (1987) "Is the futures field an art form or can it become a science?" *Futures Research Quarterly*, Spring, 27–44.

Bell, W. (1991) "Futuro," *Enciclopedia delle Science Sociale*, Vol. III, Roma, Italia.

Bennett, N.G., A.K. Blanc, and D.E. Bloom (1988) "Commitment and the modern union: Assessing the link between premarital cohabitation and subsequent marital stability," *American Sociological Review*, 53 (February), 127–138.

Berger, C. et al, (1984) "Repeat abortion: Is it a problem?" *Family Planning Perspectives*, Vol.16, 70–75.

Berkner, L. K. (1975). "The use and misuse of census data for the historical analysis of family structure." *Journal of Interdisciplinary History*, 4, 721–38.

Bernard, Jessie, 1974. *The Future of Motherhood*. New York: Dial Press.

Berne, Eric, *Games People Play: The Psychology of Human Relationships*. New York: Grove Press. 1964.

Betzig, Laura (1989) "Causes of conjugal dissolution: A cross-cultural study," *Current Anthropology*, 30. No. 5 (December), 654–676.

Bianchi, Suzanne M., and Daphne Spain, *American Women in Transition*. New York: Russell Sage Foundation. 1986.

Blake, Judith. *Family Size and Achievement*. Berkeley: University of California Press. 1989.

Blake, Judith, with J. Mayone Stycos. *Family Structure in Jamaica: The Social Context of Reproduction*. New York: Free Press of Glencoe. 1962.

Blanc, Ann Klimas, "Nonmarital Cohabitation and Fertility in the United States and Western Europe," *Population Research and Policy Review*; 1984, 3, 2, June, 181–193.

Blanc, Ann Klimas, "The Formation and Dissolution of Second Unions: Marriage and Cohabitation in Sweden and Norway," *Journal of Marriage and the Family*, 1987, 49, 2, May, 391–400.

Blaxter, M. (1990) *Health and Lifestyles* London: Routledge.

Blaxter, Mildred (1985) "Self-definition of health status and consulting rates in primary care," *Quarterly Journal of Social Affairs* 1, 131–71.

Blaxter, Mildred (1990) *Health and Lifestyles*. London: Tavistock/Routledge.

Block, Jeanne H., Jack Block, and P. F. Gjerde, "The personality of children prior to divorce," *Child Development* 57 (1986): 827–840.

Bloom, D. E. (1982) "What's happening to age at first birth in the United States? A study of recent cohorts," *Demography*, 19 (3), 351–370.

Blute, Marion, "Biologists on Sociocultural Evolutionism: A Critical Analysis," *Sociological Theory*, Vol. 5, No. 2, 1987.

Boddy, Janice. *Wombs and Alien Spirits: Women, Men and the Zar Cult in Northern Sudan*. University of Wisconsin Press. 1989.

Bohannan, Paul. ed., *Divorce and After: An Analysis of the Emotional and Social Problems of Divorce* Garden City, NY: Anchor Books, 1970.

Bohannan, Paul, review of Colleen L. Johnson, "*Ex familia; grandparents, parents, and children adjust to divorce.*" *American Ethnologist*, 19: 178–9 February 1992.

Booth, Alan, and John N. Edwards, "Age at marriage and marital instability," *Journal of Marriage and the Family*, Vol. 41, No. 1 (February 1985): 67–76.

Boss, Pauline, William J. Doherty, Ralph LaRossa, Walter R. Schuman, and Suzanne K. Steinmetz (eds.) *Sourcebook of Family Theories and Methods*. Plenum. 1993.

Bourdieu, Pierre (1962) "Célibat et condition sociale," *Etudes Rurales*, Summer.

Bradbury, Bettina. "The Fragmented Family: Family Strategies in the Face of Death, Illness and Poverty, Montreal, 1860–1885." In Joy Parr (Ed.) *Childhood and Family*. Toronto: McClelland and Stewart. 1983. Pp. 109–28.

Bradbury, Bettina, "Pigs, Cows and Boarders: Non-wage forms of survival among Montreal families, 1861–91" *Labour/Le Travail* 14 (Fall 1984): 9–46.

Brown, Bruce, W., *Images of Family Life in Magazine Advertising: 1920–1978.*. New York: Praeger. 1981.

Brown, R.H. (1977) *A Poetic for Sociology*, Chicago: University of Chicago Press.

Bruner, Edward. In Graburn, Nelson (ed.) *Readings in Kinship and Social Structure* ,New York: Harper and Row. 1971.

Brush, Linda D. (1989). "Violent Acts and Injurious Outcomes in Married Couples: New Data from the National Survey of Families and Households." Centre for Demography and Ecology: University of Wisconsin-Madison. National Survey of Families and Households Working Paper No. 6. 1989.

Buchler, Ira R., and Henry A. Selby. *Kinship and Social Organization*. New York: Macmillan. 1968.

Bumpass, Larry, L. "Bigger isn't necessarily better: A comment on Hofferth's 'Updating children's life course,'" *Journal of Marriage and the Family*, Vol. 47 (1985): 797–799.

Bumpass, Larry L., and James A. Sweet, "National estimates of cohabitation," *Demography*, Vol. 26, No. 4 (November 1989).

Bumpass, Larry L. (1987) "The risk of an unwanted birth: The changing context of contraceptive sterilization in the U.S.," *Population Studies*, 41, 347–363.

Bumpass, Larry L., James A. Sweet, and Andrew Cherlin, "The role of cohabitation in declining rates of marriage, *Journal of Marriage and the Family*, 53: 913–27, November 1991.

Bumpass, Larry L., "What's happening to the family? Interactions between demographic and institutional change," *Demography*, Vol. 27, No. 4 (November 1990): 483–498.

Burch, Thomas K. (1989) "Common-law unions in Canada: A portrait from the 1984 Family History Survey," pp. 103–119 in Jacques Légaré, T.R. Balakrishnan, and Roderic Beaujot, eds. *The Family in Crisis*, see below.

Burch, Thomas K. "Age-sex roles and demographic change, an overview." *Canadian Studies in Population*. vol. 14, no. 2, 1987, pp. 129-146.

Burch, Thomas K. and B.J. Matthews (1987) "Household formation in developed societies," *Population and Development Review*, 13, 3, September, 495-511.

Burch, Thomas K., "Family Structure and Ethnicity." In Shiva S. Halli, Frank Trovato, and Leo Driedger (eds.) *Ethnic Demography: Canadian Immigrant, Racial and Cultural Variations*. Ottawa: Carleton University Press. 1990. Pp. 199–212.

Burke, M.A. (1986) "Families: Diversity the new norm," *Canadian Social Trends*, Summer(1), 6–10.

Burke, R.J., and P. Bradshaw (1981) "Occupational and life stress and the family," *Small Group Behavior*, Vol. 12, No. 3 (August), 329–375.

Cain, M. (1982) "Perspectives on family and fertility in developing countries," *Population Studies*, 36 (2), 159–175.

Callan, V.J. (1982) "How do Australians value children? A review and research update using the perceptions of parents and voluntarily childless adults," *Australian and New Zealand Journal of Sociology*, 18, 3 (November) 384–398.

Campbell, Jacquelyn C. "Beating of Wives: A Cross-Cultural Perspective," *Victimology*, Vol. 10, No. 1–4, (1985): 174–185.

Canabal, M.E. (1990) "An economic approach to marital dissolution in Puerto Rico," *Journal of Marriage and the Family*, 52, 2, May, 515–30.

Cancian, F.M., and S.L. Gordon (1988) "Changing emotion norms in marriage: love and anger in U.S. women's magazines since 1900," *Gender and Society*, 2 (3), September, 308–342.

Caplow, Theodore (1991). *Recent Social Trends in the United States: 1960–1990*. Montreal: McGill-Queen's University Press. 1991.

Carmichael, G.A. (1987) "Bust after boom: first marriage trends in Australia," *Demography*, 24, 2, May, 245–264.

Carter, Angela (ed.) *The Virago Book of Fairy Tales*. London: Virago Press. 1991.

Carter, Gregg. *Empirical Approaches to Sociology*. Prentice Hall. 1993.

Chamberlain, K. and S. Zika, (1988). "Religiosity, life meaning and well-being: Some relationships in a sample of women." *Journal for the Scientific Study of Religion*. 27, 3, September, 411–420.

Charbit, Yves. "Union patterns and family structure in Guadeloupe and Martinique." *International Journal of Sociology of the Family*, 10, January-June, 41-66. Reprinted in Lorne J. Tepperman and Susannah J. Wilson (eds.) *Next of Kin: An International Reader on Changing Families*. Englewood Cliffs, New Jersey. Prentice Hall. 1992. Pp. 90-5.

Cheal, David, *Family and the State of Theory*. University of Toronto Press. 1991.

Cheal, David J. "Intergenerational family transfers," *Journal of Marriage and the Family*, 45: 805-13, 1983.

Chen, Pi-Chao. "China's other revolution." *International Family Planning Perspectives*, 10, 2, June, 48-57. Reprinted in Lorne J. Tepperman and Susannah J. Wilson (eds.) *Next of Kin: An International Reader on Changing Families*. Englewood Cliffs, New Jersey, Prentice Hall. 1992.

Chen, J., and T.R. Balakrishnan (1990) "Do gender preferences affect fertility and family dissolution in Canada," Discussion Paper No. 90-7. London; Ontario: Populations Studies Centre, University of Western Ontario.

Cherlin, Andrew, and Apichat Chamratrithirong (1988) "Variations in marriage patterns in central Thailand," *Demography*, 25, 3, August, 337-153. Reprinted in Lorne J. Tepperman and Susannah J. Wilson (eds.) *Next of Kin: An International Reader on Changing Families*. Englewood Cliffs, New Jersey, Prentice Hall. 1992.

Cherlin, Andrew, and Frank F. Furstenberg, Jr. (1983) "The American family in the year 2000, " *The Futurist*, June, 1983: 7-14. Reprinted in L. Cargan, and J. H. Ballantin (eds.) (1988) *Sociological Footprints: Introductory Readings in Sociology*, 4th ed. Belmont, CA: Wadsworth Publishing Company, 143-150.

Cherlin, Andrew J. *Marriage, Divorce, Remarriage*. Revised and Enlarged Edition. Harvard University Press. 1992. (Originally published 1981.)

Chesnais, Jean-Claude (1992) "The history of violence: Homicide and suicide through the ages," *International Social Science Journal*, 44, 2 (132), May, 1992, 217–234.

Chesnais, Jean-Claude, "Population trends in the European Community, 1960-1986." *European Journal of Population*, Vol. 3, No. 3/4, 1987: 277-486, July, 1988 (sic).

Clayton, Richard R., and Harwin I. Voss (1977) "Shacking up: Cohabitation in the 1970's," *Journal of Marriage and the Family*, 39 (May), 273-284.

Coale, Ansley J., and Susan Cotts Watkins, eds. *The Decline of Fertility in Europe*. Princeton: Princeton University Press. 1986

Coale, Ansley J. et al., eds. (1965) *Aspects of the Analysis of Family Structure*. Princeton: Princeton University Press.

Coale, Ansley J. "The decline of fertility in Europe from the French Revolution to World War II," pp. 3-24 in S.J. Behrman, L. Corsa, and R. Freedman (eds.), *Fertility and Family Planning*. Ann Arbor: University of Michigan Press,1969.

Cole, Sally, *Women of the Praia: Work and Lives in a Portugese Coastal Community*. Princeton, NJ: Princeton University Press. 1991.

Collins, Randall, "Love and Property" in Randall Collins (1982) *Sociological Insight: An Introduction to Non-Obvious Sociology*, New York: Oxford University Press, 119-54.

Collins, Stephen, "British stepfamily relationships, 1500-1800," *Journal of Family History*, 1991, 16, 4, October, 331-344.

Cook, Peter. "Requiem for the Welfare State: How a four-week currency crisis and global economic pressure dimmed the lights on what was once the world's most ambitious social experiment." *Globe and Mail*. October 3, 1992. D4.

Courlander, Harold. *The Drum and the Hoe: life and lore of the Haitian people*. Berkeley: University of California Press. 1960.

Currie, Dawn, "State Intervention and the 'Liberation' of Women: A Feminist Exploration of Family Law." In Tullio C. Caputo, Mark Kennedy, Charles E. Reasons, and Augustine Brannigan (eds.) *Law and Society: A Critical Perspective*. Toronto: Harcourt Brace Jovanovich. 1989. Pp. 271- 89.

Daly, Martin, and Margo Wilson, "Evolutionary Social Psychology and Family Homicide," *Science*, vol. 242, October 18, 1988: 519-24.

Dandurand, Renée et al., 1988. *Des Méres Sans Alliance: Monoparantalité et Disunions Conjugales*, Québec. IQRC (Institut québécois de recherche sur la culture). 1988.

Das, N. (1987) "Sex preference and fertility behaviour: A study of recent Indian data," *Demography*, 24 (4), November, 517–530.

Davidoff, Leonore, and Catherine Hall, *Family Fortunes: Men and Women of the English Middle Class, 1780-1850*. Chicago: University of Chicago Press. 1987.

Davis, James A., *Social Differences in Contemporary America*. New York: Harcourt Brace Jovanovich. 1987.

Davis, Kingsley (1948) *Human Society*. New York: Macmillan.

Davis, Kingsle,y and Wilbert G. Moore. "Some principles of stratification," *American Sociological Review*, 1945, 10: 242-9.

Davis, Kingsley, Mikhail S. Bernstam, and Rita Ricardo-Campbell (eds.) *Below-Replacement Fertility in Industrial Societies: Causes, Consequences, Policies*. Cambridge: Cambridge University Press. 1987.

Davis, Natalie Zemon, "Ghosts, kin, and progeny: Some features of family life in early modern France," *Daedalus*, 1977, 106, 2, Spring, 87-114.

DeMaris, Alfred, and Vaninadha K. Rao, "Premarital cohabitation and subsequent marital stability in the United States: a reassessment," *Journal of Marriage and the Family* , 54: 178-90 February 1992.

Demeny, P.G. (1987) *The Economic Rationale of Family Planning Programs*. New York: Population Council.

Devereux, M. S. (1988) "1986 census highlights: Marital status," *Canadian Social Trends*, Spring (8), 24-27.

Douglas, James W. B., *The Home and the School*. London: Macgibbon and Kee. 1968.

Duberman, Lucile, *The Reconstituted Family: a study of remarried couples and their children*. Chicago : Nelson-Hall Publishers. 1975.

Duncan, Gregg J,. and Saul D. Hoffman. 1985. "A Reconsideration of the Economic Consequences of Marital Dissolution." *Demography* 22: 485-497.

Duncan, Greg, and Ken R. Smith, "The rising affluence of the elderly: how far, how fair and how frail?" In W. Richard Scott and Judith Blake (eds.) *Annual Review of Sociology*, Vol. 15, 1989. Pp. 261-89.

Durkheim, Emile. *Suicide: A Study in Sociology*. New York: Free Press. 1951.

Easterlin, Richard A. *Birth and Fortune: the impact of numbers on personal welfare*. Chicago : University of Chicago Press. 2nd ed. 1987.

Ehrenreich, Barbara (1983) *The Hearts of Men: flight from commitment*. New York: Anchor Doubleday. 1984.

Ehrenreich, B., and D. English (1973) *Witches, nurses and midwives: a history of women healers*. New York: Feminist Press.

Ekert-Jaffé, Olivia and Christine Maugüé, "La Politique Familiale." In George Tapinos (ed.) *La France Dans Deux Generations*. Paris: Fayard. 1992. Pp. 223-56.

Elder, Glenn H., and Richard Rockwell, "The timing of marriage and women's life patterns," *Journal of Family History*, 1 (Autumn), 1976, 34-54.

Ellis, G.J., and L. R. Petersen (1992) "Socialization values and parental control techniques: A cross–cultural analysis of child rearing," *Journal of Comparative Family Studies*, 23 (1), spring, 39–54.

Ellwood, David T., *Divide and Conquer: Responsible Security for America's Poor*. Occasional Paper No. 1. New York: Ford Foundation Project on Social Welfare and the American Future. 1987.

Ellwood, David T., *Poor Support: Poverty in the American Family*. New York: Basic Books. 1988.

Emery, Robert E. "Interparental Conflict and the Children of Discord and Divorce," *Psychological Bulletin* ,Vol. 92, No. 2, (1982): 310-330.

Epstein, Joice L., "Single Parents and the Schools: Effects of Marital Status on Parent and Teacher Interactions." In Hallinan, Maureen T., David M. Klein, and Jennifer Glass (eds.) *Change in Societal Institutions* New York: Plenum Publishing Corporation. 1990. Pp. 91-121.

Espenshade, T. J. (1985) "Marriage trends in America: Estimates, implications and underlying causes," *Population and Development Review* 11 No. 2 (June), 193-243.

Fendrich, Michael (1984) "Wives' employment and husbands' distress: a meta-analysis and a replication," *Journal of Marriage and the Family*, 46, 871-9.

Festy, P. (1985) "The contemporary evolution of family formation in Western Europe," *Revue europeenne de demographie*, 1 (2–3), July, 179–205.

Finch, Janet, and Jennifer Mason, "Divorce, remarriage and family obligations," *Sociological Review*, Vol. 38, No. 2 (May 1990): 219-246.

Fine, Sean, "Motherhood too costly, report warns: National Council of Welfare urges greater support for families." *The Globe and Mail*, Tuesday, August 14th, 1990.

Finlay, Barbara Agresti, Ellen Van Velsor, and Mary Anne Hilker, "Household and Family Structure over the Life Cycle in the Industrializing South: A Comparative Historical Test." *International Journal of Sociology of the Family*, Vol. 12, No. 1 (Spring 1982): 47-61.

Fisher, Helen, E. *Anatomy of Love: The Natural History of Monogamy, Adultery and Divorce*. New York: Norton. 1992.

Fishman, Sylvia Barack, "The Changing American Jewish Family in the 80s," *Contemporary Jewry*, Vol 9, No 2, (1988): 1-33.

Flandrin, Jean-Louis, *Families in former times: kinship, household and sexuality*. Cambridge University Press. 1979 (originally published 1976).

Fox, Bonnie, "Selling the Mechanized Household: 70 Years of Ads in Ladies Home Journal," *Gender & Society*, Vol. 4, No. 1 (March): 25-40, 1990.

Fuchs, Victor R. *How We Live: an economic perspective on Americans from birth to death*. Cambridge, MA: Harvard University Press. 1988.

Furstenberg, Frank F., Jr., and Andrew J. Cherlin. *Divided Families: What Happens to Children When Parents Part?* Cambridge, MA: Harvard University Press. 1991.

Furstenberg, Frank F., Jr, "Divorce and the American family," *Annual Review of Sociology*, Vol. 16, 1990, pp. 379-36.

Furstenberg, Frank F., Jr., and Graham B. Spanier, *Recycling the Family: Remarriage after Divorce*. Beverly Hills, CA: Sage Publications, 1984.

Furstenberg, Frank F., Jr., S. Philip Morgan, and Paul D. Allison, "Paternal participation and children's well-being after marital dissolution," *American Sociological Review*, 52 (October 1987): 695-701.

Gartner, Rosemary, "Family structure, welfare spending, and child homicide in developed democracies." *Journal of Marriage and the Family*, 1991, 53: 231-240.

Gaussen, Frederic, "Les femmes et la violence islamiste." *Le Monde*, January 24, 1992.

Gerson, Kathleen, 1985, *Hard Choices: How Women Decide About Work, Career and Motherhood*, Berkeley: University of California Press.

Gerson, Kathleen, "Choosing between privilege and sharing: Men's responses to gender and family change." In Arlene S. Skolnick and Jerome H. Skolnick (eds.) *Family in Transition*. Harper Collins 8th ed. 1994. Pp. 149-56.

Gerstel, N., and H. E. Gross (1982) "Commuter marriages: A review," *Alternatives to Traditional Family Living*,: Haworth Press.

Gillis, A. Ron. "Judicial Separation, Civility and the Decline of Domestic Homicide in Nineteenth Century France." Unpublished paper. Sociology Department, University of Toronto, 1994.

Gillis, John P. *For Better, For Worse: British Marriages, 1600 to the Present*. New York: Oxford University Press, 1985.

Gittins, Diana, 1982, *Fair Sex: Family Size and Structure 1900-1939*. Hutchinson, London.

Gittins, Diana, *The Family in Question: changing households and familiar ideologies*. London: Macmillan. 1985.

Glenn, Norvall D., "Continuity versus change: sanguineness versus concern: views of the

American Family in the late 1980s. *Journal of Family Issues*, Vol. 8, No. 4, December 1987, pp. 348-354.

Glick, Paul, and Sung-Ling Lin, "Recent changes in divorce and remarriage," *Journal of Marriage and the Family*, 1986, Vol. 48, No. 4, November, pp. 737-47.

Glick, Paul C., and Arthur J. Norton (1977) "Marrying, divorcing, and living together in the U.S. today," *Population Bulletin*. Washington, D.C.: Population Reference Bureau.

Glick, Paul C., and G.B. Spanier (1980) "Married and unmarried cohabitation in the United States," *Journal of Marriage and the Family*, 42, 19-30.

Glick, Paul, "Marriage, divorce and living arrangements: prospective changes." *Journal of Family Issues*, 1984, Vol. 5, No. 1, March, pp. 7-26.

Glick, Paul, "Updating the life cycle of the family," *Journal of Marriage and the Family*, 39, February 1977, pp. 5-13.

Goldenberg, Sheldon. *Thinking Sociologically*. Belmont, CA: Wadsworth. 1987.

Goldscheider, Frances K., and Linda Waite. 1991. *New Families, No Families?* University of California Press. 1991.

Goldscheider, Frances K., and Calvin Goldscheider. 1989. "Family structure and conflict: nest-leaving expectations of young adults and their parents." *Journal of Marriage and the Family*, 51: 87-97.

Goldstein, Alice and Sidney Goldstein, "Meeting the challenge of an aging population in China." *Research on Aging*, 1986, 8, 2: 179-99. Reprinted in Lorne J. Tepperman and Susannah J. Wilson (eds.) *Next of Kin: An International Reader on Changing Families*. Englewood Cliffs, New Jersey, Prentice Hall. 1992. Pp. 340-44.

Goldthorpe, J. E. (1987). *Family life in western societies: A historical sociology of family relationships in Britain and North America*. New York: Cambridge University Press.

Goodall, Jane. *The Chimpanzees of Gombe: Patterns of Behavior*. Cambridge, MA: The Belknap Press. 1986.

Goode, William J. (1963) *World Revolution and Family Patterns* New York: Free Press.

Goode, William J. (1984) "Individual investments in family relationships over the coming decades," *Tocqueville Review*, 6, 1, spring- summer, 51-83.

Goode, William J. (1993). *World Changes in Divorce Patterns*. New Haven: Yale University Press. 1993.

Goode, William J. *Women in Divorce*. New York: Free Press. 1956.

Goody, Esther, "Separation and divorce among the Gonja." In Meyer Fortes (ed.) *Marriage in Tribal Societies*. Cambridge: Cambridge University Press. 1962.

Goody, Jack, *The Oriental, the Ancient and the Primitive: systems of marriage and the family in the pre-industrial societies of Eurasia*. Cambridge University Press. 1990.

Goubert, Pierre, "Local history," *Daedalus*, 1971, 100: 113-27.

Graburn, Nelson (ed.) *Readings in Kinship and Social Structure* ,New York: Harper and Row. 1971.

Greeley, Andrew M. (1991) *Faithful attraction*. New York: Tom Doherty Associates, Inc.

Greeley, Andrew M., R. Michael, and Tom W. Smith (1990) "Americans and their sexual partners," *Society*, Vol. 2, No. 5, 36-42.

Grindstaff, Carl F. (1984) "Catching up: The fertility of women over 30 years of age, Canada in the 1970s and early 1980s," *Canadian Studies in Population*, Vol. 11, 95-109.

Grindstaff, Carl F. (1988) "Adolescent marriage and childbearing: the long term economic outcome, Canada," *Adolescence*, Vol. 23, 45-58.

Grindstaff, Carl F., T.R. Balakrishnan, and P.S. Maxim (1989) "Life course alternatives: Factors associated with differential timing patterns in fertility among women recently completing childbearing, Canada 1981," *Canadian Journal of Sociology*, Vol. 14, 443-460.

Gross, H., and M.B. Sussman, eds. (1982) *Alternatives to Traditional Family Living*, in *Marriage and Family Review*, 5 (2). New York: Haworth Press.

Gross, Penny, "Defining Post-Divorce Remarriage Families: A Typology Based on the Subjective Perceptions of Children." *Journal of Divorce*, 1987, Vol. 10 (1,2): 205-17.

Groulx, Lionel-Henri, *Où Va le Modèle Suédois? État-Providence et Protection Sociale*. Montreal. Les Presses de L'université de Montreal. 1990.

Gunnarsson, Lars, and Moncrieff Cochran, "The social networks of single parents: Sweden and the United States." In Moncrieff Cochran et al. (eds.) *Extending Families: The Social Networks of Parents and their Children.* New York: Cambridge University Press. Pp. 105-116.

Gutman, Herbert G. *Slavery and the Numbers Game: A critique of Time on the Cross.* Urbana: University of Illinois Press. 1975

Gutman, Herbert G. *The Black Family in Slavery and Freedom, 1750- 1925.* New York: Pantheon Books. 1976.

Guttentag, M., and Paul F. Secord (1983) *Too Many Women? The Sex Ratio Question.* Beverly Hills: Sage Publications.

Guttman, Joseph (1989), "The divorced father: a review of the issues and the research," *Journal of Comparative Family Studies,* 20, 2, 247-261.

Gwartney-Gibbs, Patricia A., "The institutionalization of premarital cohabitation: estimates from marriage license applications, 1970 and 1980," *Journal of Marriage and the Family,* 48: 23-34, May 1986.

Hajnal, John, "European marriage patterns in perspective." In David V. Glass and D.E.C. Eversley (eds.) *Population in History: essays in historical demography.* London: Edward Arnold. 1965. Pp. 101-143

Hajnal, John, "Two kinds of preindustrial household formation system," *Population and Development Review,* Vo.l 8, No. 3 (November 1982): 449-494.

Hakiki-Talahite, Fatiha. *Cahiers de l'Orient,* No. 23, 3 eme trimestre, 1991.

Halliday, T.C., and A. Cherlin (1980) "Remarriage: The more compleat institution?" *American Journal of Sociology,* 86 (3), November, 630–635.

Hammel, Eugene A., and Peter Laslett. "Comparing household structures over time and between cultures," *Comparative Studies in Society and History,* 16 (1): 73-109. 1974.

Hammel, Eugene A. In Graburn, Nelson (ed.) *Readings in Kinship and Social Structure.* New York: Harper and Row. 1971.

Harden, Blaine, *Despatches from a Fragile Continent.* Norton. 1990. Pp. 333.

Haskey, John, "Trends in marriage and divorce in England and Wales: 1837-1987," *Population Trends,* Vol. 48.

Herlyn, Ingrid, and Ulrike Vogel, "Individualization: A new perspective on the life situation of women" *Zeitschrift fur Sozialisationsforschung und Erziehungssoziologie.* 1989, 9, 3, July, 162-178.

Herskovits, Melville J. *Dahomey: an ancient West African kingdom.* New York: J.J. Augustin. 1938.

Hetherington, E. Mavis. 1987. "Family relations six years after divorce." In Kay Pasley and Marilyn Ihinger-Tallman (eds.), *Remarriage and Stepparenting: Current Research and Theory.* New York: Guilford Press. Pp. 185-205.

Hill, C. D., L.W. Thompson, and D. Gallagher (1988) "The role of anticipatory bereavement in older women's adjustment to widowhood," *The Gerontologist,* 28, 6, 792-796.

Hirschi, Travis, "Family Structure and Crime," pp. 43-66. In Bryce J. Christensen (ed.) *When Families Fail: The Social Costs.* New York: University Press of America for The Rockford Institute. 1991.

Hochschild, Arlie, with Anne Machung, *The Second Shift: Working Parents and the Revolution at Home ,* New York: Viking. 1989.

Hoem, B. (1986) "The impact of eduction in modern family-union initiation," *European Journal of Population,* 2 (2), October, 113–133.

Hoem, B. (1988) "Early phases of family formation in contemporary Sweden," Centre for Demography and Ecology Working Paper 88–144. Madison: Center for Demography and Ecology, University of Wisconsin.

Hoem, Britta, and Jan Hoem, "The Dissolute Swedes: Dissolution of Conjugal Unions to Swedish Women Born in 1936-60," paper presented at the IUSSP conference, Paris, March, 1988.

Hofferth, Sandra L. "Updating Children's Life Course," *Journal of Marriage and the Family,* Vol. 47 (February 1985): 93-115.

Hofferth, S.L., and D.A. Phillips (1987) "Child care in the United States, 1970–1995," *Journal of Marriage and the Family,* 49, August, 559–571.

Hoffman, Saul D., and Greg J. Duncan, "What are the economic consequences of divorce?" *Demography*, Vol. 25, No. 4, November, 1988: 641-5.

Hoffman, Saul D., E. Michael Foster, and Frank F. Furstenberg Jr., "Re-evaluating the costs of teenage childbearing." *Demography*, Vol. 30, No. 1, February, 1993, pp. 1-13.

Hogan, Dennis P., Ling-Xin Hao, and William L. Parish, "Race, kin networks, and assistance to mother-headed families" *Social Forces*, Vol. 68, No. 3 (March 1990): 797-812.

Hossie, Linda, "Ontario cracks down on support defaulters: employers to deduct payments," *Globe and Mail*, Thursday, December 6, 1990, p. A1.

Houseknecht, Sharon K. (1982) "Voluntary childlessness in the 1980s: A significant increase?" Pp. 61–69 in Gross and Sussman, eds., *Alternatives to Traditional Family Living*. (See above.)

Howe, Neil, "America in the year 2007," *The American Spectator*, December, 1987.

Howell, Nancy. *Demography of the Dobe !Kung*. New York: Academic Press. 1979.

Huang-Hickrod, Lucy Jen, and Wilbert M. Leonard, "A quasi-longitudinal study of students' attitudes toward cohabitation," *International Journal of Sociology of the Family* 1980, 10, 2, July-December, 281-299.

Huber, John, and G. Spitze (1983) *Sex Stratification: Children, housework, and Jobs*. New York: Academic Press.

Hughes, Diane Owen. "From Brideprice to Dowry in Mediterranean Europe," *Journal of Family History*, Vol. 3, No. 3 (Fall 1978): 202-296.

Hunt, J.G., and L.L. Hunt (1982) "The dualities of careers and families: New integrations or new polarizations?" *Social Problems*, 29 (5), June, 499–510. Excerpted in Skolnick and Skolnick, pp. 275–289.

Hutaserani, S., and J. Roumasset (1991) "Institutional change and the demographic transition in rural Thailand," *Economic Development and Cultural Change*, 40 (1), October, 75–100.

Hyphantis, T., V. Koutras, A. Liakos, and M. Marselos (1991) "Alcohol and drug use, family situation and school performance in adolescent children of alcoholics," *International Journal of Social Psychiatry*, 37 (1), spring, 35–42.

Iacovetta, Franca (1992) *Such hardworking people: Italian immigrants in postwar Toronto*, Montreal: McGill-Queen's University Press.

James, S.D., and D.W. Johnson (1988) "Social independence, psychological adjustment, and marital satisfaction in second marriages," *Journal of Social Psychology*, 128 (3), June, 287–303.

Jewell, K. Sue, *Survival of the Black Family: The Institutional Impact of U.S. Social Policy*. New York: Praeger. 1988.

Jones, Carolyn C. "Split Income and Separate Spheres: Tax Law and Gender Roles in the 1940s," *Law and History Review*, Vol. 6, No. 2 (Fall 1988): 259-310.

Jones, Charles, L., Lorna R. Marsden, and Lorne J. Tepperman. 1990. *Lives of Their Own: The Individualization of Women's Lives*. Oxford University Press.

Jones, E.F., J.D. Forrest, N. Goldman, S. Henshaw, R. Lincoln, J.I. Rosoff, C.F. Westoff, and D. Wulf (1986), *Teenage Pregnancy in Industrialized Countries*. New Haven: Yale University Press.

Kagitcibasi, Cigden. (1982) "Old age security value of children and development: cross-national evidence," *Journal of Comparative Family Studies*, Vol. XIII, No. 2 (Summer), 133-142. Reprinted in Lorne J. Tepperman and Susannah J. Wilson (eds.) *Next of Kin: An International Reader on Changing Families*. Englewood Cliffs, New Jersey, Prentice Hall. 1992.

Kahn, Alfred J. and Sheila B. Kamerman, "Do the public social services have a future?" *Families in Society*, 71: 165-71, March 1990.

Kahn, Alfred J. and Sheila B. Kamerman, eds., *Child Support: From Debt Collection to Social Policy* Newbury Park, CA: Sage Publications, 1988.

Kain, Edward L., *The Myth of Family Decline: understanding families in a world of rapid social change*. Lexington, MA: Lexington Books. 1990.

Kamerman, Sheila B., and Alfred J. Kahn, "What Europe Does for Single-Parent Families." *The*

Public Interest, No. 93 (Fall 1988): 70-86. Reprinted in Lorne J. Tepperman and Susannah J. Wilson (eds.) *Next of Kin: An International Reader on Changing Families*. Englewood Cliffs, New Jersey, Prentice Hall. 1992.

Katz, Michael B. *The People of Hamilton, Canada West: Family and Class in a Mid-Nineteenth Century City*, Cambridge, MA: Harvard University Press. 1975.

Keith, Jennie, "Age in anthropological research," in Binstock, Robert H., and Ethel Shanas (eds.) *Handbook of Aging and the Social Sciences*, 2nd ed., 1985. New York: Van Nostrand, pp. 239-44.

Khoo, Siew Ean (1987) "Living together as married: a profile of de facto couples in Australia," *Journal of Marriage and the Family*, 49, 1, February, 185- 191.

Khoo, Siew Ean, "Children in De Facto Relationships," *Australian Journal of Social Issues*. 1988, 23, 1, February, 38-49.

Kiernan, Kathleen E., "The British Family: contemporary trends and issues." *Journal of Family Issues*, Vol. 9, No. 3, September 1988, pp. 298-316.

Krannich, Richard S. (1990) "Abortion in the United States: Past, present, and future trends," *Family Relations*, 365-374.

Krishnan, V. (1987b) "Preferences for sex of children: A multivariate analysis," *Journal of Biosocial Science*, 19 (3), 367–376.

Krishnan, Vijaya (1989) "Asset accumulation and family size: Insights from recursive models," pp. 417–437 in Jacques Légaré, T.R. Balakrishnan, and Roderic Beaujot, eds. *The Family in Crisis*. (See above.)

Krishnan, V. (1988a) *The effects of religious factors on childlessness: The Canadian case*, Population Research Laboratory, Research Discussion Paper No. 58, Edmonton: University of Alberta, Department of Sociology.

Ladurie, Emmanuel Le Roy. *Montaillou: Cathars and Catholics in a French Village, 1294–1324*. (Translated by Barbara Bray). London: Scolar Press. 1978.

Laing, Ronald D., and A. E. Esterson. *Sanity, Madness and the Family: Families of Schizophrenics*. London: Tavistock. 2nd ed. 1970.

Langlois, Simon, et al. *Recent Social Trends in Quebec: 1960–1990*. Montreal: McGill-Queen's University Press. 1992. (Originally pubished 1990.)

LaRossa, Ralph, "Fatherhood and Social Change," *Family Relations*, Vol. 37 (October 1988): 451–457.

Larzelere, R.E. (1986) "Moderate spanking: Model or deterrent of children's aggression in the family?" *Journal of Family Violence*, 1 (1), March, 27–36.

Lasch, Christopher, *Haven in a Heartless World: The Family Besieged*. New York: Basic Books. 1987.

Laslett, Barbara, and Johanna Brenner, "Gender and Social Reproduction: Historical Perspectives," *Annual Review of Sociology*, 15: 381–44. 1989.

Laslett, Peter (1971, 1965). *The world we have lost*. London: Methuen (University Paperbacks).

Laslett, Peter (ed.), and Wall, R. (Asst.). (1972). *Household and family in past time: Comparative studies in the size and structure of the domestic group over the last three centuries*. Cambridge: Cambridge University Press.

Laslett, Peter, "The Emergence of the Third Age," Plenary Address to the International Union for the Scientific Study of Population (IUSSP), General Conference, Montreal. August, 1993.

Laslett, Peter, *The world we have lost: further explored*. London: Methuen. 1983.

Leach, Edmund. *A Runaway World?* The 1967 Reith Lectures. New York: Oxford University Press. 1968.

Légaré, Jacques, T.R. Balakrishnan, and Roderic P. Beaujot, eds. *The Family in Crisis: A Population Crisis?* Ottawa: Royal Society of Canada. 1989.

Lemann, Nicholas, *The Promised Land: The Great Black Migration and How It Changed America*. New York: Knopf. 1991.

Lenski, Gerhard E., and Jean Lenski, *Human Societies: An Introduction to Macrosociology*. New York: McGraw-Hill. 1987.

Levine, David. *Reproducing families: the political economy of English population history*. Cambridge University Press. 1987.

Levine, E.M. (1981) "Middle-class family decline," *Society*, January-February, 1981, 72–78.

Levine, Nancy E. *The Dynamics of Polyandry: Kinship, Domesticity and Population on the Tibetan Border*. Chicago: University of Chicago Press. 1992.

Li, Peter S. (1982) "Chinese immigrants on the Canadian prairie, 1910–47," *Canadian Review of Sociology and Anthropology*, 19, 4, 527–540.

Liebes, T., and E. Katz (1990) *The Export of Meaning: Cross-cultural readings of Dallas*, New York: Oxford University Press.

Litovsky, V.G., and J.B. Dusek (1985) "Perceptions of child rearing and self-concept development during the early adolescent years," *Journal of Youth and Adolescence*, 14 (5), October, 373–387.

Lizot, Jacques. *Tales of the Yanomani: Daily Life in the Venezuelan Rain Forest*. (Originally published Paris: Seuil, 1976). New York: Cambridge University Press, 1985.

Lund, Mary. "The non-custodial father: common challenges in parenting after divorce." In Charles Lewis and Margaret O'Brien (eds.) *Reassessing Fatherhood*. Beverly Hills: Sage, 1987. Pp. 212–224.

Lupri, Eugen, and James Frideres. "The quality of marriage and the passage of time: marital satisfaction over the family life cycle," *Canadian Journal of Sociology*, 6 (3) 1981: 283–305.

Maine, Henry S. 1861. *Ancient Law*. (1955 ed.) London.

Mattessich, P.W. (1979) "Childlessness and its correlates in historical perspective: A research note," *Journal of Family History*, 4 (3), Fall, 299–307.

Matthews, Ralph, and Anne M. Matthews (1986) "Infertility and involuntary childlessness: The transition to nonparenthood," *Journal of Marriage and the Family*, 48, August, 641–649.

Mauldon, J. (1990) "The effect of marital disruption on children's health," *Demography*, Vol. 27, No. 3 (August), 431–446.

McAdoo, Harriette Pipes, "A portrait of African American Families in the United States." In Sara E. Rix (ed.) *The American Woman 1990–91: a status report*. New York: W.W. Norton and Co. 1990. Pp. 71–93.

McDaniel, Susan A. (1989a) "An alternative to the family in crisis model," pp. 439–451, in Jacques Légaré, T.R. Balakrishnan, and Roderic Beaujot, eds. *The Family in Crisis*. (See above.)

McDonald, Gerald W. "Structural Exchange and Marital Interaction," *Journal of Marriage and the Family*, Vol. 43, (November 1981): 825–839.

McLanahan, Sara, and Karen Booth (1989) "Mother-only families: Problems, prospects and politics," *Journal of Marriage and the Family*, 51 (3), August, 557–580.

McLanahan, Sara S., "The Long-Term Effects of Family Dissolution." In Bryce J. Christensen (ed.) *When Families Fail: The Social Costs*. New York: University Press of America for The Rockford Institute. 1991. Pp. 5–26.

Mead, Margaret. *Coming of Age in Samoa: A Psychological Study of Primitive Youth for Western Civilization*. New York: Blue Ribbon Books. 1932.

Melikian, Levon H., and Juhaina S. Al-Easa (1981), "Oil and social change in the Gulf," *Journal of Arab Affairs*, 1, 1, October, 79-98. Reprinted in Lorne J. Tepperman and Susannah J. Wilson (eds.) *Next of Kin: An International Reader on Changing Families*. Englewood Cliffs, New Jersey: Prentice Hall, 1992.

Menaghan, Elizabeth. 1989. "Role changes and psychological well-being: variations in effects by gender and role repertoire." *Social Forces*, 67: 693–714.

Menaghan, E.G., and M.A. Lieberman (1986) "Changes in depression following divorce: A panel study," *Journal of Marriage and the Family*, 48 (2), May, 319–328.

Meyer, Sibylle, and Eva Schulze, "Cohabitation: A Possibility for Changing Traditional Gender Relations?" *Kolner Zeitschrift fur Soziologie und Sozialpsychologie*, 1988, 40, 2, June, 337–356.

Michelson, William, "Childcare and the daily routine," *Social Indicators Research*, 23 (1990) 353–366.

Mintz, S. W., and Wolf, E. R. "Ritual Co-Parenthood (compadrazgo)," *Southwestern Journal of Anthropology*, Vol. 6, No. 4 (1950): 341–365.

Mir-Hosseini, Ziba. "Some Aspects of Changing Marriage in Rural Iran." *Journal of Comparative Studies*, 20, 2, Summer, 216–229. Reprinted in Lorne J. Tepperman and Susannah J. Wilson (eds.) *Next of Kin: An International Reader on Changing Families*. Englewood Cliffs, New Jersey: Prentice Hall. 1992.

Moen, Phyllis, *Working Parents: Transformations in Gender Roles and Public Policies in Sweden.* Madison: University of Wisconsin Press. 1989.

Mohr, James. *Abortion in America: The Origins and Evolution of National Policy, 1800–1900.* New York: Oxford University Press. 1978.

Moore, Maureen (1989a). "Female lone parenting over the life course," *Canadian Journal of Sociology*, Vol. 14, No. 3, 335–352

Moore, Maureen. "Dual earner families: the new norm," *Canadian Social Trends*, Spring, 1989, pp. 24–26.

Moore, Maureen. "Female lone parenting over the life course." *Canadian Journal of Sociology*, Vol. 14, No. 3, (Summer 1989): 335–352.

Moore, Maureen, "How long alone? The duration of female lone parenthood in Canada," *Canadian Social Trends*, Autumn, 1988: 40–2.

Morgan, S.P., and L.J. Waite (1987) "Parenthood and the attitudes of young adults," *American Sociological Review*, 52 (4), August, 541–547.

Morgan, S.P., A. McDaniel, A.T. Miller, and S.H. Preston (1993) "Racial differences in household and family structure at the turn of the century," *American Journal of Sociology*, 98 (4), January, 799–828.

Morgan, S.P., D.N. Lye, and G.A. Condran (1988) "Sons, daughters, and the risk of marital disruption," *American Journal of Sociology*, 94 (1), July, 110–129.

Moustafa, S.A. (1988) "Problematic population phenomena in Arab countries," *Free Inquiry in Creative Sociology*, 16 (1), May, 45–49.

Moynihan, Daniel Patrick, *Family and Nation: The 1985 Godkin Lectures*, Harvard University. New York: Harcourt Brace Jovanovich. 1986.

Moynihan, Daniel Patrick, *The Negro Family: The Case for National Action*. Washington DC: Office of Policy Planning and Research. U.S. Department of Labor. 1965.

Murdock, George. P. (1949) *Social Structure*. New York: Macmillan. 1949.

Nagnur, Dhruva, and O. Adams (1987) "Tying the knot: An overview of marriage rates in Canada," *Canadian Social Trends*, Vol. 6 (Autumn), 2–6.

Nagnur, Dhruva, "Rectangularization of the survival curve and entropy: The Canadian experience, 1921–1981," *Canadian Studies in Population*, 13 (1) 1986.

Namboodiri, Krishnan, "The population implosion scare," *Contemporary Sociology*, 1988.

Newcomb, P.R. (1979) "Cohabitation in America: An assessment of consequences," *Journal of Marriage and the Family*, August, 597–603.

Niemi, R.G., J. Mueller, and Tom W. Smith (1989) *Trends in Public Opinion: A Compendium of Survey Data*. New York: Greenwood Press.

Norton, Arthur J., and Jean E. Moorman (1986) "Marriage and divorce patterns of U.S. women in the 1980s," paper presented at the annual meeting of the Population Association of America, 4 April.

Norton, Arthur J., and Paul C. Glick, "One parent families: a social and economic profile." *Family Relations*, Vol. 35, January 1986, p. 16.

Ogburn, William F., and M.K. Nimkoff, *Technology and the Changing Family*. Boston: Houghton Mifflin. 1955.

Olsen, Frances E. "The family and the market: a study of ideology and legal reform," *Harvard Law Review*, Vol. 96, No. 7, 1983.

Olshansky, S. Jay, Bruce A. Carnes, and Christne Cassel, "In search of Methuselah: estimating the upper limits to human longevity. *Science*, Vol. 2501, November, 1990: 634–640.

Oppenheimer, Valerie K., *Work and the Family: a study in social demography*. New York: Academic Press. 1982.

Orubuloye, I.O. (1991) "The implications of the Demographic Transition theory for fertility change in Nigeria," *International Journal of Sociology of the Family*, 21 (2), autumn, 161–174.

Pankhurst, Jerry G., and Sharon K. Houseknecht (1986) "The family, politics, and religion in the 1980s: In fear of the new individualism." In Arlene S. Skolnick and Jerome H. Skolnick, eds. *Families in Transition*. Boston: Little, Brown. 5th ed. Pp. 578–98.

Partida-Bush, V. (1990) "The volume, age structure and rhythm of population growth in Mexico: Analysis of the effects of the demographic dynamic and consequences," *Revista Mexicana de Sociologia*, 52 (1), January–March, 223–246.

Pasley, Kay, and Marilyn Ihinger-Tallman, eds. *Remarriage and Stepparenting Today*. New York: Guilford Press. 1987.

Peres, Yochanan, and Ruth Katz (1981) "The importance of nuclear families in Israel." *Social Forces*, 59 (3): 687–704. Reprinted in Lorne J. Tepperman and Susannah J. Wilson (eds.) *Next of Kin: An International Reader on Changing Families*. Englewood Cliffs, New Jersey: Prentice Hall. 1992.

Peters, J.F. (1985) "Adolescents as socialization agents to parents," *Adolescence*, 20 (80), winter, 921–933.

Peterson, James L., and Nicholas Zill. 1986. "Marital Disruption and Behavior Problems in Children." *Journal of Marriage and the Family*, 48: 295–307.

Peterson, Peter G., and Neil Howe, *On Borrowed Time: How the growth in entitlement spending threatens America's future*. San Francisco: ICS Press. 1988.

Phillips, Roderick, *Putting Asunder: a history of divorce in western society*. Cambridge University Press. 1988.

Pillemer, K., and D. Finkelhor (1988) "The prevalence of elder abuse: A random sample survey," *The Gerontologist*, 28, 1, 51–57.

Pinot, R. *Paysans et horlogers jurassiens*. Geneva: Gronauer. 1979.

Pitrou, Agnes. (1980), "The roles of men and women in French families: change or stability in the patterns and practices?" *Research in the Interweave of Social Roles*, 1, 119–138.

Pitrou, Agnes. "Who Has Power Over Our Children—A Dialogue between the Family and the State?" *Journal of Comparative Family Studies*, 13, No. 2 (Summer, 1982), 171–183. Reprinted in Lorne J. Tepperman and Susannah J. Wilson (eds.) *Next of Kin: An International Reader on Changing Families*. Englewood Cliffs, New Jersey: Prentice Hall. 1992.

Pogrebin, L.C. (1983) *Family Politics: Love and Power on an Intimate Frontier*, New York: McGraw-Hill.

Pool, Ian, and Maureen Moore. *Lone Parenthood: Characteristics and Determinants. Results from the 1984 Family History Survey*. Catalog 99–961, Statistics Canada. Ottawa: Supply and Services, 1986.

Popenoe, David (1987) "Beyond the nuclear family: A statistical portrait of the changing family in Sweden," *Journal of Marriage and the Family*, 29, 1, February, 173–183.

Popenoe, David (1988) *Disturbing the Nest: Family Change and Decline in Modern Societies.*. New York: Aldine de Gruyter.

Prentice, Alison L., and Susan E. Houston (eds.) *Family, school and society in nineteenth century Canada*. Toronto: Oxford University Press. 1975.

Poston, D.L., Jr., and M.Y. Yu (1986) "The one-child family: International patterns and their implications for the People's Republic of China," *Journal of Biosocial Science*, 18 (3), July, 305–310.

Preston, S.H. (1987) "The decline of fertility in non-European industrialized countries," pp. 26–47, in K. Davis, M.S. Bernstam, and R. Ricardo-Campbell (eds.) *Below-replacement Frtility in Industrial Societies* (*Population and Development Review*, Vol. 12, supplement) New York: Population Council. 1987.

Pullium, Rita M. (1989) "What makes good families: Predictors of family welfare in the Philippines," *Journal of Comparative Family Studies*, XX, 1 (Spring), 47–66.

Quah, Stella R. "Sex-Role Socialization in a Transitional Society." *International Journal of*

Sociology of the Family, 10, 2, July-December. 213–231. Reprinted in Lorne J. Tepperman and Susannah J. Wilson (eds.) *Next of Kin: An International Reader on Changing Families.* Englewood Cliffs, New Jersey: Prentice Hall. 1992.

Rainwater, Lee, "Mother's contribution to the family money economy in Europe and in the United States," *Journal of Family History*, Vol. 4, 1970, 198–211.

Ramey, J. (1976) "Multi-adult household: Living group of the future?" *Futurist*, 10, 2, April, 78–83.

Rao, K. Vaninadha. (1987) "Childlessness in Ontario and Québec: Results from 1971 and 1981 census data," *Canadian Studies in Population*, Vol. 14, 27–46.

Rao, K.V., and T.R. Balakrishnan (1988a) "Age at first birth in Canada: A hazards model analysis," *Genus*, 44 (1–2), 53–72.

Risman, B.J. (1987) "Intimate relationships from a microstructural perspective: Men who mother," *Gender and Society*, 1 (1), March, 6–32.

Robinson, Barrie W., and Wayne W. McVey (1985) "The relative contributions of death and divorce to marital dissolution in Canada and the United States," *Journal of Comparative Family Studies*, Vol. 16, 93–109.

Robinson, J. (1991). Your money or your time. *American Demographics* 13 (11), pp. 22–26.

Robinson, Patricia (1989) "Women's work interruptions and the family: An exploration of the Family History Survey," pp. 271–85, in Jacques Légaré, T.R. Balakrishnan, and Roderic Beaujot, eds. *The Family in Crisis.* (See above.)

Rodgers, A. *Politics of Everyday Life—Continuity and Change in Work and the Family.*

Rodgers, F.S., and C. Rodgers (1989) "Business and the facts of family life," *Harvard Business Review*, November–December, 121–129.

Rosenthal, Carolyn J. "Kinkeeping in the Familial Division of Labor," *Journal of Marriage and the Family*, Vol. 47 (November 1985): 965–974.

Rossi, A.S. (1984) "Gender and parenthood," *American Sociological Review*, 49 (1), February, 1–19.

Rossi, A.S., ed. (1985) *Gender and the Life Course.* New York: Aldine Press.

Rossi, Alice S., and Peter H. Rossi. *Of Human Bonding: Parent-Child Relations Across the Life Course.* New York: Aldine de Gruyter. 1990.

Rothschild, N., and M. Morgan (1987) "Cohesion and control: Adolescents' relationships with parents as mediators of television," *Journal of Early Adolescence*, 7 (3), fall, 299–314.

Roussel, Louis, *La Famille Incertaine.* Paris: Odile Jacob. 1989.

Rowland, D.T. (1984) "Old age and the demographic transition," *Population Studies*, 38, 73–87.

Rowland, Robin (1982) An exploratory study of the childfree lifestyle," *Australian and New Zealand Journal of Sociology*, 18 (1), March, 17–30.

Russell, G. (1979) "Fathers! Incompetent or reluctant parents?" *Australian and New Zealand Journal of Sociology*, Vol. 15, No. 1 (March), 57–65.

Rybczynski, Witold. *Looking Around: A Journey Through Architecture.* Harper Collins. 1992.

Ryder, Norman B. (1965). "The Cohort as a Concept in the Study of Social Change." *American Sociological Review*, 30 (1965): 843–61.

Ryder, Norman B. (1979) "The future of American fertility," *Social Problems*, 26, No. 3 (February), 359–370.

Sacco, Vincent F., and Holly Johnson (1990) *Patterns of Criminal Victimization in Canada.* General Social Survey Analysis Series, Catalogue 11–612E, No. 2. Ottawa: Statistics Canada.

Sacks, Jonathan, *The Persistence of Faith: Religion, Morality and Society in a Secular Age.* The 1990 Reith Lectures. London: Weidenfeld and Nicolson. 1991.

Sandqvist, K. (1987) *Fathers and family work in two cultures* Stockholm: Almqvist and Wiksell International.

Sarantakos, S. (1982) "Getting married: Unknowingly and uwillingly," *Australian Journal of Sex, Marriage and Family*, 3 (1), February, 13–23.

Sauer, R. (1984) "Attitudes to Abortion in America, 1800–1973," *Population Studies*, Vol. 28: 53–67.

Scanzoni, John (1987) "Families in the 1980s: Time to refocus our thinking," *Journal of Family Issues*, 8, 4, December, 394–421.

Schofield, Roger, "Family structure, demographic behaviour and economic growth." In Walter, John, and Roger Schofield (eds.) *Famine, disease and the social order in early modern society*. Cambridge University Press. 1989. Pp. 279–304.

Schorr, Lisbeth B., C. Arden Miller, and Amy Fine, "The social policy context for families today." In Yogman, Michael W., and T. Berry Brazelton (eds.) *In Support of Families*. Cambridge, MA: Harvard University Press. 1986. Pp. 242–255.

Schulz, Wolfgang, "From the Institution of the Family to Differentiated Relationships between Men, Women and Children: On Structural Changes of Marriage and the Family." *Soziale-Welt*, 1983, 34, 4, 401–419.

Seager, Joni, and Ann Olson (edited by Michael Kidron) *Women in the World: an international atlas*. New York: Simon and Schuster. Touchstone Series (A Pluto Press Project). 1986.

Seltzer, J.A., and D. Kalmuss (1988) "Socialization and stress explanations for spouse abuse," *Social Forces*, 67 (2), December, 473–491.

Seltzer, Judith A. "Legal custody arrangements and children's economic welfare," *American Journal of Sociology*, Vol. 96, No. 4 (January 1991): 895–929.

Shehan, C.L., and John H. Scanzoni (1988) "Gender patterns in the United States: Demographic trends and policy prospects," *Family Relations*, 37, 444–450.

Shorter, Edward. *The Making of the Modern Family*. New York: Basic Books. 1977.

Skolnick, Arlene S., and Jerome H. Skolnick. *Family in Transition*. New York: Harper Collins. 8th ed. 1994.

Skolnick, A., and J.H. Skolnick, eds. (1986) *Family in Transition: Rethinking Marriage, Sexuality, Child Rearing, and Family Organization*, 5th ed., Boston: Little, Brown, and Company, 520–532.

Slater, Miriam, "The weightiest business: Marriage in an upper gentry family in seventeenth century England," *Past and Present*, 1976, 72, August, 25–54.

Small, S.A. (1988) "Parental self-esteem and its relationship to childrearing practices, parent-adolescent interaction, and adolescent behavior," *Journal of Marriage and the Family*, 50 (4), November, 1063–1072.

Smith, Raymond T. (ed.) *Kinship Ideology and Practice in Latin America*. Chapel Hill: University of North Carolina Press. 1984.

Smith, Raymond T. *Kinship and Class in the West Indies: a genealogical study of Jamaica and Guyana*. Cambridge University Press. 1988.

Snell, James G., "'The white life for two': The defence of marriage and sexual morality in Canada, 1890–1914." *Histoire Sociale/Social History*, 16, 31, May, 1983: 111–128.

Social Trends 19, 1989, Tom Griffin (ed.) London: HMSO.

Soloway, M.M., and R.M. Smith (1987) "Antecedents of late birth timing decisions of men and women in dual-career marriages," *Family Relations*, 36, July, 258–262.

Sorokin, Pitirim A. *The American Sex Revolution*. Boston: Sargent. 1956.

South, Scott J., and Glenna Spitze, 1986. "Determinants of divorce over the marital life course." *American Sociological Review*, 51, 583–90.

Spanier, Graham B., 1983. "Married and unmarried cohabitation in the United States: 1980." *Journal of Marriage and the Family*, 45: 277–288.

Spitze, Glenna, "Women's employment and family relations: a review," *Journal of Marriage and the Family*, Vol. 50, No. 3, 1988, pp. 595–618.

Spock, Benjamin. *Baby and Child Care*. New York: Dutton. 1985. (Originally published 1946 as *Common Sense Book of Baby and Child Care*.)

Srivastava, A.K. (1985) "Social class and parent-child relationship in urban setting," *Eastern Anthropologist*, 38 (1), January-March, 19–32.

Stacey, Judith. *Brave New Families: Stories of Domestic Upheaval in Late Twentieth Century America*. Basic Books. 1990.

Stack, Carol. *All our kin: strategies for survival in a black community*. New York: Harper and Row. 1974.

Steelman, Lala Carr, and James A. Mercy, "Unconfounding the confluence model: A test of sibship size and birth-order effects on intelligence." *American Sociological Review*, 1980, Vol. 45, August, pp. 571–82.

Steinberg, Laurence, "Single parents, stepparents, and the susceptibility of adolescents to antisocial peer pressure," *Child Development*, Vol. 58 (1987): 269–275.

Stetson, Dorothy M., and Gerald C. Wright,Jr. (1975) "The effects of laws on divorce in American states," *Journal of Marriage and the Family* (August), 537–547.

Stevenson, Michael R., and Kathryn N. Black. "Father absence and sex-role identification." *Child Development*, 1988, 59, 3, June, 793–814.

Stevenson, W. Richard, "Tough British Plan Imposes Rigid Maintenance Formula" (New York Times News Service), *Globe and Mail*, February 8, 1994.

Stolk, Y., and P. Brotherton (1981) "Attitudes towards single women," *Sex Roles*, 7 (1), January, 73–78.

Stone, Lawrence (1981) "Family history in the 1980s: Past achievements and future trends," *Journal of Interdisciplinary History*, 12, 1, Summer, 51–87.

Stone, Lawrence. *Uncertain Unions: Marriage in England 1660–1753*. Oxford University Press. 1992.

Straus, Murray A., and Richard J. Gelles, "Societal change and change in family violence from 1975 to 1985 as revealed by two national surveys," *Journal of Marriage and the Family*, Vol. 48 (August 1986): 465–479.

Straus, Murray A., Richard Gelles, and Suzanne K. Steinmetz (1980) *Behind Closed Doors: Violence in the American Family*. New York: Doubleday and Co.

Sudia, C.E. (1973) "An updatings and comment on the United States scene," *Family Coordinator*, 22 (3), July, 309–311.

Swan, G.S. (1986) "The political economy of American family policy, 1945–85," *Population and Development Review*, 12 (4), December, 739–758.

Sweet, James A., and Larry L. Bumpass (1984) "Living arrangements of the elderly in the United States." University of Wisconsin Madison: Center for Demography and Ecology Working Paper 84–11.

Sweet, James A., and Larry L. Bumpass. *American Families and Households*. New York: The Russell Sage Foundation. 1987.

Tanfer, Koray, "Patterns of premarital cohabitation among never-married women in the United States," *Journal of Marriage and the Family*, 49: 483–97, August 1987.

Teachman, Jay D., and Karen A. Polonko. "Cohabitation and marital stability in the United States," *Social Forces*, 69: 207–20, September 1990.

Tepperman, L. (1974) "Ethnic variations in marriage and fertility: Canada, 1871," *Canadian Review of Sociology and Anthropology*, 11(4), 324–343.

Tepperman, L. "Demographic aspects of career mobility," *Canadian Review of Sociology and Anthropology*, 12, 2, 1975, 163–177.

Tepperman, L., and S.J. Wilson, eds. (1992) *Next of Kin: An International Reader on Changing Families*. Englewood Cliffs, New Jersey: Prentice Hall.

Thomson, David, "I am not my father's keeper: families and the elderly in 19th century England." *Law and History Review*. 1984, 2: 265–86.

Thomson, Elizabeth, and Min Li. 1992. "Family Structure and Children's Kin." University of Wisconsin, Madison: National Survey of Families and Households Working Paper No. 49.

Thornton, Arland, "Influence of the marital history of parents on the marital and cohabitational experiences of children." *American Journal of Sociology*, Vol. 96, No. 4 (January 1991): 868–94.

Tillion, Germaine, *The Republic of Cousins: Women's Oppression in Mediterranean Society*. London: Al Saqi Books. 1983 [c1966].

Tiryakian, Edward A. (1991) "Modernization: Exhumetur in Pace (Rethinking Macrosociology in the 1990s)." *International Sociology*, Vol. 6, No. 2: 165–80.

Todd, Emmanuel. *The Explanation of Ideology: Family Structures and Social Systems*. London: Basil Blackwell. 1985.

Tomes, N. (1985) "Childlessness in Canada, 1971: A further analysis," *Canadian Journal of Sociology*, 10, 37–68.

Tourigny, Marc, in Picard, André. "Home is where the heartbreak is," *Globe and Mail*, December 14, 1993.

Trent, Katherine, and Scott J. South, "Structural determinants of the divorce rate: A cross-societal analysis," *Journal of Marriage and the Family*, Vol. 51, No. 2, (May 1989): 391–404.

Trost, Jan (1988) "Conceptualising the family," *International Sociology*, 3, 3, 301–308.

Trost, Jan, "Married and Unmarried Cohabitation: The Case of Sweden, With Some Comparisons," *Journal of Marriage and the Family*, Vol. 37 (1977): 677–682.

Trost, Jan, "Remarriage." In Cseh-Szombathy, Laszlo, Inger Koch-Nielsen, Jan E. Trost, and Iteke Weda, in collaboration with M. Bak and P. Tamasi. *The aftermath of divorce: coping with family change: an investigation in eight countries*. Budapest: Akadémiai Kiadó. 1985. Pp. 51–74.

Turner, R. Jay, and Don Lloyd (1993). Paper presented at the 1993 conference of the American Public Health Association.

Turner, R. Jay, and William R. Avison, "Assessing risk factors for problem parenting: The significance of social support." *Journal of Marriage and the Family*, November 1985, 47(4): 881–892.

Turner, R. Jay, Carl F. Grindstaff, and Norman Phillips, "Social support and outcome in teenage pregnancy." *Journal of Health and Social Behavior*, 1990, Vol. 31, pp. 43–57.

Uhlenberg, Peter (1980) "Death and the Family," *Journal of Family History*, 4: 313–20. 1980.

Uhlenberg, Peter, "Aging and the societal significance of cohorts." In J.E. Birren and V.L. Bengtson, eds. *Emergent Theories of Aging* New York: Springer. 1988. Pp. 405–25.

United Nations, UNESCO, *Families: A Global Perspective in a World of Change*. A Gaia book, with UNESCO. 1993. Doubleday.

United Nations, UNICEF. *Progress of Nations*. 1993.

van de Kaa, Dirk. (1987) "Europe's second demographic transition," *Population Bulletin*, 42, No. 1 (March), 1–59, Washington DC: The Population Reference Bureau. Reprinted in Lorne J. Tepperman and Susannah J. Wilson (eds.) *Next of Kin: An International Reader on Changing Families*. Englewood Cliffs, New Jersey: Prentice Hall. 1992.

Vasary, I. (1989) "'The sin of Transdanubia': The one-child system in rural Hungary," *Continuity and Change*, 4 (3), December, 429–468.

Vaughan, Diane (1986) *Uncoupling: How Relationships Come Apart*. New York: Vintage Books.

Veenhoven, R. *Conditions of Happiness*. Dordrecht: D. Reidel Publishing Company. 1984.

Veevers, Jean E. (ed.) *Continuity and Change in Marriage and the Family*. Toronto: Holt, Rinehart and Winston of Canada. 1991.

Veevers, Jean E., "Traumas versus Stress: A Paradigm of Positive versus Negative Divorce," *Journal of Divorce and Remarriage*, 1991, 15, 1–2, 99–126.

Walter, L.E. (1989) "Who are they? When is then?: Comparison in histories of the Western family," *Journal of Comparative Family Studies*, 20, 2, Summer, 159–173.

Walters, J., and L.H. Walters (1980) "Parent-child relationships: A review, 1970–1979," *Journal of Marriage and the Family*, 42 (4), November, 807–822.

Watkins, Susan Cotts, Jane A. Menken, and John Bongaarts, "Demographic foundations of family change," *American Sociological Review*, Vol. 52, No. 3 (June 1987): 346–359.

Watson, Roy E. L., and Peter W. DeMeo, "Premarital cohabitation vs. traditional courtship and subsequent marital adjustment: a replication and follow-up," *Family Relations*, 36: 193–7, 1987.

Weitzman, Lenore J., and Ruth B. Dixon (1980) "The transformation of legal marriage through no-fault divorce," reprinted in A. Skolnick and J. Skolnick (eds.) (1986) *Family in Transition: Rethinking Marriage, Sexuality, Child Rearing, and Family Organization*, 5th ed. Boston: Little, Brown, pp. 338–351.

Weitzman, Lenore J., *The Divorce Revolution: The Unexpected Consequences for Women and Children.* New York: Free Press. 1985.

Wellman, Barry, and Scot Wortley, "Brothers' keepers: Situating kinship relations in broader networks of social support," *Sociological Perspectives*, Vol. 32, No. 3 (1989): 273–306.

Wells, L. Edward, and Joseph H. Rankin, "Families and delinquency: A meta-analysis of the impact of broken homes," *Social Problems*, 1991, 38, 1, February, 71–93.

Westoff, Charles F. "Some speculations on the future of marriage and fertility," *Family Planning Perspectives*, Vol. 10, No. 2 (March/April 1978): 79–83.

Whicker, Marcia L., and Jennie J. Kronenfeld (1986) "Men and women together: The impact of birth control technology on male-female relationships," *International Journal of Sociology of the Family*, Vol. 16, No. 1 (Spring 1986): 61–81.

White, James M. "Premarital cohabitation and marital stability in Canada," *Journal of Marriage and the Family*, 49 (3): 641–7, August 1987. 51: and discussion, ibid. 535–44, May, 1989.

Williams, Holly Ann (1990). "Families in refugee camps." *Human Organization*. 49 (2): 100–9. Reprinted in Lorne J. Tepperman and Susannah J. Wilson (eds.) *Next of Kin: An International Reader on Changing Families.* Englewood Cliffs, New Jersey: Prentice Hall. 1992.

Wilson, William Julius, and Robert Aponte, "Urban poverty," *Annual Review of Sociology*, 11: 231–82, 1985.

Wilson, William Julius, *The Truly Disadvantaged: The Inner City, The Underclass and Public Policy.* University of Chicago Press. 1987.

Wimberley, D.W. (1990) "Investment dependence and alternative explanations of Third World mortality: A cross-national study," *American Sociological Review*, 55 (1), February, 75–91.

Wojtkiewicz, Roger A., Sara S. McLanahan, and Irwin Garfinkel (1988), "The growth of families headed by women: 1950 to 1980," Centre for Demography and Ecology Working Paper 88–31. Madison: Center for Demography and Ecology, University of Wisconsin, 1988.

Wright, Robert E., and Paul S. Maxim (1987) "Canadian fertility trends: A further test of the Easterlin hypothesis," *Canadian Review of Sociology and Anthropology*, Vol. 24, 339–357.

Wu, Lawrence L., "Age Dependencies in Rates of First Marriage," CDE Working Paper 88–35. University of Wisconsin.

Wu, Zheng, and T.R. Balakrishnan, "Attitudes towards cohabitation and marriage in Canada," *Journal of Comparative Family Studies*, 1992, 23, 1, spring, 1–12.

Wybrow, Robert J., *Britain Speaks Out, 1937–87: A Social History As Seen Through the Gallup Data.* London: Macmillan. 1989.

Xiaohe, Xu, and Martin King Whyte, "Love matches and arranged marriages." Reprinted in Lorne J. Tepperman and Susannah J. Wilson (eds.) *Next of Kin: An International Reader on Changing Families.* Englewood Cliffs, New Jersey: Prentice Hall. 1992.

Yankelovich, D. (1981) *New Rules: Searching for Self-fulfillment in a World Turned Upside Down.* New York: Random House.

Yllo, Kersti (1984) "The status of women, marital equality, and violence against wives: A contextual analysis," *Journal of Family Issues*, 5, 307–320.

Young, Michael, and Peter Willmott. *The Symmetrical Family.* Harmondsworth: Penguin Books. 1975.

Zajonc, Robert B., and Gregory B. Markus, "Birth order and intellectual development." *Psychological Bulletin*, 1975, Vol. 82, No. 1, pp. 74–88.

Zaretsky, Eli, "The place of the family in the origins of the welfare state," in Barrie Thorne and Marilyn Yalom (eds.) *Rethinking the Family: Some Feminist Questions.* New York: Longman. 1982. Pp. 188–224.

Zimmerman, C.C. *Family and Civilization.* New York: Harper and Row. 1947.

INDEXES

AUTHOR INDEX

SUBJECT INDEX